STATE GOVERNMENT

STATE GOVERNMENT

CQ's GUIDE TO CURRENT ISSUES AND ACTIVITIES
1993-94

edited by Thad L. Beyle

The University of North Carolina
at Chapel Hill

Congressional Quarterly Inc.
Washington, D.C.

Congressional Quarterly

Congressional Quarterly Inc., an editorial research service and publishing company, serves clients in the fields of news, education, business, and government. It combines the specific coverage of Congress, government, and politics contained in the *Congressional Quarterly Weekly Report* with the more general subject range of an affiliated publication, *CQ Researcher*.

CQ Books publishes college political science textbooks under the CQ Press imprint and public affairs paperbacks on developing issues and events as well as information directories and reference books on the federal government, national elections, and politics. These include the *Guide to the Presidency*, the *Guide to Congress*, the *Guide to the U.S. Supreme Court*, the *Guide to U.S. Elections*, and *Politics in America*. CQ Books recently published a three-volume encyclopedia of American government, including *The Presidency A to Z, The Supreme Court A to Z,* and *Congress A to Z*. The *CQ Almanac*, a compendium of legislation for one session of Congress, is published each year. *Congress and the Nation*, a record of government for a presidential term, is published every four years.

CQ publishes the *Congressional Monitor*, a daily report on current and future activities of congressional committees, and *Congressional Insight*, a weekly analysis of congressional action.

An electronic online information system, Washington Alert, provides immediate access to CQ's databases of legislative action, votes, schedules, profiles, and analyses.

The Library of Congress cataloged the first edition of this title as follows:

Beyle, Thad L., 1934-
    State government.

    Bibliography: p.
    Includes index.
    1. State governments—Addresses, essays, lectures. I. Congressional
Quarterly, inc. II. Title.

JK2408.B49   1985   320.973   85-9657

ISBN 0-87187-780-5
ISSN 0888-8590

Editor: Thad L. Beyle
Contributing Editor: Laura M. Carter
Cover: Paula Anderson
Index: Julia Petrakis

Congressional Quarterly Inc.

Contents

I. POLITICS IN THE 1990s

II. POLITICS: DIRECT DEMOCRACY

III. POLITICS: PARTIES, INTEREST GROUPS, AND PACS

IV. MEDIA AND THE STATES

V. STATE LEGISLATURES

VI. GOVERNORS AND THE EXECUTIVE BRANCH

VII. STATE BUREAUCRACIES AND ADMINISTRATION

VIII. STATE COURTS

IX. STATE ISSUES

Boxes, Tables, and Figures

BOXES

TABLES

FIGURES

Foreword

A new presidential administration headed by an activist, creative former governor has generated hope and even euphoria in state capitals across the country. Bill Clinton was the longest-serving incumbent governor in the nation at the time of his election as president, and few politicians in the country are as knowledgeable about the problems and needs of state governments. Unlike the last two governors elected president, Ronald Reagan and Jimmy Carter, Clinton was also deeply involved in the activities of the National Governors' Association and made common cause with state chief executives of both parties on a host of issues from Medicaid to education. It was no accident that one of the first groups President Clinton invited into the White House for lengthy and leisurely discussion shortly after Inauguration Day was his former statehouse colleagues.

But President Clinton would be the first to admit that he is in no position to solve all the states' woes. A modest increase in federal funding may help, but a massive federal debt—and the need to narrow the annual budget deficit—leave little room for dramatic action. By and large, governors and state legislatures understand this, and it is revealing that their foremost plea to Clinton is not for federal aid but fewer federal mandates that force states to spend money they often do not have.

During the Reagan-Bush era, a massive shift in the balance of federalism occurred, with enormous responsibilities—and the accompanying burdens—transferred from the nation's capital to the state capitals. The states took up the challenge, considerably expanding their activities and taking the necessary steps, however painful, to meet their obligations without unbalancing their budgets. None of this is likely to change even as the states become full partners again in a more cooperative relationship with Washington.

No scholar understands these trends better than Thad Beyle, one of the country's foremost experts in state government. He has been skillfully charting the trends that are reshaping state government and politics in this series for Congressional Quarterly. The carefully selected articles in this latest compendium recount the results of the 1992 elections for state offices, including the effects of referenda, redistricting, and campaign spending. Updates on current governors, legislatures, bureaucracies, and state courts are included, as are discussions of some overriding issues on the states' agendas, from land-use laws and state-sponsored gambling to health care reform and AIDS. News media coverage of state issues and government is also emphasized.

In a time when the federal government remains in dire fiscal straits, both the national government and the localities are looking to the states as never before for leadership. State governments are facing unprecedented challenges, and we need to be more attentive than ever to their agendas. This informative volume, the ninth in this welcome series, helps us to keep up with the states—the new cutting edge of the federal system.

Larry J. Sabato
Charlottesville, Virginia

Preface

The states have acquired considerable importance over the past decade. Their growth as measured by reach of policies and programs, size of budgets and bureaucracies, as well as overall responsibility to their citizens, is unprecedented. Their budget problems, too, are unprecedented, and the need for tax increases and attempts to avert state budget deficits are front page news.

This increased visibility and influence are tied to a major shift in how our federal system of government operates. In the late 1970s, the national government began cutting back in ever-increasing proportions on its commitment to handle the domestic issues facing the country. State governments were asked to shoulder more of the domestic policy burden while the federal government tried to cope with the national debt and issues of national defense.

The states' response to the fiscal challenges of the 1980s became an issue of national as well as local importance. It fell mainly on state governments to take up the slack created by a federal government pulling back on support for domestic programs. The states were able to meet this challenge in an expanding economy where revenue estimates were always too low and extra funds were usually available.

In 1987 Richard Nathan of the State University of New York—Albany and Martha Derthick of the University of Virginia reviewed what they saw happening in the states: "State governments are on a roll . . . they are reforming education and health systems, trying to convert welfare to workfare and building roads and bridges and other public works." They found that most elected state officials loved this new activism, often seeing governors and legislatures competing "with one another to do more, do it better, and do it faster." Even state attorneys general were coming alive "with populist flair" as they were "fighting mergers that the [U.S.] Justice Department [found] acceptable" and "challenging allegedly deceptive advertising by fast-food chains and commercial airlines." Nathan and Derthick argued that one of the most important legacies of the Reagan years would be "this increased activism in state governments" as responsibilities gravitated from both the national and local levels to the states.[1]

Toward the end of the 1980s there were signals that this build-up of budgets and programs based on an always-increasing revenue structure was coming to an end. And end it did. The 1990s brought a tough twist for state leaders to cope with as the economy went into recession. Adding to the melee, the 1992 elections saw the national government refocus its attention on deficit reduction and large-scale cutbacks in the armed forces. Cutting back on defense means base closings and fewer defense contracts, both of which have significant effects on local and state economies. The trials that state governors and legislators are facing in the 1990s verge on the impossible.

The states must handle demands for more service while seeing their revenue structures bring in much less than estimated—and needed. State expenditures are no longer easily covered. Mid-budget-year corrections (that is, budget cutbacks) have become all too common a method to cope with the fiscal crises in the states. And severe cuts in the next year's budget are becoming the norm. California, with a succession of billion dollar budget deficits, is the most well known (or notorious) state in this respect, but difficult situations have arisen equally in most other states.[2]

This fiscal situation means that state leaders have to cut back on needed programs while at the same time raise taxes just to keep basic state services going, often at a very reduced level. This is the worst possible position in which any political leader can find him- or herself: having to raise the taxes of the voters while reducing what they get for those taxes. Citizen approval ratings reflect this, as public regard for governors and legislators has plummeted in most states. Yesterday's heros are today's political targets for retribution.

Despite all this bad news, to many seeking a political career the states are where the action is and where those seeking to have an impact on government and policy making turn. The states are also important rungs on our national political career ladder, as three of the last four presidents emerged from a governor's chair.

According to Carl Van Horn of the Eagleton Institute of Rutgers University, over the past few decades state governments have undergone a quiet revolution. This revolution, in which "states reformed and strengthened their political and economic houses," now finds the states occupying "a more important role in American life" as they pioneer "solutions to some of the country's most difficult problems and demonstrate effective leadership."[3] But in the 1990s, "the stakes are higher than ever before. ... How well state political institutions and leaders handle these difficult challenges will determine how the nation is to be governed and how its citizens are to be served in the coming decades."[4]

State governments are no longer sleepy backwater operations located in far-off capitals where few people know or care what they are doing. In many ways, it might be better to look at state governments as big-time organizations comparable to some of the world's largest nations or our country's largest corporations. Using this perspective, the roles of state leaders in governing the states could be compared to those who govern large nations or run large corporations. They are large, complex organizations with a range of operations and goals—and they warrant the attention of both national and international policymakers.

For example, using 1990 data, California's gross state product would place it as the seventh largest country in the world, between the United Kingdom and Canada, in terms of gross national product, and as the fourth largest U.S. corporation, between Ford Motor Company and IBM in terms of gross sales. New York would follow closely behind as the ninth largest country, between Canada and China, and as the seventh largest U.S. company, between General Electric and Philip Morris.[5]

The 1993-94 edition of *State Government: CQ's Guide to Current Issues and Activ-*

ities includes recent articles that define and analyze these state issues and agendas. Short background essays introduce the articles and highlight developments in the states.

The organization of this book parallels that of most state government texts. First is politics: the most recent election results and the roles of direct democracy, interest groups, political parties, and the media. Next are institutions: legislatures, governors, bureaucracies, and state courts. Finally are some of the issues of primary concern to the states today: health care reform, coping with AIDS, the potential impact of a balanced federal budget, raising money through lotteries, land-use reform, and prisons. A reference guide for further study also is included.

There are many to thank for assistance in developing this book. Among them are David R. Tarr, the director of the Book Department at Congressional Quarterly, for his support, and Larry Sabato at the University of Virginia for his recommendations and kind words in the Foreword.

This is our ninth compilation of the *Guide,* and there is much we have yet to learn. Any errors you find are mine. I hope you will send your comments and suggestions so we might be able to improve the 1994-95 edition.

Notes

1. "Federalism," *State Policy Reports* 5:24 (December 1987): 23.
2. See Thad Beyle, ed., *Governors and Hard Times* (Washington, D.C.: CQ Press, 1992), for a series of specific state case studies on how leaders have tried to cope with growing problems using diminished resources.
3. Carl Van Horn, "The Quiet Revolution," in *The State of the States,* 2d ed., ed. Carl Van Horn (Washington, D.C.: CQ Press, 1992), 1.
4. Ibid., 12.
5. "How Significant Are States?" *State Policy Reports* 10:15 (August 1992): 16-17.

I. POLITICS IN THE 1990s

State officials continue to debate the timing of U.S. elections. Some argue that national, state, and local elections should be held at different times to keep separate the issues, candidates, and political concerns of each level. Following this argument, national elections for president, vice president, U.S. senators, and U.S. representatives would be held in even years, as they are now; exactly which year would depend on the length of the term—that is, representatives every two years, presidents every four years, and senators every six years. State-level elections for governor and other executive officials, state legislators, and state constitutional amendments and referendums would be held in "off-years" (nonpresidential election years) or possibly in odd-numbered years. And local elections would be at another time, preferably not in conjunction with either state or national elections.

Others advocate holding all elections at the same time to maximize voter interest and turnout and, not inconsequentially, to increase the importance of the political party as the main determinant of voters' decisions from the top of the ballot to the bottom. But there is not a single Republican party or a single Democratic party to influence voters' choices. At least fifty different Republican and Democratic state parties reflect the unique political culture, heritage, and positions of the fifty states. Add to that the increasing number of independents and other voters who split their tickets, and it is clear that this political party rationale for simultaneous elections will not hold up in the practical world of politics.

Neither side of the timing argument has predominated. During the 1992 presidential election year, forty-six states elected their legislatures, but only twelve elected their governors. Of these twelve states, New Hampshire, Rhode Island, and Vermont elected their gov-

ernors to two-year terms, which means that their gubernatorial elections alternate between presidential and nonpresidential election years. Indeed, most states hold their gubernatorial elections in even, nonpresidential years, as in 1994, when thirty-six governors will be elected, along with most legislatures; or in odd years, as in 1993, when New Jersey and Virginia are holding their state elections, and in 1995, when Kentucky, Louisiana, and Mississippi will hold theirs.

A major reason why some states have shifted their elections to nonpresidential years is because the personalities, issues, and concerns evident in presidential elections often spill over into state-level contests. While presidential elections are stirring events that bring the excitement of politics to the American populace and lead to higher turnout among voters, some state officials fear that the "coattail effect" of the national elections will change the results of their elections and, most important, obscure the state issues that voters should consider on election day.

Over the 1980s and into the 1990s women have been increasingly successful as candidates for top level state offices. In 1986, Republican Kay A. Orr of Nebraska won that state's governorship but was beaten in her 1990 reelection bid. Democrat Madeleine M. Kunin of Vermont won three successive elections for governor between 1984 and 1988. In 1990, Joan Finney (D) won in Kansas, Barbara Roberts (D) won in Oregon, and Ann Richards (D) won a hard fought campaign in Texas. While no women won a governorship in the 1991 or 1992 elections, two women are strong candidates for their party's nomination in both the New Jersey and Virginia 1993 gubernatorial races. These women can attribute their success to better fund raising, aid from other office holders who are women, more active financial support and counseling from female corporate executives, and more active support for top female candidates from men.[1]

To some observers, this set of victories by women represents the third wave of recruitment of women into state politics. The first wave, up to the early 1970s, consisted of women winning as widows, wives, or daughters of established male politicians. The second wave, through the 1970s, consisted of women active in civic affairs shifting their volunteer work and contacts into political affairs. The third wave now evident is of women who have moved up the political ladder by defeating other candidates while keeping their eyes on a higher political goal such as the governorship, much as men have. In other words, the third wave consists of upwardly mobile politicians who happen to be women.[2]

State Campaigns: 1989-92

In 1989, there were two states in which gubernatorial elections took place: New Jersey and Virginia. Voters in Virginia also were electing their legislators and New Jersey voters were electing members to their lower house, the General Assembly. The Democrats were victorious in both states: in the gubernatorial races, James J. Florio (N.J.) and L. Douglas Wilder (Va.) were elected, and in the legislative races, Democrats retained their hold over the Virginia legislature and recaptured the lower house in New Jersey.

But the focus in the 1989 elections was on abortion. In July 1989, midway through these campaigns, the U.S. Supreme Court announced a major decision on abortion.[3] In effect, the Court began the process of reversing the standard set in an earlier decision, *Roe v. Wade* (1973), which had provided women the right under the U.S. Constitution to choose an abortion within a certain time period. This earlier decision also had the effect of giving

governors and "state legislators the opportunity not to choose sides in a wrenching political debate."[4]

The impact of the decision was almost immediate as candidates for office in the states were asked their positions on the issue: were they prolife or prochoice? The governor of Florida, Bob Martinez (R), even called a special fall session of his legislature to tighten up that state's abortion laws. The legislators met, but decided not to act, much to the governor's embarrassment. This issue helped Democratic challenger Lawton Chiles defeat Martinez in his 1990 bid for a second term.

The abortion issue hurt the Republican candidates for governor in both New Jersey and Virginia since they held prolife views, in contrast to the more prochoice views of the Democratic candidates. But as the Republicans began to feel the heat of the rapidly growing ranks of the prochoice activists—even from within their own party—and as they saw the numbers in their polls rising against them, they waffled on the issue, moving away from their previous prolife stand. That strategy seemed to hurt them even more.

Virginia's gubernatorial race was significant for more than how abortion affected that state's politics. The Commonwealth's voters had the opportunity to elect the nation's first elected black governor, Lt. Governor L. Douglas Wilder (D). Wilder worked his way up through Virginia politics, winning a state senate seat in 1969, then lieutenant governorship in 1985. One other aspect of this election should be noted: even though Wilder won, public opinion polls—even polls taken as voters exited the voting booths—showed him winning by a much wider margin than was ultimately the case. This indicates that a new and subtle form of racism exists in which voters are reticent to admit that they will or just have voted against a minority candidate; hence the difference between how they say they vote and the actual vote totals.

There are two stunning messages from these 1989 elections: blacks can seek and win major offices as politicians instead of as civil rights warriors; and abortion is a major issue that can help or hurt candidates depending on their views and how they handle the abortion question on the campaign trail.

In 1990, nineteen new governors were selected and seventeen incumbent governors reelected in the thirty-six states holding gubernatorial elections. Actually, three of the new governors weren't so new, as some old hands reappeared on the scene: Walter J. Hickel in Alaska, Bruce King in New Mexico, and Richard A. Snelling in Vermont. Democrats won nineteen of these contests, bringing their hold over statehouses to twenty-eight; Republicans won fifteen races, bringing their total to twenty statehouses. What was new about the 1990 elections was that two states elected independent candidates: Hickel and Lowell P. Weicker Jr. in Connecticut. Both were former Republican office holders, but this time they ran as independents, defeating not only Democratic candidates but Republican candidates as well.

Democrats also fared well in legislative races, winning forty-three more seats across the states. But these were a very critical forty-three seats since the Democrats' control of state legislatures rose from twenty-nine to thirty states, while the Republicans dropped from controlling nine to only five state legislatures. This configuration of party wins and losses resulted in split political leadership in twenty-nine states, where the governor belongs to one party and one or both houses of the legislature are controlled by the opposing party. Split-ticket voting is very much alive and well across the states.

Again, some of the results in particular states demonstrate how wide an impact split-ticket voting can have on specific elections.

Twenty-six states had contests for both their governorship and one of their U.S. Senate seats. In only eleven states were the winners of both contests from the same party; voters in fifteen states elected a governor from one party and a U.S. senator from the other.

For example, in Alaska, where the independent gubernatorial candidate Hickel won, Arliss Sturgulewski, the Republican candidate, received 26.2 percent of the vote while incumbent Republican U.S. senator Ted Stevens received 66.2 percent of the vote—a difference of forty points! In Idaho, incumbent Democratic governor Cecil Andrus won with 68.2 percent of the vote while Republican newcomer Larry Craig won the Senate seat with 61.3 percent of the vote—a swing of nearly thirty points. In Wyoming, incumbent Democratic governor Mike Sullivan won with 65.4 percent of the vote; incumbent Republican U.S. senator Alan Simpson won his seat back with 63.9 percent of the vote—another swing of nearly 30 points.

The three states that held elections in 1991 are traditionally one-party Democratic states: Kentucky, Louisiana, and Mississippi. None of the incumbent governors were able to return to office, one due to the Kentucky state constitutional limitation allowing governors to serve only one term, the other two incumbents because they were defeated in their reelection bids. Kentucky voters did as normally expected by elevating Democratic lieutenant governor Brereton Jones to the governorship. And in 1992, they removed the one term limitation on their state level officials, so Jones will be able to seek reelection in 1995 if he chooses to.

However, in the other two states it was not politics as usual. In Mississippi, Kirk Fordice became the first Republican governor since the reconstruction era as he ousted incumbent Democratic governor Ray Mabus from office in a close race. In Louisiana, former Democratic governor Edwin W. Ed-

POLITICS IN THE 1990s

wards (1972-1980, 1984-1988) returned to office after a highly contested and nationally eyed race that saw incumbent governor Buddy Roemer, who had switched from the Democratic to Republican party during his term, defeated in the unique open Louisiana primary system. Edwards then beat Republican state senator David Duke in the runoff, a contest that saw nearly every possible Republican of note, including then president George Bush, working against Duke because of Duke's history of racial and antisemitic beliefs and activities. Edwards, a controversial and tainted political figure himself, was well known for his "Louisiana Hayride" style of governing under the Cajun-French slogan *Laissez les bons temps rouler* (Let the good times roll.)[5] The voters had to choose between his often questionable style and the notorious Duke, and opted for style over divisiveness.

Also of importance in the 1991 election results was the anger the New Jersey voters vented toward the Democrats in general and Democratic governor Jim Florio specifically. They sent back to Trenton veto-proof Republican majorities in both houses of the state legislature, houses that had been controlled by the Democrats for two decades. What was the point of this anger? Tax hikes that Florio pushed and the previous Democratic legislature adopted. Now, it was up to the Republicans to figure out how to balance the state budget and keep services and programs going. Initial indications were that it was much easier to make these arguments on cutting back state government while on the campaign trail than it was in the policy making halls of the state legislature.

The 1992 elections saw the excitement of a presidential contest dominate the political scene. Three candidates, incumbent George Bush (R), Arkansas governor Bill Clinton (D), and independent Ross Perot, vied for the top

office. Clinton's win marked only the second time in the last seven elections that the Democratic candidate was able to gain the presidency. Significantly, three of our last four elected presidents had served previously as governor—an indication of how politically potent the governorship in the states has become.[6]

The races for U.S. Senate seats were heated in California, Colorado, Georgia, Illinois, New York, Pennsylvania, and Washington state, among others. These elections sent eleven new senators, including four women, one of whom is African-American, and a native American, to the nation's capital. Part of the political calculus in a number of these races was the drive by women to gain more U.S. Senate seats in the wake of the Senate Judiciary Committee's inadroit handling of Anita Hill's allegations against Clarence Thomas during the latter's Supreme Court appointment hearings in October 1991. While not all the women seeking a seat in the U.S. Senate won, there were enough challengers for observers to label the 1992 elections as the "Year of the Woman."

Twelve gubernatorial races also occurred. The Democrats won eight of these, increasing their numbers from twenty-eight to thirty, while the Republicans dropped from twenty to eighteen. However, when Republican governor Guy Hunt of Alabama was convicted of a felony and removed from office in April 1993, he was replaced by the Democratic lieutenant governor Jim Folsom Jr. This increased the number of seats held by Democrats to thirty-one and reduced the Republicans to seventeen. Republicans do hold the governorships of some very important states, however, including California and the states in the heart of the Midwest—Illinois, Iowa, Michigan, Minnesota, Ohio, and Wisconsin. Additionally, the Republican governor of Massachusetts, William Weld, is often mentioned as a possible candidate for president in 1996.

A look at the way voters chose their candidates in the 1992 races points up how common ticket splitting is in the states. Just by noting that independent presidential candidate Ross Perot received 19 percent of the vote nationwide indicates that nearly one-fifth of the voters had to have split their ballots if they voted for anyone else in the election. In Indiana, incumbent governor Evan Bayh (D) won with 63 percent of the vote while incumbent U.S. senator Dan Coats (R) won with 58 percent of the vote—a swing of twenty-one points. In North Dakota, Edward Schafer (R) won the open governor's seat with 59 percent of the vote while Byron Dorgan (D) won the open U.S. Senate seat with 60 percent of the vote—a swing of nineteen points. Finally, in Missouri, Mel Carnahan (D) won the open governor's seat with 59 percent of the vote while incumbent U.S. senator Christopher Bond (R) won with 54 percent of the vote—a swing of thirteen points. Split ticket voting was evident in many state legislative races as well. Some 1,700 new state legislators took office in 1993. In winning thirty-two seats more than the Democrats, the Republicans increased their control of both chambers from six to nine states, while the Democrats saw a drop in control from twenty-nine to twenty-five states.[7]

The Issues

As evidenced by the 1989 New Jersey and Virginia gubernatorial races, abortion can be a very potent issue. Until 1989, issues in state campaigns varied considerably, not only from state to state but also among offices being contested. For example, campaigns for state legislative seats tended to focus on the individual candidate as he or she sought to achieve name recognition among the voters. Some candidates shied away from taking a position on specific issues, preferring instead to endorse economic development, reduction of crime, better education, and other broad issues. Others used specific issues such as antiabortion, tax repeal, or growth limits to achieve the name recognition they needed to win. On the whole, however, candidates preferred to take a position on broad issues rather than commit themselves to a specific issue that could alienate potential supporters. As *State Policy Reports* has pointed out,

> Campaigns rarely reveal candidate positions on the difficult questions of state policy. The easy question is whether candidates are for lower state and local taxes, better educational quality, higher teacher pay, and protecting the environment while stimulating economic growth. The candidates generally share these objectives. The hard question is what to do when these objectives collide as they often do.[8]

As a result, the average voter has a hard time discerning where the candidates stand on specific issues, and attempts to survey state legislative candidates on specific issues usually are not successful. One public interest organization in North Carolina does provide voters with information on how incumbents are rated by their peers, lobbyists, and the media covering the legislature in addition to information on the legislation they sponsored and their votes on key bills. However, no information of this kind can be provided on nonincumbent legislative candidates.[9]

Though the days of noncontroversial state campaigns were ended by the emergence of the abortion question, other controversial issues have intruded into state campaigns and begun to overshadow abortion as the principal issue. Not that the abortion issue wasn't important in some states; it was important and made the difference in some campaigns, and it may again depending on how future U.S. Supreme Court decisions affect the issue, and what legislation may be considered or passed by state legislatures. But, the state of the U.S.

economy and especially individual state economies became the focus of many campaigns as did the question of the need for increased taxes, as was seen in the results of the 1991 elections in New Jersey. Most recently, in the 1992 elections, the major issue in some state races was incumbency—a sort of "throw all the rascals out" perspective stemming from scandals and a realization that incumbents usually win. This drive saw successful passage of fourteen term limit referenda in the states limiting a legislator's stay in office.

This section provides articles that focus on issues of political concern in the states in recent electoral politics. First, Ines Pinto Alicea of Congressional Quarterly reviews the results of the 1992 elections. Included is a table that supplies information on gubernatorial elections over the last sixteen years. An article by Thomas Galvin of Congressional Quarterly follows that looks at the term limits movement as it played itself out in the 1992 elections. Alan Ehrenhalt, also of Congressional Quarterly, then addresses another major political concern of the states in the early 1990s: the mandatory redistricting and reapportionment efforts that followed the 1990 U.S. Census.

Notes

1. Meg Armstrong, "WSEG Campaign News," *Women in State Government Newsletter*, May 1986, 4.
2. Comments of Celinda Lake, Candidate Services Director of the Women's Campaign Fund, at a National Conference of State Legislatures seminar as reported by David Broder, "Hardearned Credentials Give Female Candidates an Edge," [Raleigh] *News and Observer*, September 15, 1986, 13A.
3. *Webster v. Reproductive Health Services* (1989).
4. Wendy Kaminer, "From *Roe* to *Webster*: Court Hands Abortion to States," *State Government News* 32:11 (November 1989): 12.
5. Bob Benenson, "The Edwards 'Hayride' Ends; Rep. Roemer to Be Governor," *Congressional Quarterly Weekly Report*, October 31, 1987, 2687.
6. The former governors are Jimmy Carter (D, Georgia, 1971-1975), elected president in 1976; Ronald Reagan (R, California, 1967-1975), elected in 1980 and 1984; and Clinton (D, Arkansas, 1979-1981, 1983-1993), elected in 1992.
7. Karen Hansen, "Election 1992: The Message is Mixed," *State Legislatures* (December 1992): 13.
8. *State Policy Reports* 2:20 (October 31, 1984): 11.
9. North Carolina Center for Public Policy Research, *Article II: A Guide to the N.C. Legislature* (Raleigh, N.C.), published biennially.

Big Themes of '92 Ignored in the Voting Booths

by Ines Pinto Alicea

Anti-incumbency and "Year of the Woman" themes worked well in some key House and Senate races, but both messages flopped in the dozen gubernatorial contests from Vermont to Washington state Nov. 3 [1992].

All four incumbent governors succeeded in their quests to hold onto their offices in Indiana, Rhode Island, Vermont and West Virginia. Former North Carolina Democratic Gov. James B. Hunt Jr. also won back his job after an eight-year absence.

And the three women candidates vying for governorships in Montana, New Hampshire and Rhode Island lost, blunting this year's string of triumphs for women congressional candidates. Women hold the governorships of Kansas, Oregon and Texas.

The gubernatorial contests largely focused on pocketbook and ethics issues. Still, the races gained less national attention than they have in recent election years.

Larry Sabato, a professor of government at the University of Virginia, said key domestic issues that usually dominate gubernatorial feuds were front-burner issues in the 1992 presidential contest.

"The end of the Cold War finally allowed Americans to put those issues—health care, education and jobs—first at the national level," Sabato said.

Democrats and Republicans were each defending six governorships, but the Democrats had the edge going into the contests because they had the four incumbents—Evan Bayh of Indiana, Bruce Sundlun of Rhode Island, Howard Dean of Vermont and Gaston Caperton of West Virginia—seeking re-election. It was the first time this century that no GOP incumbents were on the ballot.

In the post-election alignment, Democrats picked off three gubernatorial seats held by Republicans in Delaware, Missouri and North Carolina, but lost one held by a Democrat in North Dakota, giving Democrats a net gain of two governorships.

In the end, 30 state chief executives [were] Democrats, 18 Republicans and two independents.

The Democratic gains were not enough for the party to reach the more than 2-to-1 split that Democrats enjoyed in 1986. That year, Democrats held 34 governorships to the

Ines Pinto Alicea is a staff writer for *Congressional Quarterly Weekly Report*. This article is reprinted from *Congressional Quarterly Weekly Report*, November 7, 1992, 3596-3599.

16 held by Republicans.

Thirty-one states went into the election with divided governments, where the same party did not control the governor's office and both legislative chambers.

The election diminished that number. At least three states with divided governments—Missouri, North Carolina and Washington—[became] solidly Democratic in January [1993], said Susan L. Seladones of the National Conference of State Legislatures.

Overall, Democrats still hold a sizable majority in state legislatures, despite Republican inroads. . . .

While some results remained incomplete at the end of election week, Republicans seemed likely to control 30 of the nation's 99 legislative chambers in January [1993], a net gain of five. Democrats were likely to control both houses in 25 states, a net loss of four, and they control 14 other chambers. The remaining four are tied. Nebraska's Legislature is unicameral and nominally nonpartisan.

And, after brief uncertainty, the political fate of the Arkansas governorship was resolved Nov. 5 [1992]. With President-elect Bill Clinton's win, a dispute had arisen over who should succeed him because of conflicting sections in the state's 118-year-old constitution.

The constitution says a special election is necessary to fill a gubernatorial vacancy if an unexpired term has 12 months or more remaining. There [were] two years left in Clinton's term.

But a conflicting 1914 amendment says the lieutenant governor—in this case, Democrat Jim Guy Tucker—should fill a vacancy "for the residue of the term." Tucker [wanted] to succeed Clinton, but so [did] Democratic Arkansas Attorney General Winston Bryant, who called for a special election to fill the seat.

The Arkansas Republican Party, which has held the governorship for only six of the past 120 years, sided with Bryant in calling for

an election. But Pulaski County Judge John Plegge ruled that the lieutenant governor will take over. Common Cause, a nonpartisan political watchdog group, first raised the issue publicly and filed a suit seeking a clarification.

Three Democratic Gains, One Republican

In Delaware, Rep. Thomas R. Carper became the first Democrat since 1972 to win the governorship. Carper, who has eight previous statewide election victories, easily beat Republican B. Gary Scott, a real estate executive, in a bid to fill the seat of outgoing Republican Gov. Michael N. Castle.

Carper, who has represented Delaware's at-large House seat since 1982, was heavily favored to win and swap posts with the popular Castle. Barred from seeking a third term, Castle sought and won the House seat. Scott failed to douse Carper's huge popularity and reputation as an able lawmaker.

In Missouri, Democratic Lt. Gov. Mel Carnahan beat Republican state Attorney General William L. Webster in the battle to succeed Republican Gov. John Ashcroft, who also could not seek another term.

Webster had won the highly publicized 1989 Supreme Court case *Webster v. Reproductive Health Services* that upheld for the first time state-imposed restrictions on abortion.

A Democrat also was elected to replace a Republican in a nasty race in North Carolina between Hunt and Republican Lt. Gov. James C. Gardner.

In North Dakota, Republicans gained their only Democratic seat in the contest to replace retiring Gov. George Sinner.

In that race, GOP businessman Edward T. Schafer beat Democratic state Attorney General Nicholas Spaeth. Schafer, the son of the former owners of the Gold Seal Co., makers of Mr. Bubble bubble bath, won by

Table 1 Gubernatorial Elections: 1977-1992

Year	Races	Democratic winner #	Democratic winner %	Eligible to run #	Eligible to run %	Did run #	Did run %	Won #	Won %	Lost #	Lost %	Where lost Primary #	Where lost General election #
1977	2	1	50	1	50	1	100	1	100	—	—	—	—
1978	36	21	58	29	81	22	76	16	73	6	27	1[a]	5[b]
1979	3	2	67	0	0	—	—	—	—	—	—	—	—
1980	13	6	46	12	92	12	100	7	58	5	42	2[c]	3[d]
1981	2	1	50	0	0	—	—	—	—	—	—	—	—
1982	36	27	75	33	92	25	76	19	76	6	24	1[e]	5[f]
1983	3	3	100	0	0	—	—	—	—	—	—	—	—
1984	13	5	38	9	69	6	67	4	67	2	33	—	2[g]
1985	2	1	50	1	50	1	100	1	100	—	—	—	—
1986	36	19	53	24	67	18	75	15	83	3	18	1[h]	2[i]
1987	3	3	100	2	67	1	50	0	0	1	100	1[j]	—
1988	12	5	42	9	75	9	100	8	89	1	11	—	1[k]
1989	2	2	100	0	0	—	—	—	—	—	—	—	—
1990	36	19[l]	53	33	92	23	70	17	74	6	26	—	6[m]
1991	3	2	67	2	67	2	100	0	0	2	100	1[n]	1[o]
1992	12	8	67	9	75	4	44	4	100	0	0	—	—
TOTALS	214	125	58	164	77	124	76	92	74	32	26	7 (22%)	25 (78%)

Source: Thad L. Beyle, "Gubernatorial Elections: 1977-1990," *Comparative State Politics* 12:2 (April 1991): 18-21. Updated June 1993. Reprinted with permission.

[a] Michael S. Dukakis, D-Mass.   [b] Robert F. Bennett, R-Kan; Rudolph G. Perpich, D-Minn.; Meldrim Thompson, R-N.H.; Robert Straub, D-Ore.; M. J. Schreiber, D-Wis.   [c] Thomas L. Judge, D-Mont.; Dixy Lee Ray, D-Wash.   [d] Bill Clinton, D-Ark.; Joseph P. Teasdale, D-Mo.; Arthur A. Link, D-N.D.   [e] Edward J. King, D-Mass.   [f] Frank D. White, R-Ark.; Charles Thone, R-Neb.; Robert F. List, R-Nev.; Hugh J. Gallen, D-N.H.; William P. Clements, Jr., R-Texas   [g] Allen I. Olson, R-N.D.; John D. Spellman, R-Wash.   [h] Bill Sheffield, D-Alaska   [i] Mark White, D-Texas; Anthony S. Earl, D-Wis.   [j] Edwin Edwards, D-La.   [k] Arch A. Moore, R-W.Va.   [l] Two independent candidates won: Walter J. Hickel (Alaska) and Lowell P. Weicker Jr. (Conn.). Both were former statewide Republican office holders.   [m] Bob Martinez, R-Fla.; Mike Hayden, R-Kan.; James Blanchard, D-Mich.; Rudy Perpich, DFL-Minn.; Kay Orr, R-Neb.; Edward DiPrete, R-R.I.   [n] Buddy Roemer, R-La.   [o] Ray Mabus, D-Miss.

emphasizing jobs in a state that has seen its population dwindle along with jobs.

Four Survive Anti-Incumbent Tide

Two governors dueling to keep their jobs—Bayh of Indiana and Dean of Vermont—were heavily favored because of their personal popularity and records of keeping their states' economies stable during the recession.

In Indiana, Bayh, at 36 the nation's youngest governor, reminded voters that he had maintained state services without raising taxes and helped Hoosiers gain 32,600 jobs [in 1991].

His opponent, state Attorney General Linley E. Pearson, unsuccessfully attacked Bayh, son of former Sen. Birch Bayh.

Pearson warned voters of financial gloom if Bayh remained as the chief executive and accused Bayh of "cooking the books" to show the state with a budget surplus. But voters soundly rejected the claims.

In Vermont, Dean, the nation's only physician serving as governor, easily deflected a challenge by Republican state Sen. John McClaughry.

More than anything, McClaughry's chances were dashed after it was revealed that he wrote a letter to a brokerage firm urging it to take off the market a recent Vermont bond offering. In the letter, McClaughry said Dean was not committed to retiring three temporary tax increases enacted in 1991, as had been stated in the bond prospectus.

Dean took over when Republican Gov. Richard Snelling died in office, keeping Snelling's staff and adopting many of his policies. He balanced the state's budget with a combination of spending cuts and tax hikes passed under Snelling. State voters and Dean have remained on a honeymoon; one Vermont bumper sticker reads: "Dean: I Just Like Him."

The two other incumbents who won Nov. 3—Caperton of West Virginia and Sundlun of Rhode Island—were seen as more vulnerable after enduring tough primary battles.

West Virginians were angered at Caperton for reneging on a 1988 no-new-taxes pledge in 1989. But in the general election, Caperton deflected the tax issue by raising ethical questions about his opponent, state Agriculture Commissioner Cleve Benedict.

Caperton stressed Benedict's ties to the state's former three-term Republican Gov. Arch Moore, who is serving a prison term on charges of buying votes and taking illegal contributions. Benedict worked in the Moore administration.

In Rhode Island, Sundlun withstood an aggressive primary opponent, who said he had done little to help the state's recession-wracked economy. But in the general election, Sundlun emphasized his efforts to improve the state's economy and resolve Rhode Island's bank crisis.

Women Candidates Fail

Sundlun's re-election bid also tested the "Year of the Woman" theme, a trend that emerged in gubernatorial contests not only in Rhode Island but also in open seats in Montana and New Hampshire.

Sundlun's challenger, Republican Elizabeth Ann Leonard, a political newcomer and car dealership owner, appeared to be a strong opponent early in the race, having handily won a tough primary. But her campaign lost momentum, saddled by difficulties raising enough money to run an effective campaign and overcome partisan barriers in the heavily Democratic state.

Though female candidates in Montana—Democratic state Rep. Dorothy Bradley—and New Hampshire—Democratic state Rep. Deborah Arnie Arneson—launched stronger challenges, their campaigns were stanched in the end by economic issues, particularly taxes.

"The Year of the Economy overshadowed the Year of the Woman in the governors' races," said Matt Learnard, research director for the Democratic Governors' Association. "People were looking to women for change, but what it came down to was who was going to put money back in people's pockets."

Pocketbook Issues

In Montana, the decision by Republican Gov. Stan Stephens to step down for health reasons set off a major battle between Bradley, a 16-year lawmaker who campaigned on horseback, and her Republican opponent, Attorney General Marc Racicot, over how to spend funds from a proposed 4 percent sales tax.

Both candidates wanted to use the new tax revenue to lower income and property taxes and to cover the state's budget deficit. But Bradley called for more spending on education and human services, while Racicot championed tax relief and spending cuts. The voters backed Racicot.

In New Hampshire, Arneson took the bold step of advocating the state's first-ever income tax—at 6 percent—to ease local property taxes. Though early polls suggested voters were initially receptive to her, the romance was all but dead by Election Day.

Republican Steve Merrill, a former state attorney general and chief of staff for former Gov. John H. Sununu, rode to victory on a platform of no new taxes. Merrill succeeds Republican Judd Gregg, who sought and won the hotly contested Senate race.

Washington state was the site of another gubernatorial confrontation over taxes. But this time, former Democratic Rep. Mike Lowry beat Republican Attorney General Ken Eikenberry despite telling voters that a tax hike was possible. Lowry softened the message by offering to take a pay cut as governor.

The race between Lowry and Eikenberry also presented a sharp ideological contrast. Eikenberry, a former FBI agent and attorney general for 12 years, led in early polls in which potential voters initially questioned Lowry's liberal stances. But in the end, moderate Republicans and business leaders abandoned Eikenberry as too conservative for the state.

Eikenberry's chances also were hurt when the University of Washington Board of Regents President Samuel Stroum charged Eikenberry's campaign with offering "to reappoint him" to the board "in return for a $50,000 campaign contribution."

The campaign denied the charges.

Another bitter ideological struggle was staged in Utah among a liberal Democrat, lawyer Stewart Hanson; a conservative Republican, insurance executive Mike Leavitt; and an independent, Merrill Cook.

Leavitt defeated his two opponents, but Cook took second place with 34 percent of the vote. Hanson's strong support for abortion rights and his Democratic credentials hurt him in this conservative and overwhelmingly Republican state.

Leavitt also was helped by outgoing Republican Gov. Norman H. Bangerter, who tapped him as his successor.

Ethics

In Missouri, Democrat Carnahan ran ahead in pre-election polls after pounding Republican Webster for alleged ethical lapses.

Webster had entered the race as the favorite after winning the high-profile abortion restrictions case before the U.S. Supreme Court. But Webster saw his early lead slip away after Carnahan reminded voters of the attorney general's role in a troubled state workers' compensation fund.

Webster also faced criticisms for taking in hundreds of thousands of dollars in campaign contributions from lawyers hired for state business.

Webster returned some of the contributions and denied wrongdoing but was never able to regain his early lead.

In North Carolina, Hunt, a Democrat and former two-term governor who has been out of office since losing a 1984 bid to unseat Sen. Jesse Helms, faced Republican Gardner in a race dominated by heated charges and countercharges of wrongdoing. The two were vying to succeed Republican Gov. James G. Martin, who was barred by law from seeking a third term.

Gardner accused Hunt of being a liar and lacking "steel in his spine." Hunt struck back, demanding that Gardner explain hundreds of thousands of dollars in unpaid business debts and back taxes.

But Hunt managed victory by largely focusing his campaign on improving the state's economy and worker retraining programs.

Limits Score a Perfect 14-for-14, But Court Challenges Loom

by Thomas Galvin

About the only people who fared even better on election night than President-elect Bill Clinton were supporters of term limits. In a landslide of their own, they prevailed in all 14 states that had ballot initiatives to limit the service of House and Senate members. In most cases, the support was overwhelming.

Nearly 21 million Americans supported term limits, a 200-year-old concept energized in recent years by congressional scandal and public discontent with career politicians.

"There is at least one clear and unequivocal mandate from the voters this election," proclaimed Cleta Mitchell, director of the Term Limits Legal Institute. "This mandate is that we limit terms."

Counting Colorado, which approved an initiative in 1990, 181 members of the 103rd Congress will serve under the specter of term limits. In some states, House members are now required to step aside in as little as six years, while all the states limit senators to 12 years.

Fresh from their victory, term-limit supporters are looking to Congress to approve a constitutional amendment that would apply limits to members from all 50 states.

But opposition from the congressional leadership will make that a tall task. House Speaker Thomas S. Foley, D-Wash., and Senate Majority Leader George J. Mitchell, D-Maine, who oppose term limits, are likely to try to bottle up any legislation.

A court challenge also looms. A suit has already been filed to strike down an initiative in Florida on constitutional grounds, and similar challenges are being mulled in other states.

A Blowout

Although pre-election polls indicated overwhelming support for term limits, the final results startled even those pushing the initiatives. "It surprised everyone. To win all 14 is a shock," said Sen. Hank Brown, R-Colo.

Democratic consultant Vic Kamber, who worked to defeat term-limit initiatives in several states, laid the blame for his side's poor showing at the feet of Democratic congressional leaders. Foley and other members have not done enough to repair Congress' image, said Kamber, and were more interested in saving their political hides than taking on term limits. "If the leadership is not willing to

Thomas Galvin is a staff writer for *Congressional Quarterly Weekly Report*. This article is reprinted from *Congressional Quarterly Weekly Report*, November 7, 1992, 3593-3594.

defend Congress, then maybe these bozos deserve it," said Kamber.

There were competitive campaigns in only a handful of states— Arkansas, California, Michigan, North Dakota and Washington. And even in those states, the term-limit debate was often overshadowed by the presidential and congressional contests.

The closest vote was in Washington state, which rejected term limits [in 1991]. Supporters recrafted [the 1992] initiative to address criticism that the limits should not be applied retroactively. The Washington state group LIMIT raised $358,000 for its campaign, although about 40 percent of that was used up getting on the ballot.

LIMIT campaign manager Sherry Bockwinkel said the group learned from last year's mistakes, when the campaign ran out of money in the final week and a last-minute drive by Foley and other state lawmakers helped turn back the initiative.

[In 1992] Bockwinkel said the group spent most of the $190,000 it had allocated for media in the last 10 days, when most voters make up their minds. In addition, she said, "People who opposed us focused on their own election. Nobody spoke out against it like they did last year."

Karen Zytniak, state coordinator of the anti-term-limit group No on 573, attributed the loss to lack of focus by voters and to businessman Ross Perot's strong 24 percent showing in the state. A wave of new voters— perhaps inspired by Perot—went to the polls, and Zytniak said they spelled the difference in approving the measure.

Financial Support

The initiatives in California and Michigan were aided by large contributions from U.S. Term Limits, a Washington, D.C.-based group that has served as a national coordinator for the movement.

Table 1 Term Limits on November 1992 Ballot

State	Senate	House	For/against (percent)
Arizona	12 years	6 years	74/26
Arkansas	12 years	6 years	60/40
California	12 years	6 years	63/37
Florida	12 years	8 years	77/23
Michigan	12 years	6 years	59/41
Missouri	12 years	8 years	74/26
Montana	12 years	6 years	67/33
Nebraska	12 years	8 years	68/32
North Dakota	12 years	12 years	55/45
Ohio	12 years	8 years	66/34
Oregon	12 years	6 years	69/31
South Dakota	12 years	12 years	63/37
Washington	12 years	6 years	52/48
Wyoming	12 years	6 years	77/23

Source: The Associated Press.

The group parceled out over $1.1 million to state campaigns, including $364,000 in Michigan and about $600,000 in California.

Most of the money for Michigan arrived in the last 10 days before the election and could not be matched, said K. P. Pelleran, campaign manager for Citizens Against Term Limitations.

Pelleran's group spent about $400,000, with the bulk of the contributions coming from Upjohn, General Motors and other Michigan corporations.

U.S. Term Limits contributed money in 11 of the 14 states, including $135,000 in Arkansas. Term-limit opponent Barbara Pardue, campaign director of Arkansans for Representative Democracy, said the contributions should raise eyebrows. "The money coming out of Washington raises questions about whether it truly is a legitimate grass-roots effort," she said.

Other term-limit opponents have charged that the group is being secretly financed by conservative and Libertarian groups, including billionaire brothers Charles and David Koch. A survey of Federal Election Commission records indicates that while many of the 51 members of the U.S. Term Limits Finance Committee contribute to Republican causes and candidates, several are also Democratic supporters.

Putting Theory into Practice

The paradox of the term-limit movement's Election Day sweep is that while voters supported the initiatives, they continued to support their own incumbents. Defying predictions that a raft of incumbents would lose, defeats were about the average number over the past 30 years.

Former Rep. Jim Coyne, R-Pa., who heads the group Americans to Limit Congressional Terms, said the lower-than-expected number of defeats buttresses the argument for term limits. "The real news was the election of all those members—business as usual," said Coyne.

Indeed, in the 14 states that approved term limits, voters returned to Congress 70 members who have served longer than the limit mandated by the initiative.

Senate Minority Leader Bob Dole, R-Kan., said the term-limit movement's success at the polls underscores the old adage that the public hates Congress, but loves local members. "I think people would like to find a way to deal with [low turnover], but they don't want to vote against their incumbent," he said.

Dole said his support for a constitutional amendment mandating limited terms would depend on whether Kansas and other smaller states would not be stampeded by delegations from larger states.

Thomas Mann, political scientist at the Brookings Institution, said many voters do not make the connection between support for term limits and the effect on their own members of Congress. "One is a vote on Congress as an institution, and the other is a vote on what they think of their member," he said.

Mann notes that if Clinton's administration is successful in changing the public's mind about government, the momentum currently enjoyed by term-limit supporters could dissipate quickly. "What's fueling the movement is discontent with government," he said. "If that discontent eases, the term limit movement could lose steam."

Legal Challenges Ahead

Only hours after Florida approved a term-limit initiative, a suit was filed in a U.S. District Court challenging its constitutionality. And suits are expected in other states, as opponents try to do in the courts what they could not do in the polls—stall the movement.

Many legal experts say they have a very good chance. "It's hard for me to see the Supreme Court upholding it," said Georgetown University law Professor Mark Tushnet.

Walter E. Dellinger, [now general counsel at the Justice Department], said it is clear that states cannot add to the three basic qualifications for federal office set forth in the U.S. Constitution—age, residency and citizenship.

In 1969, the Supreme Court ruled in *Powell v. McCormack* that the House could not refuse to seat Rep. Adam Clayton Powell, D-N.Y., accused of abusing his office, because he met the qualifications set out in the Constitution.

Others argue that the case is not applicable, because term limits are being imposed by voters in the state, not by Congress. But Dellinger disagrees: "It's not about who makes the decision. It's about what the qualifications are."

It is unlikely that a term-limit challenge would make it to the Supreme Court for at least two years, at the earliest, says Dellinger. It would probably take over a year to work its way through the lower courts, he said, and not get to the Supreme Court until late 1994 or early 1995.

Term-limit proponent Cleta Mitchell

Table 2 Rate of Legislative Turnover in the States, 1984-1991 (percent)

Very low		Low		Moderate		High		Very high	
N.Y.	10	Ga.	16	Kan.	21	Md.	26	Okla.	31
Calif.	11	Mass.	16	Ky.	21	N.M.	26	Mont.	32
Del.	13	Ind.	17	R.I.	21	Ore.	27	Alaska	35
Pa.	13	Mich.	17	Texas	21	S.D.	27	N.H.	35
Ill.	14	Mo.	17	Wis.	21	Wyo.	27	Nev.	37
Ohio	14	Fla.	19	Ariz.	22	La.	29	W.Va.	38
Va.	14	Iowa	19	Hawaii	22	Miss.	29	Neb.	43
Ark.	15	Minn.	19	S.C.	22	N.D.	29		
		Tenn.	20	Ala.	23	Utah	29		
				Maine	23	Colo.	30		
				Conn.	24				
				Idaho	24				
				N.J.	24				
				N.C.	24				
				Vt.	25				
				Wash.	25				

Source: Adapted from *State Policy Reports* 11:2 (January 1993): 13.

Note: The average rate of turnover is 23 percent.

said the courts may not be willing to consider the issue because it is more political than legal. Even if they do, she contends, history suggests the Supreme Court will uphold state-mandated limits on congressional service.

"The U.S. Supreme Court has, through the years and through many decisions, upheld the right of the states to regulate elections, including the electoral procedures related to the candidacies of persons seeking federal office," she wrote in a brief filed last December when opponents in Florida tried to keep the initiative off the ballot.

But supporters of term limits are not likely to wait to see whether she is right. For them, it looks more like a race against time to win approval of a constitutional amendment before the courts rule that state-mandated terms are unconstitutional.

That is just what term-limit supporters plan to do [in 1993]. Sen. Brown and Rep. Bill McCollum, R-Fla., will push for votes that would send a constitutional amendment to the states for ratification. Brown said he will try to attach term limits to campaign finance legislation Democrats may take up early [in 1993]. "I'm confident we'll have some sort of vote before the year is over," he said.

Securing a vote in the House will be more difficult. House rules requiring that amendments be germane could prohibit members from attaching a term-limit bill to the House version of the campaign finance measure.

Getting a free-standing bill to the floor will be next to impossible with Foley and other congressional leaders standing in the way. Mann says he would be surprised to see a vote this year: "This is a case where the leadership will protect the members."

It is up to term-limit supporters to pressure Congress to address the issue, said former Rep. Coyne. Pressure tactics, such as the campaign that forced the House to rescind a new pay raise in 1989, will be employed. Coyne also looked to a group that sent shudders through the political establishment in this election. "There are 25 million Perot supporters looking for something to do," he said.

Redistricting and the Erosion of Community

by Alan Ehrenhalt

The 25th state House district of Mississippi slithers like a snake down the banks of the Mississippi River, south from the Tennessee border as far as the old cotton town of Clarksdale, more than 50 miles away, in the Delta. For much of its length, it is barely 100 yards wide, a strip of land along the levee where no one even lives.

It is a disjointed mess of a district, but the bulk of its residents do have one thing in common: They are white. Although the 25th runs through two overwhelmingly black counties, it includes very few of the black people who live in those counties. The mapmakers managed to draw a state legislative district smack in the heart of the Mississippi black belt with a white population of 86.1 percent.

It would be hard to do that by accident, and, of course, the 25th is no accident. It is a creature of the federal Voting Rights Act. Required under interpretations of that law to design as many districts as possible that can elect black representatives, the Mississippi legislature took its job seriously, redrawing lines all over the state to pack black voters into black-majority constituencies. The 25th District was made from the leavings of that process. After the mapmakers had done all they could to maximize black voting strength

in northwest Mississippi, they found two pockets of white voters on the cutting room floor. One was mostly suburban, near the Tennessee line, in DeSoto County; the other was rural, in distant Coahoma County. They couldn't be placed in other districts because they would lower the minority population. So the legislature drew lines around them and stitched them together as the brand-new 25th. The long strip of land along the river is nothing more than a piece of cartographic thread.

The politics of the 1990s are nothing if not ironic. Twenty-five years ago, if you had predicted that the way to comply with civil rights law would eventually be to draw a district for the Mississippi legislature that deliberately excluded blacks, you would have been fairly judged a lunatic. But there we are.

The Voting Rights Act itself did not generate all this trickery; that law, as written in 1965, was aimed simply at preventing the deliberate denial of political rights that prevailed all over the Deep South at the time. It was the 1982 rewrite of the law that estab-

---

Alan Ehrenhalt is a staff writer for *Governing*. This article is reprinted from *Governing* 5:9 (June 1992): 9-10.

What States Did to Comply with the
Voting Rights Act: North Carolina

... Most southern states were required to create new minority-majority districts for the 1992 elections. For example, Alabama and South Carolina drew their first black-majority districts and several other states sought to add to their black and Hispanic representation in Congress. The process was complicated by a requirement that the U.S. Justice Department "preclear" plans in 13 states covered by the Voting Rights Act and by political maneuvering between political parties and among Democrats. In several southern states Republicans sought to create more minority districts in order to siphon black support away from adjacent areas. White Democrats, of course, sought to protect their seats while drawing new minority-majority districts.

It is especially challenging to draw minority districts in states with large rural black populations. For example, aided by high-technology computers, North Carolina created two new black districts (1st and 12th) that are especially convoluted; virtually none of the state's 12 districts are compact.[1] It is more than 2,000 miles around the perimeter of the 1st District in eastern North Carolina and the "bug district" has a white majority.[2] The new 12th is a thin, winding district that includes parts of 12 counties as it connects black neighborhoods in several cities across central North Carolina. Commenting on the issue of community of interest in the 1st District, black candidate H.M. Michaux noted, "I don't care if you're rich or poor, you're treated the same. Some may be farmers, lawyers, or construction workers, but we've all faced the same problem ... discrimination."[3]

Source: David C. Saffell, "Redistricting for 1992: Compliance with the Voting Rights Act and the Compactness Standard," *Comparative State Politics* 13:6 (December 1992): 35-36. Reprinted with permission.

1. "North Carolina Computer Draws Some Labyrinthine Lines," *Congressional Quarterly Weekly Report,* July 13, 1991, 1916-1917.
2. *Ibid.,* 1916.
3. "North Carolina: A Common Interest," *Congressional Quarterly Weekly Report,* December 21, 1991, 3726.

lished the concept of discrimination as a "result," rather than an intent. A legislature that does not include minorities in proportion to their overall presence in the state can be in violation of the law, even if the district lines were drawn in an apparently color-blind way.

As a piece of logic, this is hard to defend. Discrimination is, by definition, an act of choice; if it is unintentional, it is something else. The results of a political system may be unexpected, paradoxical, unfortunate—even tragic. But they can't be discriminatory unless someone set out to make them that way. The whole idea of discrimination without intent is an awkward stretching of plain English usage.

Of course, when it comes to drawing districts, intent can be almost impossible to prove. It was common knowledge in Mississippi in the 1960s and 1970s that the state's congressional map was drawn to prevent the election of a black congressman, but nobody could prove it—nobody even knew how to go about proving it.

It was situations like that that led Congress to change the law in 1982 and provide that a district map could be illegal if it "results in discrimination." But even then, Congress seemed to want this new weapon used rather

Reapportionment Rules and Strategies

The name of the game in reapportionment is to maximize the number of representatives elected, given a party's likely popular vote. Imagine three districts in an area that has normal Democratic majorities of 55%-45% and a population of 1,000 in each district. Democrats have 1,650 voters and Republicans have 1,350. The appropriate Republican plan is to put 1,000 Democrats in one district and then win the other two with their 1,350 votes easily outnumbering the remaining 650 Democrats. The Democratic plan is the reverse, putting most of the Republicans in one district and easily winning the other two.

There are three major constraints on drawing strange-looking district maps to get these results. The first is that the party members expected to vote for the plan will balk when the plan reduces their likely majorities, as it must to maximize the potential for party control statewide. The second is that the other party may be able to block reapportionment by having control of a governor or one house of the legislature or by combining with dissidents who don't like the majority plan.

The third is constitutional constraints that districts be compact and contiguous. These encourage using natural boundaries, like rivers and highways, and political boundaries like counties and municipal borders. They encourage districts that look like rectangles and squares on a map rather than those that look like salamanders. *Gerrymander* was coined by the combination of *salamander* and *Gerry,* the politician associated with a particularly weird configuration of voting districts. Many such districts were created to guarantee Black representation.

Source: State Policy Reports 10:22 (November 1992): 9.

sparingly. The 1982 Voting Rights amendments state specifically that there is no "right to have members of a protected class elected in numbers equal to their proportion in the population." Elsewhere, it is suggested that the new test should be employed primarily in places where the political system "is not equally open to participation" by all races and ethnic groups.

It is the Justice Department and the federal courts that have gone on to interpret the law in a way Congress never intended— either in 1965 or in 1982. Over the past decade, the results test has been interpreted to mean that the first priority in reapportionment is to draw the largest possible number of districts that can be counted on to elect a minority representative.

In the computer age, this is fairly easy.

Each district in the Mississippi House of Representatives, for example, contains roughly 20,000 people. Mapmakers take the state's 36 percent black population and group it into as many geographical clusters as they can that will be roughly 60 to 70 percent black. That is the ideal ratio. With a smaller percentage than that, the election of a black legislator is chancy; larger than that, and minority votes are being "wasted."

Mississippi ends up with a legislative map that could well elect as many as 30 or 35 black House members, rather than its present 20. But it also ends up with monstrosities like the 25th District, clumps of voters who find themselves thrown together essentially as a by-product of the whole voting rights process.

It isn't simply a matter of black and white. In Arizona. the Voting Rights Act has been

Constitutional Doubt Is Thrown . . .

"[W]e believe that reapportionment is one area in which appearances do matter. A reapportionment plan that includes in one district individuals . . . who may have little in common with one another but the color of their skin bears an uncomfortable resemblance to political apartheid."—Justice Sandra Day O'Connor, writing for the majority.

The Supreme Court on June 28 [1993] invited a new wave of lawsuits challenging the constitutionality of districts drawn to ensure the election of minorities.

In a 5-4 ruling in the case of *Shaw v. Reno,* the court reinstated a suit by five white North Carolinians who contended that the state's congressional district map, which created two sinuous majority-black districts, violated their 14th Amendment right to "equal protection under the law" by diluting their votes. Freshman Democratic Reps. Eva Clayton and Melvin Watt this year became the first African-Americans to represent North Carolina in Congress since 1901.

In her majority opinion, Justice Sandra Day O'Connor decried the creation of districts based solely on racial composition, as well as map-drawers' abandonment of traditional redistricting standards such as compactness and contiguity.

The ruling's implications extend well beyond the narrow action taken in *Shaw.* By calling into question the constitutionality of the amorphous computer-generated entities that wriggle through areas to collect a majority of minority voters, the court gave legal standing to challenges to any congressional map with an oddly shaped majority-minority district that may not be defensible on grounds other than race (such as shared community interest or geographical compactness). . . .

The ruling triggered a debate among constitutional scholars, civil rights advocates and minority-group representatives over how effective majority-minority districts are in helping minorities attain equal representation.

It also raised questions about the viability and constitutionality of the Voting Rights Act of 1965 and its 1982 amendments.

More than anything, though, *Shaw* appeared to breed confusion over what, if any, new standards need be applied to a redistricting plan. . . .

For some, *Shaw* establishes a contradictory set of criteria for a Voting Rights Act-controlled state to meet to win federal approval of its map. While the Justice Department or a federal court must approve the state's redistricting plans, *Shaw* raises the possibility that Justice Department insistence on creating the maximum number of minority districts may be challenged on constitutional grounds.

"It's almost as if you had a speed limit sign saying, 'Maximum speed 55, minimum speed 65,' " said

interpreted to require the creation of as many districts as possible with Hispanic majorities, and the mapmakers swept through some communities block-by-block, drawing the lines carefully to cram Hispanics into one district and to place their Anglo neighbors in another.

The average Arizona House district has about 60,000 people. The town of Nogales, on the Mexican border, has fewer than 20,000, about enough to make up one-third of a constituency. But in the latest redistricting, Nogales is in three constituencies. Its Hispanic majority had to be split two ways to provide numbers for a pair of districts that were being counted on to elect a Hispanic legislator. That left a few thousand Anglos who had to be put in a third district to avoid diluting the minority percentage in the other two.

... on Bizarre-Shaped Districts

one North Carolina redistricting expert.

The court left unresolved most of the larger questions about the constitutionality of race-based redistricting.

The court did not invalidate North Carolina's map or rule in favor of the plaintiffs' 14th Amendment complaint. Rather, it reversed the decision of a three-judge panel that had granted a motion to dismiss the complaint, returning the case to the state.

(North Carolina Attorney General Michael F. Easley, one of the defendants in the case, said June 29 that he would consult with state legislators, who may elect to redraw the map rather than reargue the same one before the federal panel.)

In *Shaw*, the court asserted that the plaintiffs were entitled to raise a question of constitutionality under the 14th Amendment because the state legislature "adopted a reapportionment scheme so irrational on its face that it can be understood only as an effort to segregate voters into separate voting districts because of their race, and that the separation lacks sufficient justification."

But, O'Connor wrote, the justices "express no view" as to whether the simple creation of majority-minority districts "always gives rise to an equal protection claim." Nor did the court choose to answer the defendants' contention that "the creation of majority-minority districts is ... the only effective way to overcome the effects of racially polarized voting."

The court said that even if a map is unquestionably a racial gerrymander, it may still pass constitutional muster if a lower court determines that it is "narrowly tailored to further a compelling governmental interest." Nevertheless, the court said, the fact that a redistricting plan was drawn to comply with the Voting Rights Act does not shield it from a challenge on constitutional grounds. And it added that the question of whether Section 2 was unconstitutional if it required the adoption of North Carolina's second plan remained "open for consideration."

O'Connor's opinion did, however, signal dissatisfaction with the broad interpretation of the Voting Rights Act's mandate, as expressed in the court's 1986 ruling in *Thornburg v. Gingles,* for states to create minority districts wherever possible. ...

"If you read [the court's opinion] broadly," said North Carolina's Easley, "you could say that not only must the district meet all the other tests, but the district must be geographically compact—it must be pretty."

Source: Dave Kaplan, *Congressional Quarterly Weekly Report,* July 3, 1993, 1761-1763.

The consequences of this sort of thing are enormous. Not only will voters find it difficult to keep track of who their representatives are; the representatives themselves are going to be confused. Just whose district did the 300 block of Grand Avenue wind up in? It may take half the decade to get it all straight.

I can see some good in this. We are likely to be faced, over the course of the 1990s, with the spectacle of legislators whose districts are so muddled that they cannot measure the mood of constituents and have no choice but to decide public policy questions on their merits.

For the most part, though, it is not a development to be proud of. There is, for example, the fundamental question of public awareness. If I live in a town of 20,000 people, and I am represented in the state House of Representatives by a single member, I have a fighting chance to keep track of him or her and of what sort of representation I am getting. If the map juts in and out of neighborhoods all over town and the people across the street live in a different district, I am much more likely to give up in confusion and decide the whole enterprise isn't worth following. How do any of us evaluate the representation someone is providing when it takes a cartographic memory just to remember who represents whom?

But something else is at stake here. We have, over the past generation, witnessed the withering away of a whole range of institutions that used to provide identity and stability for communities of different sizes all across America: the locally owned bank or newspaper in a medium-sized city; the local high school or Main Street cafe in a small rural town.

The state legislator is one of those disappearing local institutions. As his district ceases to be a clear geographical entity and becomes a collection of individual voters cobbled together for purposes of racial balance and mathematical equality, he loses his identity as a leader who comes from a community and speaks for it in the corridors of the state capitol.

If you choose to treat the notion of community more broadly, as something that transcends geographical lines, then it might be said that the political process has found a new way to honor it. The black community in Mississippi will have more legislative representation in the state legislature in the 1990s than it had before; the Hispanic community will have more representation in Arizona.

Even this, however, is debatable. The number of minority faces goes up; the number of white legislators who have any political need to respond to minority concerns goes down as their minority constituents are peeled off to form the new black and Hispanic districts. Who benefits from this trade-off is a question that is going to occupy us for a long time, and should.

One thing, however, is clear: The main casualty of the tortuous redistricting process now under way is the erosion of geographical community—of place—as the basis of political representation. If a district is nothing more than two pockets of disparate white voters strung together with the Mississippi River levee in between, then it is fair to ask whether the notion of a "district" is gradually ceasing to have any geographical meaning at all.

Perhaps that is appropriate to the 1990s. Many of us are less attached to our neighborhoods than we once were; our social relationships tend to revolve more around the people we work with, or went to school with, or share interests with, regardless of where they happen to live. If that is the way we want to draw our social map in America, it is only logical that we begin to draw our political map in the same way.

Still, it seems a little disturbing that so much of this political change is coming as a byproduct of a 1965 law whose only purpose was the correcting of an obvious and long-standing evil. Nobody who wrote the Voting Rights Act ever planned or wanted anything like the 25th legislative district of Mississippi. That was an unintended consequence—or, as the Justice Department might say, an example of "discrimination by result."

II. POLITICS:
DIRECT DEMOCRACY

Voters in some states do more than choose candidates for state offices; they also vote directly on particular issues. Rather than have their elected representatives make the policy decisions, the voters themselves decide. This is called *direct democracy*. The concept of direct democracy has had a long history in the Midwest and West and at the local level in New England communities, where citizens and leaders often assemble in town meetings to determine the town budget as well as other policy issues.

There are three specific vehicles for citizens to use in states with direct democracy: *initiative, referendum,* and *recall*. In seventeen states, citizens may stimulate change in state constitutions by initiating constitutional amendments to be voted on in a statewide referendum. In twenty-four states, an initiative provision allows proposed laws to be placed on a state ballot by citizen petition; the proposal is then enacted or rejected by a statewide vote. Thirty-seven states have a referendum provision in their constitutions that refers acts passed by the state legislature to the voters for their concurrence before they become law. Most amendments to state constitutions are referred to the voters for approval; only in Delaware can the legislature amend the constitution without referring the proposed change to the people. In fifteen states, a recall provision allows voters to remove a state elected official from office through a recall election.[1]

The provisions for the initiative vary among the states, the most important difference being the role of the legislature. In sixteen states the initiative process is direct: no legislative action is required to place the proposal on the ballot once the requisite number of signatures on the petition is secured. In one other state the process is more indirect: the petition with the necessary signatures is submitted to the legislature, which has the authority to place it on the ballot. Another important difference is the number of signatures required on the petition for an initiative to be considered.[2]

Like the initiative, provisions for a referendum on state legislation vary from state to state. In nineteen states, a referendum is required on certain types of bills, usually those related to state debt authorization (bond issues). In twenty-four states, a citizen petition can place an issue on the ballot for a vote by the electorate to approve or disapprove. In practice, this usually proves to be an attempt to reject an act already passed by the legislature, although many states restrict the type of legislation that can fall under this provision. Finally, fourteen states allow their legislatures to voluntarily submit laws to the voters for their concurrence or rejection.[3]

Provisions for the recall of all elected officials are included in only fifteen state constitutions. Eight states have provisions allowing the removal of all officials, six exclude judicial officials, and Montana includes all public officials, elected or appointed. Considerably more signatures are required for a recall to be placed on the ballot than for an initiative or a referendum.[4] The success of recall efforts indicates that this vehicle for direct democracy can be more than the "loaded shotgun behind the door" to keep elected officials on their toes.

The importance of the voters' right to recall an elected official was recently demonstrated in Arizona. The words and actions of Governor Evan Mecham, elected in 1986, angered many Arizonans sufficiently so that a recall petition was circulated to remove him from office. This drive was successful and was part of the series of events that led to Mecham's removal from office in April 1988, after having served only seventeen months in office.

Mecham had won a three-candidate race by gaining only 40 percent of the general election vote. This political situation led to voter approval of a 1988 constitutional amendment calling for a runoff election should no candidate receive a majority vote in the general election—that is, no more plurality vote governors. However, the 1988 Arizona legislature failed to adopt the so-called "Dracula clause" in that state's constitution that would have barred Mecham, as an impeached official, from ever seeking or holding office again. He did seek the governorship in 1990 and drew enough votes in a third place finish to force the top two contenders into a February 1991 runoff.

Immediate Effects

The effects of direct democracy can be far reaching, affecting not only the state that has the initiative, referendum, or recall provision, but also other states and the broader political milieu in which state government operates.

When California voters adopted Proposition 13 in 1978, they sent a message to elected officials across the country. This successful initiative put the brakes on state and local governments in California by restricting their ability to fund governmental programs and services. Property taxes were reduced to 1 percent of property value (a 57 percent cut in property tax revenues); future assessments were limited to an annual increase of only 2 percent; and a two-thirds vote of the state legislature was required for the enactment of any new state taxes.

The voters' message to state and local governments was clear: "We have had enough! We want less government, fewer programs, and greatly reduced taxes. You have become our problem because of the tax burden we must shoulder. We have asked you to do

something about this; nothing has been done, so we are restricting the amount of money you can raise through taxes and placing this restriction in the constitution where you will not be able to tamper with it." This message—from what had been considered the most progressive electorate and state government among the fifty—prompted a widespread reevaluation of the goals of state and local governments. To what extent should elected officials expect the taxpayers to pay to achieve these goals?

There were other signals besides Proposition 13 for decision makers to consider. Opinion polls at the beginning of the 1980s reported that more than 70 percent of the public felt that income taxes were "too high"; only 45 percent felt this way in 1962. Those who felt that "the government wastes taxpayers' money" rose from 45 percent in 1956 to 80 percent in 1980, [5] and dropped to only 76 percent in 1986. [6] In some states, elected officials heeded their electorates' call to reduce taxes; in others, tax increases for governmental services and programs were postponed. Although Proposition 13 did not spark a nationwide tax revolt, a similar proposition did pass in Massachusetts. These events set the possibility of such an occurrence in other states high enough on state policy agendas to get the attention of politically concerned policy makers.

In the 1990s, the issue is term limits. Since 1990, seventeen states have imposed term limits on some of their elected officials in response to a general feeling that incumbents have too much of an advantage in any political campaign. Since the power of incumbency seems to be insurmountable in many states, the way to beat incumbents is not to allow them to serve more than a set number of terms or years. Starting with successes in three states in 1990 (California, Colorado, and Oklahoma), the movement spread to Washington state where in 1991 the proposal was defeated by a narrow margin. In 1992, while everyone's eyes were on the presidential race, term limits were adopted in fourteen additional states, including Washington state, where it had reappeared on the ballot a second time.[7] (For background, see "Limits Score a Perfect 14-for-14, But Court Challenges Loom," pp. 15ff, this volume.)

The vehicles used for winning these term limit victories are the initiative, which gets the issue on the ballot, and the referendum, which allows the people, not the legislature, to vote on the issue. Waiting for a state legislature to propose limits on its members' terms would appear to be fruitless, so success has been achieved through direct democracy. However, when the term limit movement meets up with states that do not employ direct democracy, it may well be stopped in its tracks unless some other vehicle can be found.

One of the most interesting aspects of the term limit effort is the level of government at which it may be directed. There is no question that citizens can vote to limit the terms of elected representatives in state and local government by amending their state's constitution. But there is a real constitutional question as to whether they can limit the terms of their national representatives to the U.S. Senate and House of Representatives. Such an action would require amendment of the U.S. Constitution, which sets only age, U.S. citizenship, and residency requirements.[8]

Presidential service was limited to two terms by the constitutionally specified route to amendment: two-thirds of both houses of Congress proposed the amendment and three-quarters of the states, through legislative action, adopted the proposed amendment. The current effort at imposing term limits on these national offices solely through state action bypasses the first step set out so explicitly in the U.S. Constitution. As such, any limits adopted by a given state on its national repre-

sentatives applies to that state *only*.

What does all of this mean? Likely, some states that have adopted term limits soon will find their U.S. congressional delegations turning over as individuals reach their personal limit of service. These states will try to recruit other states' representatives and senators to go along with proposing an amendment to the U.S. Constitution that can then be sent out to the states for ratification. As a result, there will be a series of national level representatives, and one or more of these cases will reach the U.S. Supreme Court for a decision on the issue. The ultimate answer to whether the term limits movement succeeds, then, may depend on the views of the justices of the Supreme Court.

Pragmatic Decisions

Initiatives are now being placed on state ballots and voted on at the highest rate ever. In the four decades between 1900 and 1939, there were 253 initiatives on the state ballots, or about 6.3 per year. In the next forty-year period, between 1940 and 1980, there were 248 initiatives on the state ballots, or about 6.2 per year. From 1981 through 1990, there were over 270 initiatives on ballots in twenty-four states, or about 25 per year. This has been an escalating phenomenon: in 1988, there were 55 initiatives on the ballot; in 1990, there were 64. California was the leader with 58 initiatives (21 percent), followed by Oregon with 37 (14 percent).[9]

The initiative and referenda processes are not only becoming more prevalent in the states but more complex and expensive as well. One estimate of the cost of fighting for and against the twenty-nine referenda on the 1988 general election ballot in California was $100 million, or $4 per capita![10] Initiative and referenda politics are becoming big business.

In a study of 199 initiatives acted on between 1977 and 1984, *Initiative News Re-*

port found that the vehicle was being used by interests at both ends of the ideological spectrum. Seventy-nine initiatives were backed by those on the liberal side of the political spectrum, seventy-four by those on the conservative side, and forty-six were not classifiable in ideological terms (usually because the initiatives concerned narrow, business-related issues). The approval rates for both the liberal and the conservative initiatives were about the same, 44 percent and 45 percent, respectively. However, there has been a conservative ideological basis to at least two types of initiatives that have come before the voters in the last few years: term limits and minority rights, specifically the civil rights of homosexuals and lesbians. Money, coordination, petition circulators, and other needs associated with running a successful initiative campaign have been emanating from sources on the right side of the political spectrum.[11]

In this section, Robert Stern of *State Government News* discusses the problems states now face with so many initiatives on the ballot. David Kehler of *New Jersey Reporter*, covering a state that considered adding the initiative to its constitution, discusses how the initiative and referendum can and has been used to restrict minority rights. Finally, Amanda Miller and John Culver in *Comparative State Politics* discuss one very provocative initiative being proposed: dividing California into two states.

Notes

1. *The Book of the States*, 1988-89 (Lexington, Ky.: Council of State Governments, 1988), 17, 217-220.

2. Ibid., 217.

3. Ibid., 218-219.

4. Ibid., 220.

5. Susan Hansen, "Extraction: The Politics of State Taxation," in *Politics in the American States: A Comparative Analysis*, 4th ed., ed. Virginia Gray, Herbert Jacob, and Kenneth N. Vines (Boston: Little, Brown, 1983), 441-442.

6. Survey by the *New York Times*, December 14-18, 1985, reported in *Public Opinion* 9:6 (March-April 1987): 27.

7. For an in-depth discussion of term limits, see Gerald Benjamin and Michael J. Malbin, Jr., *Limiting Legislative Terms* (Washington, D.C.: CQ Press, 1992).

8. See Article I, Section 2, clause 2, and Section 3, clause 3, of the U. S. Constitution for these requirements.

9. Joan M. Ponessa and Dave Kehler, "Statewide Initiatives 1981-90," *Initiative and Referendum Analysis*, no. 2 (June 1992): 1-2.

10. "The Long Ballot in California," *State Policy Reports* 6:15 (August 1988): 27-28.

11. Discussion with Dave Kehler, April 20, 1993. See also Stuart Rothenburg, "Transplanting Term Limits: Political Mobilization and Grass-Roots Politics" (pp. 97-113), and David J. Olson, "Term Limits in Washington: The 1991 Battleground" (pp. 65-96), in Benjamin and Malbin.

Salvaging the Initiative Process

by Robert M. Stern

In 1990, California voters sweated their way through decisions on 18 ballot initiatives, ranging from term limits to pesticide regulation.

In Santa Monica, so many state and local measures appeared on the ballot that voters had to use two booths to cast votes.

A study of the 1990 nightmare, as well as the initiative process of 22 other states, showed that changes are needed. But a study, by the California Commission on Campaign Financing, also revealed that people do not want to repeal the process. Instead, they want to improve it. The commission's report has resulted in a list of suggestions for states considering adopting the initiative process.

I recognize that most states will recoil at anyone from California suggesting improvements. But it is often from the state with the worst case scenario that some of the best lessons are learned.

Proponents in states considering the initiative process should prepare for a hard fight.

It is always difficult to convince a state to set up a fourth branch of government. The established branches tend to oppose the initiative process out of fear over how it will affect them. Legislators, in particular, are against it because ballot initiatives undercut their power.

Who supports the initiative process? Groups and individuals who trust the people to make rational decisions. Supporters include those who believe citizens should be able to counter legislative inaction on a proposal they favor. Typically, these issues include questions on campaign financing, ethics, reapportionment and term limits.

How To Set Up the Process

All states with the initiative process require those wanting an initiative on the ballot to gather enough signatures to show their proposal has popular support. Recently, however, the signature process does not seem to determine how voters really feel.

In California, as in other states, if one has a million dollars and pays enough petition circulators, almost any issue can qualify. There are examples where a single corporation qualified a measure to the ballot, such as the California lottery adopted in 1984.

The U.S. Supreme Court, unfortunately, has prohibited the problem's easy solution:

Robert M. Stern is co-director of the California Commission on Campaign Financing. This article is reprinted from *State Government News* 35:9 (September 1992): 24-25. ©1993 The Council of State Governments.

banning paid signature gatherers. So the commission has looked at the possibility of using public opinion polls to determine which ideas have enough support to make it on the ballot.

If a proposal received a minimal number of signatures, it would be eligible for a state-sponsored poll, which would take the person being polled through a mock campaign, with basic information and arguments on both sides. If a measure received enough support, it would be placed before the voters. States considering adopting the initiative process should look at this new idea or something similar.

The Legislature's Role

Initiatives are circulated and enacted only because the legislators or the governors refuse to respond to the peoples' wishes.

In some states, initiative proponents are given the option of going to the legislature with their proposal. While this is a more conservative approach, these so-called indirect initiatives have distinct advantages. They allow problems with the funding or wording of a proposal to be resolved before it is enacted into law.

The commission suggests the following procedures for states to consider:

• Require a 45-day cooling-off period after the initiative qualifies for the ballot. During this period, the legislature must hold a hearing on the proposal.

• Withdraw the initiative from the ballot if the legislature approves the initiative either in its entirety or with amendments acceptable to the proponents.

• Give proponents a chance to amend the initiative if the legislature does not accept the measure. The vote of each legislator should be publicized in the ballot pamphlet sent to each voter.

• Permit the legislature to amend the initiative once it is approved by voters. The amendments must further the purpose of the measure and must have the approval of at least 60 percent of the legislature.

The commission calls the idea the "flexible initiative."

Because it is important that the voters know what is in an initiative, each voter should be sent a pamphlet containing an impartial analysis of the measure, a summary, arguments for and against and a text of the proposal. In addition, a summary information chart should be included so that voters can quickly see who is supporting and opposing each proposition.

Such information was helpful in California in 1990 when the ballot contained several competing initiatives, including two term limit propositions, two forestry measures and three propositions affecting alcohol taxes.

In an ideal representative democracy, we would not need "direct democracy." Legislators and governors would be responsive to the wishes of the majority and would not be beholden to special interests who do not represent the views of the people. But we don't live in such a society, and thus we need the initiative process.

I & R and Minority Rights

by Dave Kehler

The adoption of initiative and referendum procedures for New Jersey state government would result in the most fundamental—and most questionable—change in the public policy-making process here since the ratification of the 1947 state Constitution.

I&R would provide alternative means, unchecked by the legislative or executive branches, for enacting laws, and, perhaps, constitutional amendments. Those who favor creation of an initiative system frame the question as a rights issue. They envision the benefits of a system in which champions of almost any cause could petition to put an idea before that fraction of the public who bother to vote. If a majority were to approve, the idea would become law, or a part of the Constitution, and could not be repealed or amended by the Legislature for at least several years.

The initiative process, therefore, is an example of raw majoritarianism. New Jersey initiative advocates believe that raw majoritarianism is fair and democratic and that it produces good public policy. But is that truly the case?

Thus far, debate on this point has been far too abstract. Majoritarian rights have been discussed at some length by initiative promoters, but what about minority rights?

A basic concept of representative government is that the rights of the minority are entitled to protection, especially at the intersection of political conflict. This concept was most eloquently expressed by James Madison in *The Federalist*, No. 10. Far too often, though, the initiative device has been used by election-day majorities in other states to attack minority rights. This unfortunate legacy is ironic, as the progressives who developed the initiative concept early in this century thought the process would only be used to expand liberty.

It is true, of course, that for a time, initiatives were used to promote minority rights. Women's suffrage, for example, was originally enacted by initiative in such states as Arizona, Colorado and Oregon. On a few recent occasions, principally involving gun ownership, the initiative has been used to protect individual rights.

But, it is also true that initiatives have been used to suppress minority rights and personal freedoms on numerous occasions:

In California, voters approved Proposi-

Dave Kehler is president of the Public Affairs Research Institute of New Jersey, Inc. This article is reprinted from *New Jersey Reporter* 22:2 (July/August 1992): 55, 62.

tion 1 in 1920 to restrict Japanese from purchasing land in that state.

A few years later, during a wave of anti-Catholic hysteria, Oregon voters adopted an initiative (later invalidated by the U.S. Supreme Court) to prohibit private schools.

In 1950, the California electorate enacted a constitutional amendment requiring local voter approval for the location of low-rent, state-funded housing projects.

In 1956, in the midst of the confrontation between President Eisenhower and racist Gov. Orval Faubus over the integration of Little Rock Central High School, Arkansas voters approved an initiative instructing the state Legislature to use any constitutional means to preserve school segregation.

In 1964, California voters approved Proposition 14, striking down the state's newly enacted fair-housing law. Although this initiative was invalidated in a court challenge, its passage led to a loss of popularity in California of the use of the initiative process, a trend that persisted until 1972.

During the remainder of the 70s, however, antibusing initiatives were adopted by voters in California as well as in Colorado and Washington, with the latter measure ultimately ruled unconstitutional.

Native Americans' fishing rights were targeted by Initiative 456 in Washington in 1984, as voters approved a measure to request that Congress abrogate treaties providing for commercialized steelhead fishing by native Americans. While this question may seem murky to New Jerseyans, opponents of that initiative claimed in their ballot pamphlet statement that it "would destroy the basic culture and heritage of native Americans. . . ."

Federal elected officials also were petitioned by California voters in 1984, when that state's electorate approved Proposition 38 requesting repeal of a 1975 federal law providing for multilingual ballots. The opposition to this initiative was led by Latino-American and Asian-American members of Congress who argued that multilingual ballots encourage assimilation through political participation. Proposition 38 was sponsored by a Michigan-based organization called U.S. English. This group seems to concentrate its initiative activities in states where there is growing Latino political power, sponsoring initiatives to declare English the official language in Arizona (1988), Colorado (1988), Florida (1988) and California (1986). All four measures were approved by voters, although their actual impact has been unclear.

On yet another front, state funding of abortion was prohibited by initiatives passed by voters in Arkansas in 1988 and in Colorado in both 1984 and 1988.

In considering minority-rights issues, it is important to recall that legislatures also have enacted laws over the years in various states that were racist, sexist, bigoted against religious minorities or otherwise abhorrent. However, in recent years, as more women and people of color have been elected to state legislatures around the country, these representative institutions have become much stronger forces for equal treatment of all citizens. Even with the most bigoted of ideas, a legislative body provides a buffer between conflicting groups.

On the other hand, the initiative system seems to invite raw group-against-group conflict.

Consider recent events in Oregon. The Oregon Citizens Alliance grew out of a failed primary challenge to Republican U.S. Sen. Bob Packwood. In 1986, the Alliance sponsored an unsuccessful constitutional amendment initiative to prohibit state funding of abortions. In 1988, it was the successful sponsor of Ballot Measure 8, which revoked then-Gov. Neil Goldschmidt's executive order banning sexual orientation discrimination in state government employment. In 1990, the Alliance ran an independent candidate to succeed Goldschmidt, in the process aiding in the defeat of the Republican candidate, Attorney General Dave Frohnmayer. That same year, the Alliance also sponsored another unsuccessful anti-abortion ballot measure. These days, the Alliance is circulating petitions for an anti-rights initiative that equates homosexuals with necrophiliacs and bestialists.

The initiative process has provided the Alliance with an organization-building focal point. In fact, the Alliance's initiative activities have been so provocative that an opposing organization has been formed: The Campaign For A Hate-Free Oregon.

New Jersey is a state with a very diverse population. We need to develop political structures and organizations to work to build consensus on key issues. Garden State initiative advocates are well-meaning, neither bigots nor racists, and they are profoundly frustrated with the quality of state governance.

But citizens need to recognize that this proposed reform has some very negative aspects, and one of them is that the initiative is a potent vehicle for those who wish to attack minority rights.

California: One State or Two?

by Amanda Miller and John Culver

Elections in California attract national interest as much for the issues on the ballot as the contestants. For the first time in recent memory, there were no statewide initiatives in the June 1992 primary election. (There were two educational bond measures, which were approved, and one constitutional amendment to postpone property tax increases for low-income homeowners, which was defeated.)

Among the various county and municipal initiatives that were on the primary ballot, however, was a non-binding advisory measure to divide the state. Proposed by Stan Statham, a conservative Republican assemblyman from northern California, the measure appeared before voters in 31 of the state's 58 counties. The 31 counties are all largely rural except for San Francisco, the only city-county in the state. As it turned out, the three Bay Area counties rejected the idea as did one county in the central valley. The other 27 counties endorsed the measure by up to 80 percent of the popular vote.

Statham described his ballot measure as "a referendum on state government." As he said to the Commonwealth Club in San Francisco a month before the primary, "Your state government is broken, and it is broken beyond repair." Statham's solution to the problem—splitting California into two states—is not a new one. While his rationale for the division was not the same as those marking previous efforts, sentiment for division surfaced soon after California entered the Union in 1850 as the 31st state.

The earliest move to divide the state was initiated in 1859, when the sparsely populated counties to the south felt threatened by the fast growing north. This proposal made it to Congress, although it stalled because of the Civil War. Three other attempts to divide the state were launched in the late 1800s, and five efforts were made between 1907 and 1941. A contemporary effort to split the state on a north-south basis occurred in 1965. And five years later, a northern California state senator proposed dividing the state on an east-west basis. This proposal died quickly as did a subsequent proposal in 1975 to create three states out of California. What one finds in the history of these proposals to create little Cali-

---

Amanda Miller is a recent graduate in political science from California Polytechnic State University in San Luis Obispo. John Culver is professor of political science at California Polytechnic State University. This article is reprinted with permission from *Comparative State Politics Newsletter* 13:5 (October 1992): 17-20.

Secession and Dividing States

Dividing nations has become a hot world topic. Examples are the USSR, Yugoslavia, and serious discussion of independence for Scotland and Quebec. Secession hasn't drawn any interest in the U.S. since the 1980s when Alaska voters approved a statehood commission to reexamine whether becoming a state was a good idea. Historically, a few American states split from other states, as Maine did from Massachusetts. The last example was the division of West Virginia from Virginia when the old Commonwealth of Virginia couldn't agree on which side to take in the Civil War.

The latest move is to split Northern California from the rest of the Golden State. . . .

The parallel move in the 1980s was to split Michigan's Upper Peninsula away from the Lower Peninsula. The move received some study, but never serious consideration. The purpose was to dramatize alleged neglect by state government. The same thought is behind T-shirts appearing in Southwest Kansas. They show a tornado lifting the geographic area out of Kansas and say, "Toto, We're Not In Kansas Anymore!"

Source: State Policy Reports 10:12 (June 1992): 22.

olds v. Sims (1964) meant that representation in the upper house of the state legislature had to be based on population, not on geography. At that time, the majority of the state's counties were rural, with small populations. As a result, power in the upper house rested with senators from the rural counties. The *Reynolds* decision, however, eviscerated the power of the rural interests and transferred it to representatives from the urban areas of the state. Second, in 1978, voters throughout California approved Proposition 13, the property tax cutting initiative. At first, the impact of Proposition 13 appeared quite positive as homeowners saw their property taxes cut by about 50 percent, and a $4.4 billion state surplus was distributed to local governments to compensate for the lost property tax revenues over several years. Other tax cutting initiatives and legislative bills also were approved during the next 10 years. The net impact of this was a loss of discretionary revenues available to local governments. The state's surplus was exhausted, but local spending for state mandated programs continued to increase.

Local government officials and a good number of citizens in the rural areas of the state increasingly felt their needs were not being addressed by lawmakers in Sacramento and that their low tax bases could not finance the programs required by the state. One northern rural county was on the verge of declaring bankruptcy in 1989 before the legislature provided partial relief. In reality, most counties, rural and urban, are in dire economic shape. But the urban counties have more diverse tax sources and more latitude in deciding where programs can be reduced than do the rural counties.

The recent explosion was ignited by Lassen County's perception that the government in Sacramento is unresponsive and nonrepresentative. Life in the rural north bears little resemblance to what occurs in metropolitan

fornias out of the big one is the familiar north v. south split. The more recent rural v. urban dichotomy is an extension of this geographical division that also has a north-south dimension.

Two factors, one legal and the other economic, are tied to the roots of the rural-urban hostility. First, the "one man, one vote" decision of the U.S. Supreme Court in *Reyn-*

California. This does not present a problem when decisions made in Sacramento recognize the different situations that face rural and urban governments and their constituencies. When these differences are ignored, however, resentment and dissent build.

In 1990, the county-elected board of supervisors in Lassen County pledged not to make further reductions in public services such as health, law enforcement and public libraries and to continue spending for such services until the county ran out of money. This would shift responsibility to the state to determine whether or not to dissolve the county. The county board also proposed that the county become part of the neighboring state of Nevada. Out of this revolt in Lassen County (1990 population was 27,500, a figure slightly less than the number of students attending the University of California, Berkeley) came Stan Statham's two-state measure.

Despite the skepticism expressed by some Californians, many believe the recent vote will at least command the attention of Sacramento decision makers. And, of course, some will continue to press for dissolution. If conflict occurs among this group, it will likely be over the boundaries for the new state. Some advocate dividing the state so that the Bay Area and Sacramento are in the north, but the more long-standing north-south demarcation has been just above Los Angeles. Under this latter scheme, northern California would have most of the geography and resources, but southern California would still dominate in terms of population.

As attractive as splitting the state may be to some, the two-step process of obtaining legislative approval and then congressional approval for a division is formidable. Only the 1859 proposal made it past the first hurdle. Public opinion on a division has been lopsidedly in opposition over the years. Yet, buoyed by the support for a new state in the 27 northern counties, Statham [has introduced legislation in the 1993 legislature to carve the state into] three states.

The rift between the urban and rural counties is based on a combination of politics and economics. The legislature could attempt to heal the situation by emphasizing regional approaches to resolving issues of a regional nature, but this concept of regional government is still in the planning stages.

III.   POLITICS: PARTIES, INTEREST GROUPS, AND PACS

Politics in the American states is changing. Political parties, once the backbone of the U.S. political system and the chief force in state government, are becoming less influential, or so say many observers. As Malcolm Jewell and David Olson point out, "It has become a truism that party organizations are declining in importance, and there is no reason to anticipate a reversal of that trend." [1] Other political scientists, however, argue that parties "are an adaptable and durable force" in the states as "they remain the principal agents for making nominations, contesting elections, recruiting leaders, and providing a link between citizens and their governments." [2] Whether they are in decline or have just assumed new roles, most observers agree political parties are not what they used to be in our political system.

But what are political parties? This question must be addressed before the reasons for these different interpretations can be understood. Are they the organizations from precinct to national convention—*the party in organization?* Are they the individuals who run, win, and control government under a party label—*the party in office?* Or are they the voters themselves, who identify more with a particular party and vote accordingly—*the party in the electorate?* Political parties are all three, diverse in definition, and ever changing in their impact on state government.

Perhaps the clearest signal that parties sway voters less than they once did is the rise of split-ticket voting. In state and local elections in 1956, only 28 percent of the voters who identified themselves as either Democrats or Republicans did not vote the straight party line but split their ticket by voting for candidates of both parties; in 1980, 51 percent split their ticket. [3] In 1986, 20 percent of those identifying themselves as Democrats and 17 percent of those identifying themselves as Republicans voted for the U.S. Senate candidate of the opposing party. [4] This divided party voting and its impact is discussed in further detail in the introduction to Part I.

What's Happened to the Parties?

Various explanations have been offered for the decline of political parties. Direct primaries—the means by which party voters can participate directly in the nomination process rather than have party leaders select candidates—certainly have curtailed the influence of party organizations. By 1920 most of the states had adopted the direct primary. [5] No longer could party organizations or party bosses rule the nominating process with an iron hand, dominate the election campaign, and distribute patronage positions and benefits at will. The ability to circumvent official party channels and appeal directly to the electorate greatly increased the power of individual candidates. A candidate's personality has taken on new importance as party affiliation has become less influential in determining voting behavior.

In the political environment of the 1990s, parties are challenged by the mass media, interest groups, independent political consultants, and political action committees—vehicles that perform many of the historic functions of the political party. Public opinion polls, rather than party ward and precinct organizations, survey the "faithful." Today,

> . . . [P]olitical consultants, answerable only to their client candidates and independent of the political parties, have inflicted severe damage upon the party system and masterminded the modern triumph of personality cults over party politics in the United States. [6]

One analyst argues, however, that the rise of the political consultant has opened up the political process through the use of polls and other techniques. Now candidates can talk about the issues voters are concerned about without the "party communications filter." [7]

Candidates have also changed, and some of these changes do not help the parties. For example, we are seeing more independent candidates running for office. These independents are no less political than other candidates, they are simply independent of the two major parties. At the national level, the 1992 presidential run by Texas billionaire Ross Perot is an example of this phenomenon. At the state level, two current governors, Walter Hickel of Alaska and Lowell Weicker of Connecticut, both ran and are now serving as independents. There are others.

More important is the rise of the self-starting candidate with both fiscal and political resources of his or her own. These candidates can afford to run for office on their own, needing the party only for its nomination to get on the ballot. Such "candidate-centered campaigns are becoming more prevalent at the state level," and as they do, "party-line voting is declining." [8] Alan Ehrenhalt argues that "political careers are open to ambition now in a way that has not been true in America in most of this century.[9] He believes these self-starting candidates are motivated by their personal ambition, which drives their entry into politics. Because they can "manipulate the instruments of the system—the fund raising, the personal campaigning, the opportunities to express themselves in public—[they] confront very few limits on their capacity to reach the top." [10]

Changes in government itself are another explanation for party decline. Social welfare programs at the federal, state, and local levels of government have replaced the welfare role once played by party organizations. Those in need now turn to government agencies rather than to ward and precinct party leaders, even though domestic cutbacks during the Reagan-Bush years, and projected future cutbacks tied to a weakened economy, have reduced the ability of government agencies at all levels to meet those needs.

To most citizens, parties are important only during the election season. Our system is unlike that of most European countries, where there are rigid election schedules in which campaigning is limited to a specific time period. The American state and local government election season is generally thought to start around Labor Day in early September and run until election day in early November. Cynics believe that this is too long, and that in most voters' minds, the season really begins at the end of the World Series in late October. Of course, the candidates have been at work for months, even years, getting ready for this unofficial election season, but the impact of other events, such as the World Series, often conspires to distract the electorate.

Ehrenhalt makes another intriguing observation on the fate of the major political parties in the minds of the citizens. He argues that "solutionists" have become our new majority party. Those with "fuzzy optimism" promise that we can solve any of our problems and that "everything is possible" if we set our minds on a solution. "Voters, who are routinely informed by candidates that their problems can and will be solved, have a right to turn cynical when the same problems are still on the table . . . years later." [11] Such cynicism quickly turns to apathy and nonparticipation in politics, regardless of party affiliation.

Signs of Party Resurgence

Yet not everyone is ready to declare the parties moribund. As noted, the party process is still the means of selecting candidates for national, state, and, in some cases, local office. Control of state legislatures is determined by which party has the majority, with the sole exception of Nebraska. Appointments to state government positions usually go to the party colleagues of state legislators or of the governor.

Although party in organization and party in the electorate are weaker than they once were, party in office may be gaining strength, argues Alan Rosenthal of the Eagleton Institute of Politics at Rutgers University. Legislators are increasingly preoccupied with winning reelection. The "art of politicking" may be superseding the "art of legislating." [12] Party caucuses have begun to play an important role in selecting the legislative leadership, assigning committee and other responsibilities, and establishing positions on issues. In fact, the party in organization may not be as weak as many think. Since the 1960s, budgets and staffs have grown in size, staffs have become more professional, party services and activities have increased, and elected leaders may be even more involved in party affairs. [13]

Regional Differences in Party Politics

Of course, party politics differ in each state. As Samuel C. Patterson writes, "In some places parties are strong and vigorous; in other places, they are sluggish; in yet others, moribund. But, on balance, the state parties appear remarkably vibrant." [14]

New York appears to be content with its four-party structure of Conservative, Republican, Democratic, and Liberal parties; Nebraska operates on a nonpartisan basis for many of its elections; Wisconsin still has deep ties to populism; and California, once represented by a liberal northern half and conservative southern half, is expanding to include the strengthening Hispanic and Asian minorities. The political growth and impact of these minorities are increasing as they learn how to play the game of politics by American rules. The geographical split in the Golden State is even leading some to advocate splitting the

state into two states, as discussed in Part II.

Today, few states are consistently dominated by one party. This is true even in the South, which for many years was the Democrats' stronghold. Southern states now see growth around urban centers shaking up old party lines as "yuppies," northern corporate executives, and retirees join the "Bubbas" and presidential Republicans of old to create more competitive two-party systems.

At one time, being a Democrat was practically a necessity to vote and hold office in southern states. Party primaries decided who would be elected; general elections were simply ratifying events. But the old one-party dominance is fast eroding as is the role of the primary in determining who will govern. In some Southern states, the Republicans are now finding themselves in contested, sometimes even nasty, party primaries. Why? With an increasing possibility of winning against the Democrats in the general election, being the Republican candidate is more attractive than it once was.

While still a political minority, the Republicans' winning trend is causing southern Democrats to question the political "sanity" of continuing to hold divisive party primaries in which Democrats battle with each other when seeking the party nomination, only to have their Republican challengers use these same arguments to defeat them in the general election. In effect, the primaries expose weaknesses in the Democratic candidates that the Republicans exploit. In fact, the North Carolina legislature recently reduced the percent of the vote needed to win in the first primary from 50 percent to 40 percent in an attempt to forestall divisive second primaries.

Not all of these Republican wins are beneficial to the party: in February 1989, the former grand wizard of the Ku Klux Klan and organizer of the National Association for the Advancement of White People, David Duke, won a seat in the Louisiana legislature as a Republican. In a bitter and often racist campaign, Duke defeated John Treen, a longtime Republican party functionary and brother of the first Republican governor of Louisiana in this century. Treen had the strong support of newly elected president George Bush and former president Ronald Reagan—an unprecedented national-level intrusion into a local race. Within three months, Duke not only had become a folk hero for many Louisianans, but his "avowed racism in an area that's racially polarized" intensified the state's problems.[15]

In 1990 Duke challenged Democratic U.S. senator J. Bennett Johnston and received over 40 percent of the vote in Louisiana's unique "you'all come" primary in which everyone runs in the same primary for the nomination and election. In 1991, Duke unsuccessfully sought the governorship and came in a close second in the open primary behind former governor Edwin Edwards and ahead of incumbent governor Buddy Roemer, who had recently switched to the Republican party for his reelection effort. Edwards easily bested Duke in the runoff election. Duke was finally halted in spring 1992 when he reached for the Republican nomination for the presidency only to find that conservative columnist Pat Buchanan had caught the attention of dissatisfied Republican voters. The final nail in his effort was driven by the independent presidential candidacy of Ross Perot who many saw as the "real" political outsider.

Interest Group Politics

Are interest groups an evil that must be endured or are they a necessary part of the governing process? Is their impact on state government primarily beneficial or harmful? Perhaps most importantly, do the interests that groups seek to advance or protect benefit the whole state or only the lobbies themselves? State officials, pressured by a myriad of interest groups, wrestle with these questions and reach different answers.

Interest groups' influence on the political process varies from state to state. Business groups are by far the most predominant; the influence of labor groups pales in comparison. Thus, the interest group structure of most states is business oriented and conservative. Lately, however, groups representing government employees, local government officials, and the public interest (for example, Common Cause and environmental protection groups) have increased their visibility and effectiveness in state politics. According to a fifty-state study by Clive Thomas and Ronald Hrebenar, there are nine states in which interest groups have a dominant impact vis-à-vis other political bodies on public policy, and eighteen states in which interest groups are complementary to other political bodies; that is, they must "work in conjunction with or are constrained by other parts of the political system." Eighteen other states fall between these two categories of strength, and five states appear to have interest groups that are at best complementary if not subordinate to these other political institutions.[16]

An interest group's effectiveness depends on the representatives it sends to the state legislature and executive branch agencies—the so-called professional lobbyists. Who are these people? Usually they have served in government and are already known to those they seek to influence. Their ranks include former agency heads, legislators, and even governors in private law practice who have clients with special interests. Some of the most effective lobbyists represent several interests. In North Carolina, a survey of legislative lobbyists found that the three most influential lobbyists in the 1991 session represented fifteen, sixteen, and seventeen clients, respectively.[17]

The relationship between political parties and interest groups in the states tends to follow a discernible pattern: the more competitive the party system, the weaker the interest group system. More specifically, "the stronger the parties, the less leeway to operate and the less influence interest groups have." [18] This apparently symbiotic relationship between parties and interest groups largely determines who controls state government.

Theoretically, in a competitive, two-party state, the stakes are more likely to be out in the open as one party fights the other for control. Conversely, in the noncompetitive, one-party state, the stakes are less easy to see as interest groups do battle with each other to maintain or change the status quo. Again, in theory, the power of the party flows from the voters through their elected representatives; the power of interest groups is derived from their numbers, money, and lobbying skill. But in practice the relationship is not as clear as this explanation would suggest. In fact, once the parties organize state government, state politics usually become the special quarry of interest groups—except, of course, on distinctive, party-line issues (such as selecting the leadership), or when there are other institutions with political strength, such as the governor or the media.

The Role of State Governments

State governments have two main roles vis-à-vis the other actors in state politics: they set the "rules of the game" in which parties and interest groups operate, and then they regulate their financial activities. The rules govern the nomination and election processes and the ways in which interests are allowed to press their demands. However, the rules change at a glacial pace because those who know how to play the game fear that change will upset the balance of power—or at least their spot in the power system. In fact, it often takes a lawsuit by someone outside that power system to change the rules or a scandal to tighten financial reporting requirements.

Laws regulating campaign finance have been on the books for almost one-hundred years. In 1892, New York and Massachusetts adopted laws in reaction to the corruption of the day requiring candidates to report how they spent their campaign money. Other states followed with a variety of "publicity laws," restrictions on corporate contributions, and limits on campaign expenditures. By 1925, a majority of states had some restrictions on their books, but these often were not enforced. [19]

Recently, the states have adopted policies that increase their regulatory role regarding political parties. Public disclosure and campaign finance laws are more strict, and political action committees (PACs) are monitored with a more watchful eye due to their increased activity. Some of these regulations have been successfully challenged in the courts. For example, the Republican party of Connecticut won its fight to allow some nonparty members, that is, independents, to vote in their primary despite a contrary state law, and California found its ban on pre-primary party endorsements invalidated. [20]

Part III provides some insight into politics at the state level. Rob Gurwitt of *Governing* explores the "mirage" of campaign reform in the states. Amy Young of Common Cause looks at the problems associated with getting out the vote. And Herbert Alexander, Jeffrey Schwartz, and Eugene Goss in *State Government News* look at one of the more interesting experiments in the states: public financing of political campaigns.

Notes

1. Malcolm Jewell and David Olson, *American State Political Parties and Elections* (Homewood, Ill.: Dorsey Press, 1982), 280.

2. John F. Bibby, Cornelius P. Cotter, James L. Gibson, and Robert J. Huckshorn, "Parties in State Politics," in *Politics in the American States,* 5th ed., ed. Virginia Gray, Herbert Jacob, and Robert B. Albritton (Glenview, Ill.: Scott, Foresman, 1990), 120.

3. David E. Price, *Bringing Back the Parties* (Washington, D.C.: CQ Press, 1984), 15.

4. Survey by ABC News, November 4, 1986, reported in *Public Opinion* 9:4 (January-February 1987): 34.

5. Price, *Bringing Back the Parties,* 32.

6. Larry Sabato, *The Rise of Political Consultants: New Ways of Winning Elections* (New York: Basic Books, 1981), 3.

7. Walter DeVries, "American Campaign Consulting: Trends and Concerns," *PS: Political Science and Politics* 12:1 (March 1989): 24.

8. Stephen A. Salmore and Barbara G. Salmore, "The Transformation of State Electoral Politics," in *The State of the States,* 2d ed., ed. Carl Van Horn (Washington, D.C.: CQ Press, 1993), 51.

9. Alan Ehrenhalt, *The United States of Ambition* (New York: Times Books, 1992), 272.

10. Ibid., 273.

11. Alan Ehrenhalt, "Solutionists': America's Majority Party," *Congressional Quarterly Weekly Report,* September 20, 1986, 2251.

12. Alan Rosenthal, "If the Party's Over, Where's All That Noise Coming From?" *State Government* 57:2 (Summer 1984): 50, 54.

13. Timothy Conlan, Ann Martino, and Robert Dilger, "State Parties in the 1980s: Adaptation, Resurgence, and Continuing Constraints," *Intergovernmental Perspective* 20:4 (Fall 1984): 23.

14. Samuel C. Patterson, "The Persistence of State Parties," in Van Horn, 169.

15. Associated Press, "Former KKK Head Wins La. Election," [Raleigh] *News and Observer,* February 19, 1989, 1A. Jason Berry, "In Louisiana, the Hazards of Duke," *Washington Post National Weekly Edition,* May 22-28, 1989, 25.

16. Clive S. Thomas and Ronald J. Hrebenar, "Interest Groups in the States," in *Politics in the American States,* ed. Virginia Gray, Herbert Jacob, and Robert B. Albritton (Glenview, Ill.: Scott, Foresman, 1990), 147-148.

17. Kim Kebschull Otten, *Article II: A Guide to the 1993-1994 N.C. Legislature* (Raleigh: North Carolina Center for Public Policy Research, forthcoming).

18. Clive S. Thomas and Ronald J. Hrebenar, "Interest Groups in the States," in Gray, Jacob, and Albritton, 127.

19. Kim Kebschull, et al., *Campaign Disclosure Laws* (Raleigh: North Carolina Center for Public Policy Research, 1990), 20.

20. Patterson, "The Resistance of State Parties," 197. The cases were *Tashjian v. Connecticut* (1986) and *Secretary of State of California v. San Francisco Democratic Central Committee* (1989).

The Mirage of Campaign Reform

by Rob Gurwitt

Let's start with a short test.

Imagine a state somewhere in the Midwest. The public's disgust with politics has boiled over. A small band of reformers, arguing that campaign money has been corrupting the legislature, seizes the moment and puts a measure on the ballot to stifle the influence of private interests in the campaign process.

They propose setting aside enough public money every two years to give every candidate with a serious campaign as much as it takes to conduct it. Private funding would be legal, but everything possible would be done to discourage it; if your opponent took private funds, you would get public funds to match.

The campaign gets raucous. Some opponents of the measure argue that public funds have no place in campaigns. Others bombard radio talk shows with complaints that taxpayers' money shouldn't go to support politicians. The reformers counter that only when there's enough public funding to run a full-scale campaign will candidates stop bellying up to the special-interest bar. Even better, they say, candidates won't have any incentive to turn to fat cats in a close race because all it would do is generate more public money spent against them.

Throughout the fall, polls show a cynical electorate going back and forth on the question. Half the streets in the state are festooned with bright blue signs reading, "We Deserve Better. Yes on Public Financing," and red signs countering, "Your Money? For Politicians??? Vote No!" A to-do erupts when newspapers reveal that the opposition is being funded by the state's major corporations, but it quiets down after a report that the other side has been tapping the liberal Democratic network in Hollywood. Finally, Election Day rolls around. Early returns show the measure going down narrowly, but it pulls ahead when the numbers start flowing in from the cities, and finally passes.

Here's the question. It's now 2002, a decade later. Which of the following has happened?:

(A) The reform law has served mainly to create a multimillion-dollar industry of consultants, pollsters and campaign professionals, all of them skilled at running "independent expenditure" campaigns for the corporations, unions, trade associations and ideological groups that just want to "participate" on

Rob Gurwitt is a staff writer for *Governing*. This article is reprinted from *Governing* 5:11 (August 1992): 48-52, 55.

behalf of their favored candidates. The Supreme Court says it is unconstitutional to prohibit these expenditures. Because of them, special interests are as powerful in the state as ever.

(B) Legislators, faced with tight budgets, seem chronically unable to find enough money to fund the provision guaranteeing extra public funding for candidates whose opponents use private contributions. So the public money turns out to be nothing more than a floor. When a campaign is really close and hard-fought, private funding is what makes the difference.

(C) Campaign costs, which were supposed to go down after the reform law passed, keep going up. Candidates with rich friends believe their chances of winning go up if they spend every dollar of private money they can raise, even if their opponents are given public money to match them. The reform law not only hasn't controlled costs—there is talk that it is going to bankrupt the state.

(D) Nobody really knows what the reforms would have accomplished, because the Supreme Court has thrown them out. The court said that the provision matching public money against excess private funding violates the free speech rights of the person who wants to spend the extra private money.

(E) The reformers were right: The system survives all its court challenges, it wrings private money out of campaigns and holds costs down, it allows candidates to spend their time campaigning rather than raising funds, and it gives legislators the freedom to cast their votes without worrying about their campaign budgets. All in all, it is a tonic for democracy.

And now that you've made your choice, here's the real question: Why did you just snicker when you got to E?

It has been almost 20 years since the campaign reform movement built up its first real head of steam in the aftermath of Watergate. At the time, there was a widespread feeling of optimism, a belief that effective reform was just a matter of legislating the appropriate limits and disclosure laws. Congress passed them, states passed them, and now it is hard to find anyone who believes it's that simple anymore. A problem that seems as though it ought to be solvable—how to keep campaign money from influencing the decisions of government—is proving an enormously frustrating puzzle.

True, the country has made some progress since Watergate. There was a time when it was next to impossible to find out where candidates got their money. Now, every state requires disclosure of the amounts and sources of campaign contributions, although some—Ohio, for example—make gathering the information an unpardonable endurance test for the public.

In addition, some 20 states prohibit candidates from accepting direct corporate donations, and more than half the states have tried to curb the undue influence of any one contributor by limiting individual donations; a smaller number limit giving by political action committees. Twelve states provide direct public financing to individual candidates, although several of those systems have proved irrelevant in practice.

Still, it is hard to find people who think the system is significantly better; many insist it is worse. Private money is ubiquitous in all its forms—direct contributions, independent expenditures, "soft money," "bundled" donations—and the routes it travels to candidates only multiply with each new effort to restrict them. Campaigns continue to become more expensive. Legislators complain that the pressure of raising money is giving them less and less time for legislating or engaging voters. Donors complain that they are under increasing pressure to give to legislators who preside over their interests.

Perhaps most important, the voters themselves are increasingly cynical about the role of money in elections. They are convinced that monied interests can buy whatever they need in the legislative process, and they believe that the elections system perpetuates the status quo. "Most people perceive that politicians become careerists because the campaign finance system gives them the advantage as incumbents," says Gary Moncrief, a Boise State University political scientist.

In short, it's hard to escape the feeling that much of the campaign reform effort has been a waste of time. "The terms of the debate have not changed much since the early 1970s, when I first got into it," says Daniel Lowenstein, a law professor at UCLA and the first chairman of California's Fair Political Practices Commission. "And to the extent they have, they've changed for the worse: More prominence is being given to even more simple-minded ideas."

That may stem from simple frustration. If anything, the past two decades of campaign finance reform have given the country a lesson in the difficulties of legislating change. They have demonstrated that good intentions have little to do with actual results, that it's hard to keep reform efforts from falling prey to political maneuvering, that Republicans and Democrats diverge fundamentally in the way they view the issue, and that beyond a certain point no one seems able to agree even on what they want to accomplish.

Above all, they have made it clear that trying to force the system to conform to some preconceived set of ideals is doomed to fail. "We live in a democratic and pluralistic society, and you just cannot structure a regulatory system that will cover everything," says Herb Alexander, a campaign finance specialist and director of the Citizens' Research Foundation in Los Angeles.

The elections process is like a minor ecosystem; changing one small part of it can yield entirely unforeseen results elsewhere. Wisconsin, for instance, is one of three states that provide public financing for state House and Senate campaigns (the others are Minnesota and Hawaii). The idea was to level the playing field for incumbents and challengers, and to cut reliance on PAC contributions. But the system has gone off-kilter. Not only have legislative candidates been ignoring it routinely in close contests, opting to forego public money in exchange for freedom from spending limits, but the parties have been using it mainly to subsidize nuisance challenges to incumbents on the opposing side.

"If you want to keep an incumbent busy in some seat," says Democratic state Senator John Medinger, "you get a sacrificial lamb. He or she gets $8,000 or so of public money and keeps the incumbent home, and then the parties target the eight or nine seats where they're willing to blow the limits." Those eight or nine crucial elections, of course, are fought out with private funding.

"Public financing is a nice ethical thing to do," says Medinger, who is retiring this year, "and it's certainly good government. It just may not be good politics in every case." What has happened in Wisconsin is certainly not what the state's reformers had in mind.

One reason reforms can be counted on to produce unanticipated consequences is that campaign money is remarkably protean, not unlike the liquid-metal robot in *Terminator 2*. Just when you think you've dealt with it, it rises from the floor behind your back.

Take Arizona. The state has the strictest contribution limits in the country, $240 per candidate for individuals and most PACs in 1992. (The amount is indexed for inflation.) With contribution ceilings so low, you'd think that no legislator would feel a debt to any individual donor, and that interests trying to influence the legislature would look for some means other than campaign giving. You

Searching for the Cheap Seats

If you're hoping to break into politics with a run for the state legislature, you might want to think about heading for someplace as sparsely populated as Montana or Idaho. House seats in both states are flat-out bargains—winning one consumed less than $5,000 on average four years ago, and hasn't gone up much since.

There are plenty of other states where campaign costs haven't risen beyond the reach of ordinary folk, but identifying them can be difficult. Because the states treat campaign disclosure forms differently, it's almost impossible to compare legislative campaign costs for all 50 of them. The accompanying chart shows average and median costs for state House seats in 11 states—those covered in a joint project led by political scientists Anthony Gierzynski of Northern Illinois University and Gary Moncrief of Boise State.

In all cases, the average cost is higher than the median, or the mid-point of all campaigns, because a few high-spending contests have pulled the figure up.

Different costs among states can be traced to anything from varying district sizes to the expense of media markets to the degree of campaign professionalization that has taken place. It would be unthinkable, for example, to run for the California Assembly without paid staff, consultants and pollsters; in Montana, where legislative careerism has yet to take hold, you'd probably be laughed out of the state for using them.

There are other forces at play as well. Minnesota and Washington are close to each other in number of people and professionalization, but it costs a fair bit less to run in Minnesota. The reason probably is Minnesota's public financing law, which generally keeps spending down.

The escalation of campaign expense varies within states as well. Moncrief has found, for instance, that the cost of winning a House seat in Washington state grew by about 25 percent between 1980 and 1990, controlling for inflation. But the cost of a Senate seat rose by an inflation-adjusted 300 percent. The reason: The House remained under firm Democratic control during the decade, while the Senate became the crucial battleground between the parties.

The Cost of Running: State House Campaign Expenditures, 1988

State	Average	Median
California	$370,722	$302,128
Idaho	4,425	2,244
Minnesota	13,244	13,144
Missouri	9,618	6,921
Montana	2,692	2,265
New Jersey	48,033	33,670
North Carolina	12,085	10,025
Oregon	35,982	30,333
Pennsylvania	18,462	13,944
Washington	25,811	20,145
Wisconsin	14,868	11,812

Sources: Created by Anthony Gierzynski from data collected in a joint project with David Breaux, William Cassey, Keith Hamm, Malcolm Jewell, Gary Moncrief and Joel Thompson.

Source: Rob Gurwitt, "Searching for the Cheap Seats," *Governing* 5:11 (August 1992): 50.

would, of course, be wrong.

For one thing, political committees don't sit still once they've given all they can to candidates. Instead, some mount independent expenditure campaigns—that is, campaigns on behalf of or against a particular candidate that are separate from the candidate's own campaign. In the 1990 elections, for example, the political action committee run by US West Corp. gave maximum contributions to the candidates it was supporting, and still had half of the money it had raised left over. But there were about a dozen key races that would decide the majority in each house, so the PAC mounted independent campaigns in several of them, trying to help the GOP win control. "I refused to sit back and not have the opportunity for US West to participate in the political process," says Barry Aarons, the PAC's director.

At the same time, Arizona's strict contribution limits have hardly wrung individual influence brokers out of the system. Since putting a viable campaign together in $240 increments is hard work, anyone who can convince others to contribute to candidate X is bound to become a pretty valuable friend of X's. In fact, some candidates are bypassing PACs altogether and searching out people—somehow, many of them turn out to be lobbyists—who can persuade donors who might have contributed to a PAC to contribute directly to the candidate instead. As one Arizona lobbyist points out, "Some candidates make a great to-do about the fact that they don't accept PAC contributions, but then they solicit individual PAC members for direct contributions."

The problem is by no means unique to Arizona: Donors and candidates all across the country have shown endless inventiveness in getting around contribution limits. A few years ago, the *Charlotte Observer* in North Carolina told the story of a party activist who reported being handed an envelope containing $15,000

in checks from optometrists to a statewide candidate. Each check was for less than $100, the level at which it would have had to be reported; the total amount, however, was well in excess of the $4,000 to which an optometrists' PAC would have been limited. The head of the state optometric association saw nothing wrong with that sort of "bundling." "The Optometric Society has not functioned politically as a group," he said. "If we were, we would be organized legally as a PAC."

In essence, says Alexander, "some of these laws just exchange the big giver for the big solicitor." Or as Paul Gillie, research director for Washington State's Public Disclosure Commission, puts it, "Money is like water: It will find its way no matter what obstacles it encounters."

This would be a sobering thought even under the most statesmanlike of circumstances, with incumbents committed to improving the system regardless of the impact on their own careers and parties willing to ignore partisan advantage in the interest of doing the right thing. But of course, we don't have those circumstances. We have incumbents who don't want to do anything to help challengers, and Democrats and Republicans whose main goal in legislative life is to achieve—or to keep—majority status.

That shouldn't be very surprising. "If you're in political office and like it and want to get reelected, why should you help your opponent?" asks Alan Rosenthal, director of the Eagleton Institute at Rutgers University. "There aren't many areas in which we believe that people should encourage their competition—we don't believe that Johnson & Johnson should go out and help Merck."

That applies to parties at least as much as it does to individuals. Democrats control most state legislative bodies in this country. They want the leaders of those bodies to continue to be able to shift money from their own campaign funds—stocked with PAC donations—to the campaigns of Democratic allies. Republicans have no trouble raising money from individual private donors. They do not like the idea of limiting the amount of money in private contributions that a candidate will be allowed to accept. "Campaign finance is a cutthroat business, and each party will try to devise a system that helps it best," says Ran Coble, who directs the North Carolina Center for Public Policy Research.

That dynamic [was] on display [in 1992] in Washington State, where two separate campaign reform initiatives [were] proposed for the November [1992] ballot. One of them, backed by the GOP, qualified after a petition campaign in which people were paid to gather signatures—a new practice in Washington. The other, supported by a coalition that includes the League of Women Voters, Common Cause and a variety of prominent Democrats, collected barely enough signatures to qualify.

The Republicans' measure [would place] limits on the size of contributions, [prohibit] transfers between candidates, and [require] unions to get the written permission of members before using their payroll deductions to fund a PAC. It in no way [tried] to restrict spending, or the overall amount a candidate [could] raise.

The rival measure, on the other hand, would involve spending limits. Candidates would not have to abide by them, but if they did, they would be given the reward of being allowed to take larger contributions. In addition, no candidate could get more than a third of his or her money from PACs and party caucuses.

[The Republican measure passed handily, while the Democratic measure was defeated.]

No one knows whether variable contribution limits could pass constitutional muster—the Supreme Court essentially equates political

spending with free speech—but Mark Brown of the Washington Federation of State Employees insists that spending limits are vital. "Campaign finance reform without expenditure limits will clearly favor Republicans," he says. That is because, he argues, the groups that support Democrats are currently being priced out of the market. "The labor movement in recent years has come to realize that we simply cannot remain competitive in the political arena with the cost of campaigns skyrocketing as they have," Brown says.

There are some problems with spending limits quite apart from the constitutional questions. There is evidence, for instance, that spending limits tend to hurt challengers. "Over the years," says Daniel Lowenstein, "we have found out that spending a substantial amount of money is more crucial to challengers than it is to incumbents. So spending limits are more of a problem than they may once have seemed." Moreover, as Herb Alexander once pointed out, "It is altogether impossible to prevent a savvy election lawyer from finding a hole in expenditure ceilings wide enough to drive a campaign message through."

The debate over spending limits, though, does serve to highlight a basic conflict between equally respectable political values: Trying to keep the barriers to entering politics as low as possible, versus giving challengers the freedom to spend whatever they need in order to win.

But there is another conflict that goes even further to explain the frustrations of campaign finance reform, and that is the discord between its fundamental aim—removing the influence of special interests from the legislative process—and the notion that everyone ought to be able to participate in elections by giving money to his or her candidate of choice. "The problem in campaign finance," says Larry Sabato, a political scientist at the University of Virginia, "is that people will not accept the fact that we can't have it all. We want completely clean elections

Anatomy of a Campaign

When Ray Moore of Seattle celebrated his first election campaign victory in 1978, he had no inkling that just 12 years down the road he would be setting an unenviable record in Washington state politics. Running for a state Senate seat against an incumbent in 1978, he had to spend $40,000.

Senator Moore's bid for reelection in 1982 cost $65,000. In 1986 the cost went up steeply, to $110,000. But even that did not prepare him for 1990, when he set a record for a state legislative race in Washington—$286,867. Even adjusted for inflation, that's an increase of 357 percent in 12 years.

"It's a record I would prefer not to hold," he says.

Where does the money go in a state legislative campaign that costs more than a quarter of a million dollars?

In Senator Moore's campaign, the largest single item was for a direct mail promotion, which accounted for 30 percent ($86,059) of the total expenditures. Costs for the mail program included printing, postage and mail house service for approximately 20 mailings. Direct mailings are important in the senator's district because it is an urban area that includes many large apartment buildings where doorbelling—one of Moore's favorite campaign tactics—is impossible.

Consultant services were the next most expensive item at $64,615—23 percent of the campaign's total cost. The consultant category included $16,062 for polling.

Administrative items—campaign staff salaries, office equipment, phones, rent, postage, office supplies and miscellaneous costs came to $43,687—15 percent of the total.

TV and radio advertising were fourth most expensive at $27,741.

Senator Moore holds fund-raising events throughout his four-year Senate term, and the expenditures for these fund raisers are included in the cost of his next campaign. From 1987-1990, 17 fund-raising events cost the 1990 campaign $18,486. His other major campaign cost was $16,474 for contributions to other candidates and issue campaigns.

The balance of the expenditures for Senator Moore's campaign—$29,805—went for phone banks, a doorbelling program, billboards, yard signs and travel and meals. The campaign wound up with a surplus of approximately $1,200.

Senator Moore says that he would like to see spending limits for campaigns, "but I'm not sure the general public cares how much is spent. When I raised and spent the most money in a legislative race in this state's history, there was no outpouring of public outrage. Only the media grumbled," he observed.

And given past experience, he is not certain that campaign reform would accomplish its goal.

"Campaign reform?" he asked. "In this state we've resisted that, plus other reforms. And when we do try campaign reform, it only seems to make things worse. Public disclosure hasn't deterred special interest financing. Its only notable result is another mountain of paperwork and another bureaucracy," he said, "and still the public doesn't know who's really buying elections."

The senator said that he does hear sharp criticism about the quality of campaign tactics and the length of campaigns. "Perhaps legislative efforts would be better spent in these areas," he says.

Source: Tommy Heal, "Anatomy of a Campaign," *State Legislatures* 18:5 (May 1992): 20.

with no tainted money, and we want full and unfettered rights of free speech and association. You cannot have both. If you're not going to tinker with the First Amendment, you have to accept the fact that you can't dam the flow of political money."

Does that mean that effective campaign finance reform is a dead end? Given the conflicts between basic political values, the fluid dynamics of political money and the difficulties inherent in asking legislators and political parties to tackle the matter, it's understandable that many people think so. But despite all the disappointments and unpleasant consequences of the campaign reform movement over the past two decades, the fact remains that there is still useful work to be done.

At the very least, it is time to recognize that in this field, as in many others, there are limits to what government regulation can accomplish—that "good enough" is the best we can hope for. That is not to say that reform efforts are pointless. There are regulations, such as contribution limits and even public financing, that have helped temper some of the grossest excesses of the past, and proposals for free television time and cut-rate mailing costs may also help. But it's naive to expect new legislation to produce a perfect system, especially since campaigns have evolved to the point where every new limit seems to hurt as much as it helps. Boosting individual contributions at the expense of "special interest" donors, for example, has obvious public appeal, but it may also harm groups, such as teachers or anti-abortionists or women's rights advocates, whose ability to have an impact on a campaign rests in pooling many small donations. In the long run, legislation that works to keep the various sources of funding in balance, rather than trying to eliminate one or another, may prove the most stable reform.

It may also go the farthest toward protecting the one element of reform that seems most in need of safeguarding: the system's openness. With strong disclosure laws, the system at least has a chance to correct itself. As Larry Sabato once wrote, disclosure "is the greatest single check on the excesses of campaign finance, for it encourages corrective action, whether by the politicians themselves, by the judiciary through prosecution in the courts, or by the voters at the polls."

"You've got to let the voters see what's going on, and then let them make their own decision," says Kent Cooper, a longtime official of the Federal Elections Commission. "If they want to reelect a guy who's representing a cash constituency more than them, fine: If they make an informed choice, the system's not corrupt." Perhaps the most basic reform mechanism, in other words, is to make it as easy as possible for the public to find out who's getting money from whom, and to avoid reforms that force money underground.

That seems like an obvious idea, but you couldn't tell by looking at its reception in many legislatures. Most states require all candidates for statewide and legislative office to file campaign disclosure reports in a central state office, although a few—Ohio, North Carolina, Vermont and Nevada—do not. But only 20 states require listing the occupation and principal place of employment of contributors, and only five—Florida, Louisiana, Maryland, Ohio and Wyoming—require all contributions to be itemized, regardless of the amount. There are even some states—Ohio and Wisconsin, for instance—that allow so-called "conduits," which are set up by special interest groups to funnel contributions by their members to candidates; the group can take credit for the money, but all that gets reported is the individual's contribution.

Even more important, in those states that have watchdog disclosure agencies, they are treated like poor stepchildren. They rarely have the staff or resources to analyze what is happening to the campaign finance system as a whole, to perform specific audits of candidates' returns or even to make the data available in a form that allows people to figure out, say, how much the dairy industry has contributed to a particular candidate. Even the most highly regarded campaign disclosure agencies—New Jersey's Election Law Enforcement Commission and California's Fair Political Practices Commission, for example—have had to withstand severe budget cuts over the past few years. "We were like a thin man entering a famine as we went into this recession," says Fred Herrmann, director of New Jersey's ELEC. Until states get serious about disclosure, nothing else they do will amount to much.

That is especially true because, short of outlawing all private money—which the Supreme Court would not allow—money will always be a factor in elections. Reform legislation can force it further underground, or it can pull it into the open, but, as Cooper says, "the schemes will be there and the people operating in the gray area will be there." Disclosure is no ideal answer; it may simply be the best one we have.

Getting Out the Voters

by Amy E. Young

President Bush may have vetoed the National Voter Registration Act in June, but state legislatures have made important strides toward getting more citizens registered to vote. Connecticut, Kansas and New York recently enacted motor-voter registration laws, under which the motor vehicles department is authorized to distribute voter registration forms when citizens renew or receive driver's licenses.

The United States has one of the lowest voter turnouts among major democratic nations. Barely 50 percent of eligible voters participated in the 1988 presidential election—and one culprit is restrictive registration laws, according to a 1988 *New York Times*/CBS post-election poll of non-voters.

Registration laws vary from state to state and often involve complicated identification procedures, deadlines far in advance of Election Day or inconvenient hours and locations. In addition, some state registrars practice "selective purging"—the removal of previously registered voters from state rolls for failure to vote and other reasons.

Voter registration is a key factor in participation rates. While only 50 percent of eligible voters went to the polls in 1988, more than 80 percent of registered voters partici-

pated, according to the U.S. Census Bureau. To reach the more than 70 million Americans not yet registered, many CC [Common Cause] state organizations have lobbied successfully for motor-voter registration, mail-in registration, deadlines closer to Election Day and increased funding for election boards.

Among the reforms, motor-voter registration has been the most successful since it reaches nearly every eligible voter—especially hard-to-reach groups such as young people—and more efficiently tracks changes of address or name. The program can be "staff-active" as when agency staff ask citizens to register and assist with filling out forms, or "passive," when the forms are simply distributed with other agency documents.

Motor-voter systems are also cost-effective. The League of Women Voters (LWV) estimates that voter registration using deputy registrars costs between $1 and $15 per transaction while motor-voter systems cost between 3 and 33 cents.

Michigan established the first motor-voter system and, partly as a result, has

Amy E. Young is a staff writer at *Common Cause Magazine*. This article is reprinted from *Common Cause Magazine* 18:3 (Fall 1992): 37.

registered 86 percent of its eligible citizens. Currently, 28 states and the District of Columbia have some form of motor-voter registration and have met with similar successes. In 1984 Colorado's registration level was 59 percent; in 1988, after motor-voter was established, it rose to more than 80 percent.

In Connecticut more than 600,000 citizens are not registered to vote. To correct that, CC/Connecticut joined a coalition with the LWV, the state Civil Liberties Union, the state machinists union and others, and lobbied successfully for the motor-voter system. State registrars initially opposed the bill, says CC/Connecticut Executive Director Eric Lorenzini. "They worried that the bill would dilute their authority, create more work or encourage fraud," he explains. Prepared with success stories from other states' programs, the coalition quickly put those fears to rest.

When the bill takes effect January 1, 1994, Lorenzini expects a "dramatic increase" in the number of registered voters. Changes of names and addresses will be handled more efficiently, he adds.

After more than three years of lobbying by CC/Kansas, Gov. Jean Finney signed a motor-voter bill in July. The law also takes effect January 1, 1994.

Michael Woolf, CC/Kansas executive director, says traditional registration methods ignored the needs of Kansas's rural population. "This should reach well over 90 percent of the population and give people an opportunity they might not have had before," he says.

CC/Kansas's efforts were aided by the *Wichita Eagle*'s reporting project "Your Vote Counts," an experiment in election coverage. During recent state and municipal elections, the newspaper analyzed issues in depth, along with candidate positions and political ads. The editors also gave space to readers' questions and the candidates' responses. Post-election polls found that readers had a clearer understanding of the issues and felt a greater sense of participation in the process.

New York Gov. Mario Cuomo also signed motor-voter legislation [in 1992], but with a disappointing provision. The law stipulates that while agency personnel will distribute voter registration forms, they aren't allowed to give verbal assistance in completing the form.

"The availability of the forms should increase registration, but the gag rule will reduce the law's impact," laments CC/New York Executive Director Julian Palmer, noting that there are five million unregistered voters in the state.

Meanwhile, CC/West Virginia, which successfully lobbied for motor-voter legislation last year, recently joined forces with the state LWV to promote First Vote, a school-based program to introduce high-school students to voting. The program, developed by People for the American Way, explores in six lessons citizenship and the history and importance of the right to vote. It culminates with in-class voter registration. CC/West Virginia Executive Director John Barrett has introduced the program to two classes at a Lincoln County high school.

State Experiments with Public Financing

by Herbert E. Alexander, Jeffrey Schwartz, and Eugene R. Goss

States have experimented with ways to funnel money into politics since the inception of public financing systems in the 1970s.

Like so many scientists, the states have covered a spectrum of approaches.

In Hawaii, for example, all local and state legislative candidates qualify for public funding—but only for $50 per election.

Then there's New Jersey, which provides generous public funding but only for gubernatorial contests. In 1989, New Jersey allocated up to $1.35 million to gubernatorial candidates in the primary election and $3.3 million to gubernatorial candidates in the general election.

The goals of public financing are to reduce the fund-raising advantage of incumbents, to lessen the advantage of self-contributions by wealthy candidates and to provide alternate sources of funds. In an age of high campaign costs, public financing provides a system under which candidates agree to campaign spending limits. And it is designed to increase participation in the political process and minimize the influence of special-interest groups.

Along with tax-assisted funding for candidates and political parties, public financing originated at the state level in 1973, gaining momentum in the aftermath of Watergate. The system generally held its ground in the 1980s, adding a few states in the middle and late years of the decade. In the 1990s, two states—Kentucky and Rhode Island—expanded public funding programs.

Of the 23 programs in operation, 20 states raise money through their income tax system. There are two ways to do this.

The first is the tax check-off, which allows taxpayers to earmark a small portion of their tax payments for a special political fund. This is the same method the federal government uses to collect funds for the Presidential Election Campaign Fund. Because the check-off does not increase the taxpayer's liability, the funds in effect are appropriated by the

Herbert Alexander is a professor of political science and director of the Citizens' Research Foundation at the University of Southern California. Eugene R. Goss and Jeffrey A. Schwartz have served as research assistants to the Citizens' Research Foundation. This article is reprinted with permission from *State Government News* 35: 9 (September 1992): 21-23, 26.

state, thus providing a public subsidy.

The second is the tax add-on, which requires the taxpayer to add to his or her tax liability. This method is considered public funding only because it uses the tax system to solicit small, voluntary contributions that are distributed according to a legal, often intricate, formula administered and enforced by the state.

Twelve states use a tax check-off, and nine use a tax add-on, with North Carolina employing both. Florida, Indiana and New Hampshire use neither.

Because the add-on increases the taxpayer's liability, and the check-off does not, the two systems elicit different participation rates. In 1984, the average participation rate in state tax check-off programs was 21 percent. This compared favorably with the participation rate in the federal systems, which was 23.7 percent for the same year.

Yet by 1990, the average participation rate dropped to 14.5 percent, more than five percent below the federal level for the same year. This represents a precipitous decline from highs in the 1970s and 1980s, when states such as Hawaii reached above 50 percent.

Low participation rates in the tax check-off—like low voter turnout—may be caused by increasing skepticism about the political process. Also, the programs are no longer new, and concerns have been raised about whether tax dollars should be spent for politics. With respect to the tax add-on, skepticism is compounded by increased tax liability.

The states' experience with the check-off stands in sharp contrast to the participation rate with the add-on. In no state do more than 2 percent of taxpayers choose to add on. The average participation rate in 1990 was 0.8 percent.

A few examples illustrate the difficulties faced by the tax add-on. When Montana switched from a check-off to an add-on in the late 1970s, the participation rate plummeted from 16.4 percent to 1.5 percent. The most recently enacted add-on program, in Arizona, registered taxpayer participation rates of 0.45 percent and 0.41 percent in 1989 and 1990 respectively. And in California, the small number of taxpayers contributing to the political fund dropped by 31 percent when the number of other special funds activated by an add-on were increased from four to six in 1987.

States distribute public funding in a variety of ways. Some give matching funds. Others have flat grants or channel money to candidates through political parties, while other states allocate funds directly to the parties with few or no restrictions on their spending. Some states provide public financing for both primary and general elections, but the majority of states provide funding for only the general election.

While some states fund all statewide candidates, others limit funding to candidates for governor. In Minnesota, candidates for the U.S. House and Senate may receive public financing—although the program is under legal challenge.

Twelve states distribute money to candidates. This includes Minnesota, North Carolina, Rhode Island and Kentucky, where public funds are distributed to both candidates and political parties. Of the 12 states that provide funds directly to gubernatorial candidates, eight provide assistance to candidates for other offices. However, in only three of these states—Minnesota, Wisconsin and Hawaii—are legislative candidates eligible for public funds.

Strengthening the Parties

Fourteen states distribute money to political parties. This includes Rhode Island, which gives money to political parties and statewide

59

Big Spending in the Quest for the Governor's Chair

Gubernatorial campaigns are increasingly expensive as the stakes in running in the states continue to escalate. At least three trends seem to be driving these increasing stakes. First is the decline of the federal government's involvement in the domestic agenda, which places more responsibility and problems on the states, and on their governors. The action has moved to the states and the governors.

Second is the political decline of certain sources of presidential candidates, i.e. the U.S. Senate and House, and the interest in turning toward governors as a cadre of potential presidential candidates. In the five presidential elections since 1976, six of the ten major party candidates for president were current or former governors.

Third is the transformation of our political process from a party based system to an individual candidate/media based system, a system that is driven by money. Despite an apparent leveling off of expenditures in the most recent elections,[1] a great deal is still spent in these contests. Since 1977, the 202 separate campaigns cost on average $8.18 million (in 1991 dollars), but with a range between $.24 million (Vermont, 1978) to $55 million (California, 1990).[2]

What are the prospects for the 1990s? We will probably see more rather than fewer expensive gubernatorial campaigns over the next few years. This will be especially true in those elections held in the non-presidential years, and in the most populous states. And the premium will continue to be on candidates who have their own money to spend or have access to considerable financial support. Gubernatorial campaigns in the states are a big business, and like any big business you need money to get into the game.

[1] See "Total Cost of Gubernatorial Elections, 1977-1991," in *The Book of the States, 1992-93* (Lexington, KY: The Council of State Governments, 1992), 35.
[2] All dollar figures are in 1991 equivalent dollars.

Source: Thad Beyle, "Big Spending in the Quest for the Governors' Chair," *Spectrum: The Journal of State Government* 65:3 (Summer 1992): 15, 20. Reprinted with permission.

office candidates; North Carolina, where money from the check-off goes to political parties, while money from the add-on goes to candidates for governor; and Kentucky, which sends check-off revenue to political parties and appropriates money from the general fund to the slate of governor and lieutenant governor.

Also included are Minnesota, which distributes money to political parties and candidates, and Indiana, where money from the sales of personalized license plates goes to the parties.

In the majority of states where the taxpayer may designate the recipient political party, the Democratic Party has received more funds than the Republican Party, in some cases by as much as 2-to-1. The Democratic edge has led some observers to be concerned about the implications for Republican state parties, which tend to be weaker than the national party in many states.

However, in Iowa and Idaho the amount collected by the Republicans surged ahead of the Democrats at the outset of the 1980s, reversing a trend prevalent throughout the 1970s. In Utah, Arizona and Alabama, the Republican Party has done well, and in Minnesota, where party check-offs favored Democrats by 3-to-1 in 1978, the margin had been cut to 51-49 by 1989.

The Impact of Funding

With some exceptions, public financing of state elections has not significantly affected the campaign process. This is because of the insufficient amounts of money provided and because funds given to political parties are used to support party programs and operations that diffuse the impact on candidates.

Among the major exceptions are the New Jersey gubernatorial general election in 1977 and the Michigan gubernatorial general election in 1978. Taxes substantially funded both. Here, public financing affected campaign strategy and the traditional campaign process, particularly in the areas of campaign spending and debts. New Jersey's experience in 1981 was another exception, when the program was extended to cover primary campaigns, and 16 candidates received public funds that year.

The New Jersey gubernatorial general election of 1977, publicly funded for candidates who qualified, illustrated the problem of finding an equitable spending limit. Both major party candidates raised the maximum amount in private contributions, about $500,000, and received public funds, a little more than $1 million, which brought them close to the spending limit of $1,518,576.

This worked to the disadvantage of the challenger, state Sen. Ray Bateman, who was unable to change strategies and revise campaign themes late in the campaign and still stay within the spending limit. Incumbent Gov. Brendan Byrne won the election.

In this case, spending limits rigidified the system. Subsequently, the New Jersey Election Law Enforcement Commission has recommended four times that expenditure limits be repealed.

In Michigan, the major party candidates in 1978 each received $750,000, which represented 75 percent of the $1 million general election spending limit. However, low spending limits once again worked to the advantage of an incumbent, Gov. William Milliken, who was able to capitalize on wide recognition.

As these two cases illustrate, spending limits tend to work to the advantage of candidates who are better known, who have the backing of a superior party organization or who have the ability to enlist volunteers. In some states, such as Minnesota and Wisconsin, some candidates have refused public funds, preferring not to be held to restrictive spending limits. But these are arguments against spending limits, not against public funding.

The Evolving Laws

State election laws not only cover the collection, distribution and expenditure of public or tax-assisted funds but also include public disclosure, contribution limitations, bipartisan election commissions and expenditure limits.

Forty-eight states require pre- and post-election disclosure—South Carolina and Wyoming require only post-election disclosure. States differ as to threshold amounts required for reporting. Florida, for example, requires itemization of all contributions. Other states, such as Maine, Mississippi and Nevada, set this limit as high as $500. Twenty-one states limit individual contributions.

Every state has provisions for the organization of political action committees, and half limit the amount they may contribute. Twenty states prohibit direct corporate contributions, and 18 limit the amount corporations can donate. Twenty-one states limit labor union contributions, and nine states prohibit such contributions to candidates.

Thirty states have independent authorities that administer some aspects of campaign finance law. In the remaining 20, election law

---

Momentum for Campaign Reform Picks Up Speed:
Georgia and Rhode Island

Under Georgia's first lobby disclosure law, which passed in the legislative session's final hour, lobbyists must disclose what they spend on gifts, entertainment and travel for elected and appointed state officials. In addition the law lowers campaign contribution limits from $3,500 per election for any candidate to $2,500 per election for statewide candidates, and $1,000 per election for legislative and local candidates. Finally, the law bars statewide candidates from accepting donations or honoraria from businesses they would oversee if elected.

[Common Cause/Georgia Executive Director Melissa] Metcalfe credits *The Atlanta Constitution* for exposing lawmakers' behind-the-scenes maneuvering when the bill was under consideration. The newspaper's coverage, which was accompanied by a list of legislators' phone numbers, provoked citizen outrage and an outpouring of calls to lawmakers.

The reform wave sweeping Rhode Island crested when Gov. Bruce Sundlun signed campaign finance legislation that strengthens existing public funding provisions and expands the program to cover all statewide candidates. The formula now encourages small donations: Contributions of $250 or less will be matched with doubled funds while those greater than $250 will be matched dollar for dollar.

The law also provides publicly funded candidates free air time on public and cable television, bans direct corporate contributions, reduces individual contribution limits from $2,000 to $1,000 per year per candidate and prohibits personal use of campaign funds.

[Common Cause]/Rhode Island Executive Director Phil West says the new legislation "is the culmination of more than four years of work and significantly strengthens" a law enacted in 1988. It was pushed by a broad-based coalition of business, community and religious leaders.

Source: Amy E. Young, "Momentum for Campaign Reform Picks Up Speed," *Common Cause Magazine* 18:2 (April/May/June 1992): 36.

---

continues to remain under the purview of the secretary of state, except for Utah, where the lieutenant governor retains such authority.

Twelve states have imposed expenditure limits that are constitutional if associated with public funding, in accordance with *Buckley vs. Valeo,* the 1976 U.S. Supreme Court decision that upheld the practice of public funding. Massachusetts and Montana offer public funding without expenditure limits, and New Hampshire imposes spending limits without providing public funds. Additionally, Vermont has recently imposed spending limits, though there is no public subsidy in the state.

Existing tax-assistance programs, especially tax check-offs, have worked effectively and have not fallen into abuse or partisanship. However, in a period of tight budgets and fiscal austerity, it will be increasingly harder for state legislatures to justify spending tax dollars in support of candidates and political parties. Additionally, individuals are less inclined to increase their tax liability in periods of economic lag.

IV. MEDIA AND THE STATES

The media—in all forms—have become important actors in state politics and government. This is especially true given the changes that have been occurring in politics, such as the decline of political parties and the rise of individual, media-oriented campaigns. Every candidate for statewide office and many candidates for local offices now have to count a media consultant among the consultants they must hire. The rapidly increasing costs state and local political candidates incur are, in great part, tied to the rapidly escalating costs of running media-oriented campaigns.

But this is only part of the reason that the media are important in the states. With the demise of the old political organizations and machines, the means of government-citizen communication have changed. In many cases, it is the media that carry the messages between government and citizens.

The media have no formal powers per se, but they are protected by the First Amendment's free speech clause. This allows a certain freedom of action for the media; they cannot be constrained by governmental action. However, part of the media is regulated by the federal government through the licensing of radio and television stations. Among the license stipulations are the equal time and public service provisions.

The equal time provision protects an individual or a group by assuring them an opportunity to respond to attacks or critiques; it is sort of a "letters to the editor" space required of radio and television. This provision is especially important for political campaigns because it may affect what will be allowed on the air. In fact, several political campaigns report that stations are becoming much more critical of what is contained in political ad-

vertisements, and some have refused to air what they regard as ads with questionable content. The public service provision calls on the licensee to devote a certain amount of air time to public affairs.

Types of Media

"The media" is a broad term that needs to be broken into its components for us to better understand how the media operate in the states. There are the print media, the daily and weekly newspapers we read; the television stations, which provide local and national news; the radio stations, which offer a large variety of formats; and the wire services, which provide the backbone of news stories to the other media.

In fact, it is the wire services and the daily newspapers that set the agenda for television and radio, although TV and radio stations pick and choose what they want to cover. Look at your state's or city's major morning paper and compare the main stories on the front page with what you hear on the early morning radio news. Go into any radio or television station and watch how closely they follow and use the information coming over the wire services. A recent study indicates that state elected officials find newspapers and the wire services the two most politically significant media in the states. This is in contrast to the general perception that newspapers and TV are the most important media at the national level.[1]

There are assets and liabilities to each medium. For example, the newspapers can cover a broad range of items and concerns, making them attractive to many readers. In fact, some critics argue that the newspapers may be covering too many types of stories and may be losing their focus and concern over larger public issues. Television is a "hot" medium because stories are expressed through pictures, which is an easier way for most people to absorb the news. However, TV is limited by its own technology since it depends on pictures to carry the message; how does one take a picture of taxes? A study conducted in the mid-1970s of forty-four newspapers and television stations in ten cities found that newspapers allocated more space to stories on state government than did television stations. Newspapers also gave stories on state government greater prominence (front page location) than did the television stations (lead story status).[2] But Bill Gormley, the study's author, argued that even with this newspaper coverage, "few give it [state government] the kind of coverage it needs."[3]

Gormley cited the comments of others who had misgivings about the media's coverage of the states. Political scientist V. O. Key, Jr. argued in 1961 that the media "may dig to find the facts about individual acts of corruption but the grand problems of the political system by and large escape their critical attention."[4] Former North Carolina governor Terry Sanford (D, 1961-65) questioned, "Who, in some 40 states or more, can say he begins to understand state government by what he reads in the newspapers?"[5]

State Media Structures

There is great variety in the media structures across the states just as there is great variety in population size, population centers, and economic complexity. For example, New Jersey sits within two major media markets—the northern part of the state receives broadcasts from the New York City metropolitan area, and the southern part receives broadcasts from the greater Philadelphia metropolitan area. Radio, TV, and cable stations emanating from those major markets dominate what is seen or heard in New Jersey, and there are no strong New Jersey-based media outlets to

combat this. News about New Jersey must fight for a spot in these media outlets.

West Virginia also faces this problem: much of the state is served by media markets in Cincinnati, Pittsburgh, and Washington, D.C. West Virginia lacks its own major media outlet because its terrain makes it impossible for any station to reach all parts of the state. In his 1980 reelection bid, Governor John D. "Jay" Rockefeller IV (D, 1977-85) spent a lot of money on outlets in these large cities in order to reach potential voters in remote areas of the state. There were stories of voters in Washington, D.C., going to the polls to vote for Rockefeller because they had seen his ads on TV so often.

Then there are states that have many media markets within the state's own boundaries. California clearly is the leader in media markets because there are so many large communities to be served in the state, ranging from San Francisco and Sacramento in the northern part of the state to Los Angeles and San Diego in the southern part. And there are many other markets in between. Texas also has many media markets, as does Florida, New York, and North Carolina.

At the other extreme are states with only one major media market that dominates the state. Examples are Colorado with the Denver media market, Georgia with Atlanta, and Massachusetts with Boston. In fact, the Boston media market spreads well into Rhode Island, southern New Hampshire, and southwestern Maine, making it difficult for residents there to get a clear understanding of what is happening in their own states. One New Hampshire state legislator worried that "most citizens in the lower one-third of the state get their news from Boston TV, so we have a very distorted view by many citizens of what is happening in state government."[6] When one such market or major city dominates the state, there is little chance for those in the remainder of the state to voice their own particular interests. A rural-urban or rural-suburban rift in the state's media coverage is the rule.

Some comparative figures also indicate the wide variation between the states in media markets. In 1990, there were 1,611 daily newspapers in the United States, or an average of 32 per state, but they were not distributed equally. There were 116 daily newspapers in California, but only 2 in Delaware. Texas had 98, whereas Hawaii and Utah had 6 each. The other states ranged between these extremes.[7]

This means some states' residents have a greater opportunity to read local newspapers than do residents of other states. In 1987, the daily newspaper circulation per one-hundred residents was forty-four in New York and forty-two in Virginia, compared to fifteen each in Maryland and Mississippi. The rate was thirty-six in Massachusetts and thirty in both Nebraska and Rhode Island, compared to seventeen in Utah and eighteen each in Alabama, Georgia, Kentucky, and Louisiana.[8]

The number of television stations also varies by state, although with the expansion of cable systems across the United States the actual number of stations available to a household through cable may be in the twenty-five to forty (or more) range. But even among those cable systems and their many channels, there is considerable variation in the number of local stations available. In June 1990, there were 1,419 television stations in the United States, or an average of 28 per state, but again they were not distributed equally. Texas had 108 stations and California had 92 stations, compared with Delaware with 3 and Rhode Island with 4. Florida had 67 stations and Ohio had 50, Utah had 10 stations and New Hampshire and Vermont had 16 between them.[9]

Radio is a considerably more ubiquitous form of media; in June 1990 there were 10,578 stations in the United States. If the stations were distributed equally across the states, there would have been an average of 212 stations per state. In actuality, there were 689 radio stations in Texas and 628 in California, compared with 21 in Delaware and 30 in Rhode Island. Florida had 428, Pennsylvania had 420, and New York had 416, whereas Hawaii had 54, and Vermont had 56.[10]

Much of the variation in the data noted above is tied to the size of the state in terms of land area and population. But some of the variation is related to population diversity: some newspapers and radio stations target specific populations.

How the Media Work in the States

There is almost a definite pattern in how the media cover state politics and state government. During political campaigns, when candidates are vying for nominations and election to office, the media are involved selectively. Being involved can mean several things. First, the media cover some of the campaigns on a day-to-day or week-to-week basis, especially those campaigns with the greatest appeal in terms of what the media feel will sell papers or draw listeners and viewers.

In the 1990s, there is a perceptible decline in the coverage given to politics and government in the newspapers. For example, the political reporters in one large southeastern city were directed to cover only the presidential, congressional, gubernatorial, state legislative, and maybe one or two other contests. This meant the readers in that newspaper's market did not read anything about the other contests they would be voting on unless there was a scandal or major news event attending one of those races. There weren't, so in making their decision, the voters had to fall back on party identification, knowledge of the incumbent's name, or skip voting in that race entirely.

Second, the media have become the major

vehicle for political messages—the paid fifteen- or thirty-second campaign ads that we see on TV and hear on the radio and the printed advertisements we see in newspapers. In fact, a major new approach in getting messages to the voters is use of drive time radio, when potential voters are trapped in their cars and have to listen to what is coming at them from the car radio.

Third, some of the media become part of campaigns when they conduct public opinion polls, which delineate the important issues in the race and show which candidate is ahead. The media also become part of campaigns when they sponsor debates between the candidates and endorse candidates through editorials. A new role some newspapers have adopted is that of a monitor or critic of political campaign ads, especially those shown on television. In monitoring the ads, the papers have a reporter present the text of the political ad (often negative in tone and style), then match that with the facts of the situation. Then there is an analysis of the differences, if any.

For their part, candidates and their campaign organizations develop ways to obtain "unpaid media"—getting candidates and their names on TV or in print to increase their name recognition. Knowing when the major TV stations must have their tapes "in the can" for the nightly news can determine when a candidate makes an appearance or holds a press conference.

Fourth, the media become a part of the calculus by which decisions are made and actions are taken in politics and government. The best example of this is the pervasive influence that the *Manchester Union Leader* has on New Hampshire government and politics. This newspaper runs very conservative editorials on the front page for all to see. An observer of the state wrote in the 1960s that "[m]any state officials said they feared personal and vindictive editorial reprisal on the front page if they took exception to one of the paper's policies." [11] These officials felt "the paper has created an emotionally charged, reactionary atmosphere where new ideas are frequently not only rejected but fail to appear in print for public discussion." [12] In the 1980s, a political scientist observed that this paper "still profoundly shaped politics in the state," [13] and in the 1990s, one state legislator grumbled that "political bias [is] demonstrated consistently in [its] stories as well as editorials." [14] This may or may not be an exception to how most papers operate. Sometimes such an atmosphere or situation can be created in more subtle ways than front page editorial attacks but exist nonetheless.

Other media organizations have acted in a more responsible manner over the years. These organizations have worked with those in government and politics to help their readers understand what is happening. For years, the *Louisville Courier-Journal* did this for Kentucky and for parts of adjoining states. [15] As one newsman argued, "Publishers have a responsibility to the public to do more. Call it public service, if you will . . . but the press has the responsibility to enlighten and serve." [16]

A second pattern to media coverage and activity in the states has to do with the timing of state legislative sessions. There is an adage that when the legislature is in town, no one is safe. More to the point, when the legislature is in town, so are the media of the state. Not only do the capital press and media corps regulars cover general legislative activity, but specific newspapers and TV stations send reporters to cover the representatives from their city or county. Also, if there is some legislation that will have an impact on a particular section of the state, there most certainly will be media from that section to monitor what is happening.

This leads to some interesting observations by those who have watched this "cover-the-legislature-at-all-costs" phenomenon. First, coverage of other state government activities, programs, and individuals often is neglected as a result. Why? "[I]t's a lot easier to cover the legislature. . . . Stories are easy to get. Legislators seek out reporters, doling out juicy quotes and swapping hot rumors." Plus, editors want their reporters to be there. "When reporters aren't there, editors want to know why not." [17]

Second, there have been changes in the nature of the capital press corps. There tend to be fewer gray beards than in the past and more younger reporters. The tradeoff seems to be youth, vigor, and inexperience versus age and experience; hence the coverage may not be as good as in the past even though there may be more media folk involved. For example, the capital press corps in one state capital once operated under the following set of rules for new reporters: "(1) Don't fall down; (2) Don't get sick; and (3) Don't *ever* look like you don't know what you are doing." [18] No one knows what the rules might be now.

Another major factor influencing how state governments and politics are covered by the media is the location and size of the state capital. In some states, the capital city is not the largest city; instead, it seems to be a "compromise" city between two large urban centers. Examples of this include Springfield, Illinois, located about two-thirds of the way from Chicago toward St. Louis, Missouri; Jefferson City, Missouri, located midway between St. Louis and Kansas City; and Trenton, New Jersey, located closer to the Philadelphia metropolitan area than to the New York area.

Some other state capitals are near the geographic center of the state, such as Little Rock, Arkansas; Des Moines, Iowa; Oklahoma City, Oklahoma; and Columbia, South Carolina. However, several capitals are in what seems to be out-of-the-way locations,

including Sacramento, California; Annapolis, Maryland; Albany, New York; and Carson City, Nevada. Still other states put their capital in the largest city, where most of the action takes place. Some examples of such capitals are Denver, Colorado; Atlanta, Georgia; Boston, Massachusetts; and Providence, Rhode Island.

When the state capital is in an out-of-the-way location, the media may find it more difficult to cover events since the government may be the only game in town. When there is not much action—or when the legislature adjourns—many in the press return to their home cities, leaving state government uncovered. When the state capital is located in the state's largest and most active city, there may be better coverage of state government, but that may be drowned out by the coverage of all the other activities in the city.

The National Media and the States

How does the national media treat what goes on in the states? One quick answer is that the national media doesn't cover the states unless a disaster occurs. Media specialist Doris Graber calls the national media's coverage of state issues "flashlight coverage." [19] She argues that there are basically two types of news in the eyes of the national media: high priority news and low priority news. The former is news that "has been judged in the past as intrinsically interesting to the audience by the usual news criteria. . . . [It is news that is] exciting, current, close to home, about familiar people, and audiences are likely to deem it relevant to their life." On the other side of the coin is low priority news, which "has been judged intrinsically uninteresting although it may be important." [20]

Graber argues that state news traditionally has been in the low priority news category, with only an occasional "entertainment or convenience item" receiving "a brief spotlight" in the news. However, when state news can be tied to high priority news, such as national elections, coverage increases.[21]

A recent study of the media coverage of the 1989 Virginia gubernatorial election is instructive of another aspect of what national coverage can mean during a state-level election.[22] This race was in an off-presidential year, which meant there wasn't too much political news. In addition, the Democratic candidate, L. Douglas Wilder, was vying to become the nation's first elected black governor. The study showed how two "local" papers covered the race (the *Richmond Times-Dispatch* and the "Metro" section of the *Washington Post*), and how the national media covered it (included were articles from the *Christian Science Monitor, Los Angeles Times, New York Times, Wall Street Journal, Newsweek, Time,* and *U.S. News and World Report*).

The results are revealing. The national coverage focused narrowly on the historical aspect of the race, and on the fact that Wilder was prochoice on the abortion issue while his opponent was prolife. The local papers focused more broadly on the substantive issues, and provided candidate and voting group profiles. The national media obviously concentrates on the aspects of a story that appeal to a broad audience; however, this treatment does not ensure coverage of the whole story—or even the correct story.

Working with the Press

There is another side to the media-government relationship: how those who serve in state government react to the role of the media. Most governors, some state agencies, and a growing number of legislatures have established press offices to work with—and even cater to—the media and its needs. This means

each governor has a press secretary or communications director. Recently, state legislators have realized the need for a media liaison who works either for a party caucus or the party leadership. Many agencies in state government also are developing offices that work with the press.

For press offices, working with the media on a daily basis usually entails distributing press releases and answering queries. But press offices are also responsible for making sure that their bosses handle themselves properly with the media corps. At the 1982 New Governors Seminar sponsored by the National Governors' Association, newly elected governors were given the following advice on dealing with the media:[23]

• Good press relations cannot save a poor administration, but poor press relations can destroy a good one.

• Never screw up on a slow news day.

• If you don't correct an error immediately, in the future you'll be forced to live with it as fact.

• Never argue with a person who buys ink by the barrel.

• When you hold a press conference and are going to face the lions, have some red meat to throw them or they'll chew on you. It should be something of substance, as long as the governor isn't the Christian.

• Never make policy at press conferences.

At the 1990 New Governors Seminar, the newly elected governors were advised that selecting a press secretary or director of communications was a key position that should be filled quickly. And in selecting that individual, "the main objective is to have someone who has the respect of the media and knows what is happening, and does not lie or misrepresent the Governor."[24]

Part IV provides some perspectives on the media in the states. Michael Aron in *New Jersey Reporter* analyzes the impact of the demise of a newspaper. Deborah Howell in *Spectrum: The Journal of State Government* discusses some problems, or in her words, sins, of political reporters. And Mark Rozell in *Comparative State Politics* reports on a survey of Virginia journalists and how they define professional objectivity.

Notes

1. Thad L. Beyle and G. Patrick Lynch, "The Media and State Politics." Paper presented at the annual meeting of the Midwest Political Science Association, Chicago, April 1991.
2. William T. Gormley, Jr., "Coverage of State Government in the Mass Media," *State Government* 52:2 (Spring 1979): 46-47.
3. Ibid., 47.
4. V. O. Key, Jr., *Public Opinion and American Democracy* (New York: Alfred Knopf, 1961), 381.
5. Terry Sanford, *Storm Over the States* (New York: McGraw-Hill, 1967), 51.
6. Response by a New Hampshire state legislator to a 1990 survey question sent by the author.
7. Bureau of the Census, "Daily and Sunday Newspapers—Number and Circulation by State, 1990," Number 901, in *Statistical Abstract of the United States, 1992* (Washington, D.C.: Government Printing Office), 558.
8. Table A-40, "Daily Newspaper Circulation per 100 Residents, 1987," *State Policy Data Book, 1989.*
9. Bureau of the Census, U.S. Department of Commerce, "Cable Television, Broadcasting Stations, and Newspapers," *State and Metropolitan Area Data Book, 1991,* 4th ed. (Washington, D.C.: Government Printing Office), 280.
10. Ibid.
11. Sanford, 50.
12. Ibid.
13. Richard F. Winters, "The New Hampshire Gubernatorial Election and Transition," in *Gubernatorial Transitions: 1982 Election,* ed. Thad Beyle (Durham, N.C.: Duke University Press, 1985), 304.
14. Response by a New Hampshire state legislator to a 1990 survey question sent by the author.
15. Sanford, 51.
16. Quoted in ibid., 52.
17. Jack Betts, "When the Legislature's in Session, Does Other News Take a Back Seat?" *North Carolina Insight* 12:1 (December 1989): 63.
18. Jack Betts, "The Capital Press Corps: When Being There Isn't Enough," *North Carolina Insight* 9:2 (September 1986): 48.
19. Doris A. Graber, "Flashlight Coverage: State News on National Broadcasts," *American Politics Quarterly* 17:3 (July 1989): 278.
20. Ibid., 288.
21. Ibid., 288-289.
22. Mark J. Rozell, "Local v. National Press Assessments of the 1989 Virginia Gubernatorial Campaign," *Polity* 24:1 (1991).
23. Thad L. Beyle and Robert Huefner, "Quips and Quotes from Old Governors to New," *Public Administration Review* 43:3 (May/June 1983): 268.
24. Thad Beyle, "Organizing the Transition Team," *Management Note* (Washington, D.C.: Office of State Services, National Governors' Association, 1990), 15.

What's Lost When a Paper Dies?

by Michael Aron

It's a credit to New Jersey's newspapers that you really can't see what a terrible year they had in 1991. The news and editorial content have not visibly suffered. But talk to publishers and editors and you hear real tales of woe. "I've heard comments to the effect that this has been the worst year since the Depression," says John O'Brien, executive director of the New Jersey Press Association, a trade group representing the state's newspapers.

The public got an inkling of the trouble Jan. 3 [1992] when the Elizabeth *Daily Journal* folded after 212 years of continuous publication. The closing got a lot of publicity because it involved the state's oldest paper and because its death occurred during the slow New Year's holiday week. Nine months earlier, the Hudson *Dispatch* had folded. There were also layoffs at four New Jersey papers in '91—138 at *The Record* of Hackensack (9 percent of the work force), 52 at the Record-owned *News-Tribune* of Woodbridge, 43 at the *Asbury Park Press,* and 33 jobs cut at the Atlantic City *Press* by layoff, early retirement and attrition.

Advertising revenues are way off at all the papers. Through October of '91, line inches of advertising were down 15 percent from the preceding year at the Newark *Star-Ledger,* 16 percent at the *The Record* and 37 percent at the *Asbury Park Press.* 1990 was not a good year, either. The best years were in the mid-80s. The economy was booming and classified advertising in particular went through the roof. Classifieds are fueled by help-wanteds, real estate and automobiles, all of which were hot in the 80s. Classifieds went from 30 percent of the ad-revenue stream to 50 percent at some papers. But now there are fewer jobs to be advertised, the real estate market is in a slump, and classified advertising has collapsed. *The Record's* ad revenues for '91 were down by $30 million compared to 1988, and $22.6 million of that was in classifieds. In late December, *Record* publisher Byron Campbell was induced to resign by the paper's board of directors, and board chairman and principal owner Malcolm Borg reassumed control. A week later, *The Record* raised its daily price from 35¢ to 50¢. Borg says the layoffs last summer "were the first since 1931-32, when my grandfather did it," and that they were very painful.

The Record would like to acquire the

Michael Aron is a senior political correspondent for New Jersey Network News. This article is reprinted from *New Jersey Reporter* 21:5 (January/February 1992): 55, 60.

Central Jersey *Home News,* another newspaper in trouble. Editor Dick Hughes says the *Home News* is still making money but volunteers that the news staff has been reduced by attrition from 90-plus to 70 over the past few years. *Home News* chairman William Boyd wants to sell the paper. Borg would like to buy it, and merge it with *The News Tribune* (which is not making money). But ambitious expansion plans during the heady 80s saw the *The Record* borrow $120 million to build a new color printing plant in Rockaway. Borg's bankers wouldn't finance his purchase of the *Home News* last year, and Borg is now trying to sell his printing plant for $35 million and lease it back so that he can refinance his loans and gain the money needed to buy the *Home News.*

"1991 was just a really, really, really terrible year in terms of advertising," Borg says. "Businesses like Crazy Eddie, Newmark and Lewis, and automotive dealers that used to do a lot of business with us, they're out of business." Borg says one Paramus auto dealer, Wild Bill, used to spend $1.3 million a year on advertising in *The Record.* But Wild Bill went out of business, and his successor "doesn't spend $500,000."

The *Asbury Park Press,* which was highly profitable in the 80s, has also been hurt. *Asbury* was described by one industry source as having once been like "a license to print money." Apparently it boomed as the populations of Ocean and Monmouth counties boomed. Now, industry sources say, it has a color printing press that cost $12 million sitting in a warehouse unused. The paper had expected to expand but is now looking for a buyer for the color press. *The New York Times* recently reported that, according to one unnamed newspaper executive, the *Press* itself is being quietly shopped around by its owners, Jules Plangere Jr. and the E. Donald Lass family. But a corporate spokesman insists that's not true.

How then is it that we readers haven't noticed the newspapers' pain? First of all, because papers tend to fire newsroom personnel last. And when it happens, they target the soft sections of the paper: entertainment, travel, television, things they can replace with wire service features. *The Record,* for example, laid off a film reviewer and now carries Roger Ebert's syndicated reviews. At the *Home News,* says Dick Hughes, "we've given up frills. That means we have fewer feature writers, less coverage of culture and entertainment outside our immediate area and less sports travel. We do cover every out-of-town Rutgers game, men and women, but not the pro teams anymore. If it doesn't go to our immediate area of coverage, we don't do it."

"Everybody is trying like hell to give the best product we can within the resources available," says Borg.

Less advertising does mean smaller news holes. Customarily the ad-to-edit ratio is about 50-50 at smaller papers, closer to 60-40 at large metropolitan dailies. So the papers are a little thinner, but that's not something the average reader notices.

Financial bottom lines are closely kept secrets at most New Jersey papers, most of which are still owned by families or privately-held companies. So unless they tell you, it's impossible to say for certain which ones might be losing money. Most are said to be still profitable. As John O'Brien of the NJPA put it, "You talk to a publisher who's used to a 30 percent profit—he's down to a 10 percent profit and he's ready to slit his throat."

Some publishers are upbeat about the second half of '92. They say they've gotten their houses in order by cost-cutting, and that when economic recovery comes they'll be better off for having tightened their belts. The two leading papers in South Jersey seem less battered by the recession than papers in the North, where more bank failures and bank-

73

Statehouse and State Issues Coverage

It may sound strange, but the new kid on the block is *The New York Times*. The paper is covering New Jersey again in a very noticeable way. Last November [1991], the day before the Republicans swept the legislative elections, the *Times* unveiled its new "Metro" section. Like any change, the redesigned section with its geographical banners was jarring at first. But after six months, it's become a welcome addition to the New Jersey media scene.

For years, the *Times* had more or less neglected the region it served. It strived to be a national paper. Its local coverage was oriented to the city. Four years ago, Max Frankel became executive editor and began a process of internal reassessment. With the help of managing editor Joseph Lelyveld, assistant managing editor David Jones, and the recently elevated heir-apparent publisher Arthur Sulzberger, Jr., a decision was made to beef up regional coverage. Most *Times* people believe it was a journalistic decision first, a business decision second. The paper has more readers in the suburbs now than in the city. Clearly the advertising department would like to attract more suburban advertising. But few think this was the advertising tail wagging the editorial dog. The *Times* has never operated that way, says one *Times* man, reciting a part of the paper's mythology.

So now, where we used to get one Jersey story per day in the *Times*—if that—we get three, and sometimes four. On a recent Saturday, for example, there were pieces about the Linden incinerator proposal, a murder in Hackensack, an analysis piece on the Statehouse sales-tax wrestling match, and a long feature on the arcane subject of municipal-level public defenders.

What we're getting, the rest of the New York metropolitan region is also getting. The paper has gone from one reporter in Connecticut to four; from two in Westchester to four; from one on Long Island to five; and from three in New Jersey to seven. The space they're given, the "newshole," has been expanded from about 20 columns per day (six columns equals one page) to about 30. In New York, the paper has beefed up its editing staff to deal with this additional material from the provinces. Computers, cellular telephones and fax machines have been shipped out to the bureaus, and there's a new bureau in Newark.

The upshot is that here in New Jersey we're getting a little more hard news from the *Times* than we're accustomed to, more daily Statehouse stories. On top of that, we're getting the "broad-gauge" features, as one editor calls them, that the *Times* is pretty good at. From a New Jersey perspective, the *Times* can never replace the *Star-Ledger* or other solid local papers. But it's become a stronger supplement to them, and if you can only get to the *Times* on a given day, chances are now that you'll at least get the big state story of the day ("Sales Tax Cut Passes Senate," "Guarini Becomes Third N.J. Congressman to Quit").

The beefed-up Metro section comes at a time when the other great out-of-state paper, *The Philadelphia Inquirer*, seems to have pulled back on its Statehouse and state issues coverage. A year ago the *Inquirer* was king around the Statehouse in some people's eyes, but in the winter and early spring of '92 it seemed to go almost into hibernation. The new Metro section also underscores how flaccid and old-fashioned the *Times*' Sunday New Jersey Weekly section is—but that's okay, because there's already too much to read and watch on Sundays here in the media crossroads of the Middle Atlantic.

Source: Michael Aron, *New Jersey Reporter* 22:1 (May/June 1992): 60-63.

ruptcies have occurred. The *Courier-Post* of Cherry Hill just built a new wing with new presses for $50 million. And publisher Jim Hopson of the Atlantic City *Press* thinks his current staff level of 375 full-time equivalents—15 percent lower than 1988 levels—won't have to shrink any more in 1992. "Our actions to get costs under control, plus recovery, can ultimately produce reasonable profitability again," he says.

Others are a bit more gloomy. "I don't know that the newspaper business will ever come back up to what it was four to five years ago," says John Kolesar, who recently retired as managing editor of the *Courier-Post*. He notes that the state has lost 20 percent of its daily newspapers in the past half dozen years—the *Millville Daily*, the *Dover Advance*, the merging of the *Paterson News* and Passaic *Herald News* into the North Jersey *Herald & News,* plus the Hudson *Dispatch* and Elizabeth *Daily Journal,* leaving 20 where there were once 25. "The survivors will do fine, but there'll be fewer of them," Kolesar says.

What's lost when a paper dies? Newspaper people tell you that the big loss is community coverage. Another paper may spread into a neighboring market and fill a void, but it won't be inclined to focus on local affairs at the level of depth a local paper does. Kolesar argues that the people of Paterson and Passaic were better served when each city had its own paper, and he asks, "Who will cover Elizabeth anymore? Will anyone cover Elizabeth politics the way the *Daily Journal* did? That was their franchise."

Publishers are worried about a new law enabling New Jersey Bell to deploy a fiberoptics cable system, which they fear will give the phone company an unfair advantage in the future. Some are also worried that older readers are not being replaced by enough younger readers. And they believe fervently that newspapers are important to society. "We do important things nobody else will do," says Hopson of the Atlantic City *Press.* "Enterprise reporting. Detailed community reporting. I don't think people recognize how important newspapers are. Cable TV, weekly shoppers—they don't have that kind of commitment."

The Four Deadly Sins of Political Reporters

by Deborah Howell

First, I should say that I love politics, government, public affairs and journalism. It was my career ambition to be a political reporter and I was well on my way when my career came to an abrupt end. But more about that later.

I've spent 30 years being a reporter and editor, covering the University of Texas Student Government; Corpus Christi, Texas, City Hall; Minneapolis City Hall; the University of Minnesota; St. Paul City Hall; the Minnesota Legislature; and now the federal government.

I've covered big city councils and small village councils, county boards, sewer boards, school boards and legislatures, state and national. And I've supervised the coverage of all of them.

I've lived on both sides of journalism and politics. Besides being a journalist all my adult life, I also am the widow of a prominent Minnesota legislator. I know intimately the frustrations of public and political life: I'm the only editor I know who used to roll over in bed to an angry reader in the morning.

I can sympathize with politicians who see incomplete or inaccurate stories about themselves. I've had my own share of frustrations with colleague journalists.

But they're my own kind, and I have always vociferously fought for their right to find out what our readers deserve to know. How many of you have had knock-down, drag-out arguments with your spouse over whether conference committees should be open to the press?

And all of that experience has gone into what I believe about public affairs reporting and shaped what I'm doing as a Washington bureau chief.

My message is simple: Reporters should emphasize the public in public affairs reporting.

Let me tell you what I think are the four deadly sins of political reporting. And I have committed them all.

1. Writing for sources. I don't know a reporter who hasn't at one time or another. The problem is when the reporter wants compliments more from a politician than from readers. Even good reporters sometimes align with the people they cover and forget they're the public's watchdog. They go easy on sources who are friends. Sometimes so do their editors.

Deborah Howell is Washington Bureau Chief for Newhouse News Service. This article is reprinted from *Spectrum: The Journal of State Government* 66:1 (winter 1993): 60-63. ©1993 The Council of State Governments.

It's important to see that doesn't happen often.

2. Writing too many quarter-turn stories, especially at the legislature and city hall and on the campaign trail. Readers don't need to know two paragraphs of new information followed by 10 paragraphs they already know. Save the space, the newsprint and the trees for something more important.

3. We don't write what we know. We keep the wrong secrets. I'm not talking about the one-night stand of some legislator and boozy lobbyist after a 3 a.m. committee meeting. I'm talking about the powerful senator who is drunk half of the time. I'm talking about the house speaker who's in the back pocket of a special interest. Or the city council member who's genuinely acting like the Minnesota state bird—that's the loon.

4. We don't look behind the vote, the bill, the amendment and explain to readers why it is there and who benefits and why they should care. We get to know the system so well that we forget that most people don't. We also understand the way the system really works, but we don't always report it.

So, what should we be doing?

My golden rule: Write for readers.

After that, my eight public reporting commandments:

1. Report, report, report. Write about what's behind and between the for and against. Political stories often have too few facts and too many opinions—especially too many anonymous opinions.

2. Context, context, context. We write too many stories as if there isn't any context. We need to relate issues to readers' lives.

3. Don't make sense of what politicians say, when they don't make sense. Report they don't make sense. Democracy is messy. Don't pretty it up.

4. Report what public officials do—or have done—not what they say they do or have done.

5. Hit the streets. Talk to people, not reporters. There is no news in the newsroom. Call home if you want to find out what's going on. Ask your mother.

6. Write about what people are worrying about. There's an old aborigine saying: "We must keep our ears to the ground or we will lose our way."

7. Tell readers something they don't already know. I have added new beats at my bureau—family, children and education; race relations; religion; ethics and morality; social trends. We even have a humorist on the staff.

8. Stay in touch with readers. Reporters should also keep our ears to the ground outside city hall, the state capitol and the White House.

I had an interesting conversation recently with Tom Gordon, the *Birmingham News* political reporter. Tom went from being a political reporter to working in the Features Department, a move he didn't ask for. After a year in the Features Department, he went back to being a political reporter—but with some regret. He felt like he learned a lot.

Tom told me, "I talked to real and honest people who do meaningful things. They had no hidden agenda, they spoke for themselves. It was very refreshing."

Those "real honest folks" that Tom talked to? We need to move closer to the people that we write for—the voters and the potential voters.

It is their concerns we ought to report and it is their questions we ought to see are answered. But first, we have to do a serious reporting effort to determine what the questions are. We have to be plugged in to the people we're writing for.

I look back at my own mistakes; I know I was too close to some people I covered. I once baby-sat for the school superintendent's kids when I was covering the schools. It's not wrong to be friendly with people we cover, but

Political Protocol Part I

A reporter stops by your desk and asks questions about the political investigation into agency operations. You are privy to inside information that will soon be announced publicly. Should you tell the reporter that you just don't know?

Telling the reporter that you just don't know, when you do know, is lying. There's no question that you should not reveal inside information unless authorized to do so, but it is not advisable for you to lie. Lies should be used only as a last resort, rather than as a common technique. And on occasion lying may be required, principally to protect people to whom the truth would do needless damage. But this is not such an occasion. It is easy to just tell the reporter that whatever information you have cannot be disclosed until publicly announced. Even reporters can understand that.

Despite my advice to the contrary, you may be tempted to ask yourself just what the reporter has done for you in the past and what he or she will do for you in the future. That, after all, is the way of the world. Has the reporter mentioned you favorably in the press, or, better still, invited you to appear on a television panel? Wouldn't such largesse count for a lot? It also may occur to you that the disclosure of information about the political investigation into your agency would likely hurt someone else's career, thus promoting your own. A real incentive to blab. But, no matter, mum's the word. Get ahead some other way.

Source: Alan Rosenthal, *State Government News* 35:8 (August 1992): 38. Reprinted with permission.

when we get too friendly, we ought to bow out.

I know whereof I speak. I covered the Minnesota Legislature in the 1970s, and it was there I met the man who ended my political reporting career—the late Nicholas Coleman, the Democratic Senate majority leader, whom I married in 1975.

My biggest piece of advice to Nick and to all public officials: Never lie to the press. We always find out and we never forget.

Fat lot of good the advice did for Nick. On the last night of one long legislative session, I went off to Washington, D.C., to city editor school at the American Press Institute.

I was awakened to a call from one of our political reporters asking me if Nick had kicked in the glass door of the Capitol at 4 a.m. She had called him and he had told her it wasn't him—but she wasn't sure.

My instincts told me she was right and he was lying like a rug. He had a hot Irish temper. Add a few pops and the frustration of not getting everything he wanted in the session—I could hear the glass breaking myself. But I told her the truth: I didn't know.

Nick was already on a plane to join me. I met him in the lobby of the Sheraton Reston with fire in my eyes and one big question on my lips: "Had he lied?" The look on his face told me everything I needed to know.

I blew. My blast went something like this: "@#$%&**! If you are going to lie, don't you ever do it to one of my reporters!!" He called her from the lobby, told the truth and apologized—before he got inside my room.

Not that I was without sin. He once swore me to secrecy at the dinner table and told me what the compromise tax bill was going to look like. I couldn't help myself. The next morning I got a reporter to confirm the details and it was in the paper by the afternoon.

Years later, he didn't tell me for a week that he was thinking of running for Congress. "Didn't want to see it in the paper," he said, as I winced.

So, as much as I loved political reporting, I got out. I became an editor instead.

As an editor, I've worked for years to give excellent public affairs coverage to readers. I'm frankly tired of hearing that readers don't care about how they're governed and that all public affairs news is boring. That's simply not true. If we report well what is of interest to voters, then they will read us more.

The news is boring if we let it be boring. Readers respond to good reporting about issues of importance in their community. In St. Paul, I had two reporters spend six months investigating the Metropolitan Waste Control Commission. Is that a boring subject or what? After we finished with the sewer board— misspent money, pollution, nepotism, malfea-sance, misfeasance, no feasance—the publisher came in my office and proudly said, "Everybody in town is talking about the series."

It seems to me that public affairs reporting is getting more complex as politicking is getting more simpleminded.

We can't always make the complex simple, but we must make it understandable and try our damndest to make our stories so interesting that people will read them and be moved to care and then to vote.

The decline in newspaper readership seems to mirror the decline in people voting, and we can't afford either any longer.

If we report the things that people care about—and not on insider quarter turns—we might be able to bring people back to the voting booths.

At least, I for one am giving it a shot. I want to be part of the solution, not part of the problem.

Professional Objectivity in State and Political Reporting: Where Do Journalists Draw the Line?

by Mark J. Rozell

During the Persian Gulf War, a most contentious issue concerned the extent to which U.S. journalists had an obligation to be objective in reporting a war in which their country was involved. Cable News Network (CNN) anchor Bernard Shaw refused debriefing by U.S. officials after leaving Baghdad because he believed that he had to remain "neutral" in the conflict.[1] His colleague, reporter Peter Arnett, insisted that a reporter's first duty is to journalistic professionalism— defined by objective reporting—and not to nationality.[2] At the same time, *Atlanta Journal* columnist Jim Wooten advocated U.S. jamming of CNN broadcasts to protect national interests.[3] ABC News Washington Bureau Chief George Watson said, "U.S. reporters can't be on both sides of a war in which the United States is a combatant."[4] It became clear from this controversy that, even during wartime, the journalistic profession is not of one mind on the debate over professional objectivity. There are no universally accepted professional standards of journalistic conduct in this area. Individual news organizations and journalists develop rules for their own conduct.

The Persian Gulf War brought out into the open, if only temporarily, an important issue in journalistic professionalism. Unfortunately, it took a war being covered by celebrity journalists to draw attention to an issue that deserves more serious, regular inquiry. Where do journalists draw the line when it comes to their involvement in the partisan activities on which they are reporting? Do journalists understand, as professionals, what kinds of partisan activities they must avoid? Or do they just make the rules up as they go along? Why do certain partisan activities, in the views of these journalists, constitute a breach of professionalism when other such activities do not?

Journalists do not need a war, or some other extraordinary event, to be aware of this issue. They confront it almost every day. The purpose of this analysis is to provide a "source's-eye-view" of the conflict between journalists' partisan activities and their professional objectivity.

Methodology

To develop insight into where journalists draw the line in determining partisan activities in which to engage, I surveyed the members of

Mark J. Rozell is associate professor of political science at Mary Washington College in Fredericksburg, Virginia. This article is reprinted with permission from *Comparative State Politics* 13:5 (October 1992): 1-9.

the Capitol press corps in Virginia. In late December 1991-early January 1992, I mailed anonymous surveys asking a series of questions about journalists' involvement in partisan activities—as well as their backgrounds, political views, voting and policy views—to the Capitol correspondents (or Virginia politics reporters), Virginia politics news assignment editors, and editorial page editors of Virginia newspapers. I consulted the most recent edition of the *Bacon* directory of newspapers to identify the correct people to whom to send the surveys.[5] I checked that information against an updated listing of members of the Virginia Capitol Correspondents Association.[6] Of the 95 surveys mailed, I received 60 responses for a response rate of 63.2 percent.[7]

The journalists responded either "yes" or "no" to each of the following nine questions:

1. Do you ever sign petitions for political candidates or causes?

2. Do you ever make donations to political candidates, political parties, or partisan organizations?

3. Do you ever display personal political views by, for example, wearing a campaign button, displaying a political bumper sticker on your automobile or a political sign on your lawn?

4. Do you ever get involved in any candidate's campaign for public office?

5. Do you ever vote in party primary elections at the national level?

6. Do you ever vote in party primary elections at the state and local levels?

7. Do you ever vote in general elections for the presidency?

8. Do you ever vote in general elections to congressional offices (Senate and House)?

9. Do you ever vote in general elections to Virginia public offices both statewide and local?

In cases of journalists answering "no" to questions, they were asked to explain (in the space provided) "why not?" I tallied the "yes" and "no" responses and then coded the "why not?" explanations according to categories of common explanations.

Results[8]

The survey results reveal that there is substantial journalistic disagreement regarding the kinds of partisan activities in which members of the press may engage. The most notable exception is voting in general elections, although other activities (i.e. openly displaying partisan views, making donations, campaigning) are generally considered unacceptable. Primary voting and petition signing cause the most dissension. [*See Table 1.*]

Not every journalist who answered "no" provided an explanation for his or her response. Of those journalists who did respond, their explanations usually fell into two categories: (1) "Such activities compromise my ability to be objective"; (2) "Such activities are unprofessional because of appearances." The distinction between these two categories is important. In the first instance, the journalist believes that his or her partisan activities

Table 1 Partisan Activity

	Yes		No	
Question	N	%	N	%
1. Sign petitions	25	(41.7)	35	(58.3)
2. Make donations	11	(18.3)	49	(81.7)
3. Display partisan views	7	(11.7)	53	(88.3)
4. Campaign activities	7	(11.7)	53	(88.3)
5. Vote in national primaries	30	(50.0)	30	(50.0)
6. Vote in state and local primaries	35	(58.3)	25	(41.7)
7. Vote in presidential elections	59	(98.3)	1	(1.7)
8. Vote in congressional elections	59	(98.3)	1	(1.7)
9. Vote in Virginia elections	60	(100)	0	(0.00)

Table 2 Why Partisan Activity Should Not Be Engaged In

| Question | Answered "no" | | Written response | | Responses | | | | | |
| | | | | | Objectivity | | Appearance | | Other | |
	N	%	N	%	N	%	N	%	N	%
1	35	(58.3)	25	(71.4)	15	(60.0)	10	(40.0)	0	(0.0)
2	49	(81.7)	35	(71.4)	12	(34.3)	16	(45.7)	7	(20.0)
3	53	(88.3)	41	(77.4)	15	(36.6)	22	(53.7)	4	(9.8)
4	53	(88.3)	42	(79.2)	14	(33.3)	27	(64.3)	1	(2.4)
5	30	(50.0)	23	(76.7)	8	(34.8)	14	(60.9)	1	(4.4)
6	25	(41.7)	20	(80.0)	7	(35.0)	12	(60.0)	1	(5.0)
7	1	(1.7)	0	(0.0)	0	(0.0)	0	(0.0)	0	(0.0)
8	1	(1.7)	0	(0.0)	0	(0.0)	0	(0.0)	0	(0.0)
9	0	(0.0)	0	(0.0)	0	(0.0)	0	(0.0)	0	(0.0)

undermine the ability to report or comment objectively on events. In the second instance, the journalist believes that he or she is perfectly capable of both participating in the process and then writing about it in an impartial manner. Yet, this journalist decides not to participate to protect his or her professional credibility and that of the newspaper.

Journalists offered the explanations [in Table 2] for their "no" answers.

Analysis

On the first question, a relatively weak majority (58.3 percent) believe that it is wrong for any journalist to sign a petition. With a good many journalists saying that they do sign petitions (41.7 percent), it becomes clear that journalists and newspaper organizations are deciding for themselves the appropriate professional standard. Two of the "no" respondents explained that, whereas signing petitions for partisan groups is unprofessional, they would consider signing petitions for any internationalist group that they believe to be "nonpartisan" (they cited such examples as Greenpeace and Amnesty International). That means that 45 percent of the respondents either do sign petitions for "candidates or causes" or consider such a practice acceptable.

The disagreement among journalists in this area is highlighted by their specific survey comments. One editor said, "I do not want to be identified with any cause or special interest. Aim: to protect reputation for analytical fairness." A reporter wrote, "while we have no written policy that prohibits this, I have a personal policy against signing anything that would indicate a bias on my part as a reporter." Another reporter explained that "doing so would show a preference and destroy objectivity and credibility. In the case of petitions, the problem would be more one of perception, but still a problem." Nonetheless, one journalist—both an editor and reporter for a small newspaper—participates in many partisan activities and responded as follows: "I am a citizen of the United States of America; therefore, I participate in the political process. My preferences, however, do not color my objectivity as a reporter."

Journalists are substantially less willing to make political donations (81.7 percent answered "no") than to sign petitions. The journalists' specific explanations for not making donations included an editor's statement that "I observe the process. My job and ethics dictate that I stay above the fray." A reporter editor for a small newspaper will not make

Who Was to Blame?

Bob Braun of the *Star-Ledger* has been in the business long enough to know its power. He has been education writer for the *Ledger* for at least two decades. He is one of the paper's stars, one of those reporters given a wide berth and encouraged to spew forth opinion as well as fact. He is dogged, persistent, and provocative. Moreover, it's amazing he hasn't gotten bored with the education beat—one of the deadliest subjects a journalist can be asked to cover, with its mushy language and bland jargon.

Braun is very much engaged with his subject. At times he speaks as *the* conscience of the education system in the state. At times he speaks as the lone defender of "the kids of the state." ("The children of New Jersey—deprived of a strict monitoring system, concerned leaders, even state aid payments—have gained nothing but indifferent silence from . . . the state school board.") He functions almost as a shadow education commissioner, commenting on what the real commissioner does in a way that sets the agenda or flames the debate for everyone interested in education in the state. It's a combination of his paper's influence and his personality—his drive to be the pace-setter.

Braun not only shadowed John Ellis, he cast a pall over Ellis' tenure in Trenton. Shortly after Ellis arrived in July 1990, Braun started writing about Ellis' willingness to bend to the whims of his "puppeteers" in the Governor's Office and in the Democratic legislative caucus rooms. . . .

As Braun told it, Ellis was the pawn of Florio's chief education advisor Tom Corcoran, and together they presided over the "transformation" of the Education Department from "a professional department" to "a cog in the partisan machine.". . .

The headlines on Braun's columns pulled no punches: "Politics of patronage destroys integrity of commissioner's post"; "Spending controls are swept aside by Ellis regime"; "Ellis' exit, like his tenure, replete with politics.". . .

Whether or not Braun was on target about Ellis, I really do not know. I do know that Ellis thinks he got a raw deal from Braun and that he thinks Braun basically drove him out of the state. Ellis told me so about two weeks before he left the state for good.

. . . If Braun was right about the harm Ellis was inflicting on the Education Department (and by extension "the kids"), Braun deserves an award for public service, because he was the only reporter in the state who saw it and uncovered it. Right or wrong, I admire his willingness to criticize and make enemies. We need reporters like that.

It is difficult for the reader, however, to know whether he can trust a reporter who is so consistently negative about the main subject of the reporter's beat. . . .

In his "farewell" column on Ellis, Braun offered this warning: "If the department continues to be viewed simply as a cog in the partisan machine, even true achievements won't be believed. They will be dismissed as mere political grandstanding because the administration has made the department so political." I agree with Braun. Believability is important.

Source: Michael Aron, *New Jersey Reporter* 22:5 (January/February 1993): 40, 46.

donations because he tries "to maintain some objectivity." This person, nonetheless, signs petitions and votes in primaries. Another editor said that making donations "would be compromising—at least in perception—personal and professional interests." Despite an overwhelming majority of "no" responses to this query, the fact that as many as 18.7

percent of reporters and editors admit to making political donations might be cause for concern among journalistic professionals. Furthermore, four journalists (6.7 percent) said they don't make political donations only because they cannot afford to. That [suggests] 25 percent either make political donations or believe that it is acceptable to do so.

On the next two questions, displaying political views and campaigning for candidates, there is equally widescale agreement (83.3 percent answering "no") that such activities are inappropriate. Just slightly more than one in 10 journalists (11.7 percent) engage in such activities. Journalists offered some strong statements about why they do not engage in such activities, for example, (1) "Never! I don't think it should be done, period. Reporters have enough to contend with—why aggravate the situation?" (2) "It would be a grotesque display of partisanship and destroy whatever small amount of objectivity the public still believes the press retains." (3) "It's bad form for a reporter to cover a politician while wearing a button ballyhooing the politician's opponent." (4) "Once I was asked to be someone's press secretary and I laughed. [Journalists] can get caught up in campaigns, but shouldn't. I just don't get involved. Period." (5) "It's one thing to demonstrate support for a candidate privately. Getting publicly involved violates any chance of maintaining objectivity. It looks bad." (6) "I'd get fired."

As with signing petitions, there is no consensus among the journalists as to whether it is proper to participate in party primaries. For national party primaries (held in Virginia in 1988 but not in 1992), an equal number of journalists (50 percent) participate as do not participate. For party primaries at the state and local level, 58.3 percent participate and 41.7 percent do not. As with all of the above categories, the most prominent reasons given for not participating included compromising objectivity and professional appearance. The latter reason gets the most attention from journalists, probably because in Virginia voting lists identifying in which primaries individuals voted are public information and used by party organizations for mailing lists and political telecommunications. As to journalists' specific answers why they do not vote in primaries, one reporter said, "Even though I am Democratic leaning in philosophy, I prefer not to be identified with the party." An editor does not participate in primaries, so that his "personal political choices are not seen as a reflection of the newspaper's choices." Another editor explained, "I do not want my party affiliation on record."

The one activity that causes no concern among the journalists is voting in general elections. Only one journalist said that he or she does not vote in national general elections. Every journalist votes in Virginia general elections. A reporter explained, "I vote because it is a private activity; any other partisan activity would be public and improper for a journalist." An editor agreed: "Voting is the only way journalists have to exercise their political power at a personal level."

Conclusion

The above data reveal that, for the most part, journalists want to avoid the taint of being identified with any partisan cause. In their view, such a taint either compromises their objectivity or undermines their professional reputations, or both. Nonetheless, there is disagreement among journalists as to the kinds of partisan activities in which they may engage without threatening their professionalism.

The journalists agreed that voting in general elections is acceptable. Such voting constitutes a purely private act. The journalist can protect his or her reputation given the secret ballot.

Because the assurance of complete anonymity in primary voting does not exist—public voting records in Virginia identify the primaries in which individuals vote—the journalists are split in their opinions as to whether such a partisan act is professionally acceptable. Some journalists avoid this activity completely, protecting themselves from having even the slightest taint of partisanship. Others will not forgo the right to vote, even in party primaries. That is not altogether surprising because the journalists voting in primaries can credibly claim that they are casting ballots only for the best qualified candidates, regardless of party affiliation.

For the most part, journalists said that such publicly visible partisan activities as campaigning, displaying one's views and making donations do not constitute appropriate professional conduct. Nonetheless, a not insubstantial minority of respondents admitted to engaging in such activities. This minority insisted that citizens do not give up their convictions and right to act on such views merely because they chose journalism as a profession. They perceive no conflict between various partisan activities and the goal of journalistic objectivity.

The journalists generally were split in their assessments of whether it is appropriate to sign petitions for candidates or causes. It could be speculated that those who do sign petitions believe that they will never be publicly identified with the candidate or cause being promoted. For many people, petitions have the appearance of protecting anonymity because of the typically large number of signatures that appear on such lists.

What emerges from the above data is a portrait of a profession not certain about some of its most basic standards of conduct. The differences are nitpicking. Some of the journalists in the survey stated most strongly that rules of professional ethics and conduct require that press corps members engage only in private partisan activities (i.e., voting in general elections). Other respondents offered as much conviction in asserting that partisan activities and journalistic professionalism can be separated and that journalists have the same democratic rights to participate in the process as any other citizen. Like the big name journalists covering the Persian Gulf War, press people at the state level must confront more openly the issues raised in this survey analysis, especially if journalists are concerned about their professional credibility with news consumers.

Notes

1. John Corry, "TV News and the Neutrality Principle," *Commentary* (May 1991), p. 24; Jeff Kamen, "CNN's Breakthrough in Baghdad: Live by Satellite (censored)," *Washington Journalism Review* (March 1991), p. 28.
2. Walter Goodman, "Arnett," *Columbia Journalism Review* (May/June 1991), p. 31.
3. Goodman, p. 29.
4. "Journalists In a War of Strict Press Rules," *Broadcasting,* January 28, 1991, p. 23.
5. Bacon's *Publicity Checker: Newspapers* (vol. II), 40th ed., Chicago: Bacon's Information Inc., 1992.
6. I thank the Virginia Capitol Correspondents Association membership director, Richard Reale (WWBT-Richmond), and its president, Mike Anderson (*Lynchburg Daily News*), for providing me with the membership list. That list provided as well the names of current Associated Press and United Press International state politics reporters not listed in *Bacon's Directory.*
7. A response rate of 63.2 percent is more than adequate to establish validity, according to Babbie, who describes a response rate of 50 percent as "adequate" and 60 percent as "good." See Earl R. Babbie, *Survey Research Methods.* Belmont, California: Wadsworth Pub. Co., 1973, p. 165.
8. The findings of this study are strengthened by similar results attained in the survey of Illinois journalists in Kevin Finch, "The Press and Illinois' Political Process: Does Objectivity Limit Journalists as Citizens?" *Illinois Issues* 16 (August/September 1990), pp. 40-41.

V. STATE LEGISLATURES

In theory, state legislatures fulfill the representative democracy function in state government. Each legislator represents a particular district with particular interests. Legislators then meet in the state capital to meld the interests of the districts they represent with the interests of the state as a whole. The results of this tugging and hauling are the state budget, state policies, and occasionally a constitutional amendment.

In practice, however, state governments operate somewhat less democratically. Not everyone can afford to run for a seat in the state legislature, nor can many afford the time and loss of income that a legislator faces while serving in the legislature. So there tends to be a bias in just who serves based purely on economics: those who can afford to serve do, those who cannot don't. The resulting shortfall deprives a legislature of well-rounded representation of all the people of the state.

Further, subject-area specialists both within and outside the legislatures have an inordinate amount of power over legislators, especially those legislators who chair or are on money committees: finance or revenue, and appropriations. Because of their heavy workload, individual legislators increasingly must rely on these experts—their peers and lobbyists—for guidance on how to vote. Thus, in the basic operating processes of the legislature, some individuals, both inside and outside the legislature, wield more power than others.

Finally, once the legislation has been signed into law, the governor and the administrators of state agencies and programs are largely on their own to interpret and implement the laws. The courts often become important in helping define what a legislature really meant in passing certain legislation when conflicts arise. Or they can determine that the legislature was wrong in what it

decided and declare a legislative act unconstitutional or void. In effect, the state legislature is only the starting point for action in the states. Once legislators have made their decisions, it is up to others to interpret, carry out, and resolve the issues created by legislation.

One Person, One Vote

Until the 1960s, everyone in a state was not equally represented in the legislature due to geographical bias. State legislatures determined how district lines were drawn and thus who would be represented in the legislature and to what extent. Legislatures used various devices such as the gerrymander (excessive manipulation of the shape of a legislative district to benefit a certain incumbent or party) or silent gerrymander (district lines were left intact despite major shifts in population).[1] Both types of legislative legerdemain resulted in underrepresentation of minorities and those living in the cities.

As a result of this misrepresentation, the U.S. Supreme Court ruled in the landmark decision *Baker v. Carr* (1962) that federal courts had the power to review legislative apportionment in the states. Two years later, in *Reynolds v. Sims,* the Court ruled that both houses of a state legislature must be apportioned on the basis of population—that is, "one person, one vote." And in the *Davis v. Bandemer* case (1986), the Court gave political parties standing in court suits over apportionment if a particular political party felt gerrymandered unfairly. And which party won't feel treated unfairly if it does not get the legislative apportionment plan that helps it the most? In *Colgrove v. Green* (1946), the Court indicated that it wanted to stay out of the "political thicket" of apportionment; forty years later it jumped squarely into that thicket.

State legislatures have now finished the

process of redrawing congressional and state legislative district lines required by the 1990 census. Redistricting is always one of the most politically charged issues that state legislatures find on their agendas, since it directly affects the legislators themselves and is so overtly political. Each party tries to maximize its potential strength in future elections, and concurrently reduce the power of the opposition.

In this latest round of redrawing the lines, several of the states were compelled to create districts with enough minority strength to ensure that a minority representative would be elected. The result has led to a new legislature computer game called "shapes," which replaces the older and neater game of "blocks." [2] "Blocks" used counties, townships, cities, and voting districts as the building units (or "blocks") for creating districts. In "shapes," computers are used to create new districts that maximize the representation prospects of minorities.

While use of blocks usually resulted in neat, box- or rectangularlike districts, the latest shapes to emerge from the computers are considerably more difficult to define. The Texas legislature created what looks like a snowflake district in Houston and the Illinois legislature developed a district that has been likened to an earmuff in Chicago. The North Carolina legislature added the so-called "I-85" district that sits astride an interstate highway running from Durham to Charlotte that defies any characteristic description at all.

While this game metaphor may seem overly cute, it does capture the nature of how legislatures have been trying to cope with some difficult constraints on redistricting. The basic game remains the same: trying to provide equal representation for all citizens. But in some cases the legislatures must now work overhard to ensure that some citizens do get the representation they should have. Without such torturous and directed line-drawing activ-

ities, some minorities would remain submerged in majority-dominated districts. Put simply, their candidates would never win.

In April 1993, the U. S. Supreme Court heard a case challenging the North Carolina "I-85" district. Those who have been involved in the redistricting struggles of the 1990s are now waiting to see if legal constraints are to be altered yet again or allowed to stand as they are. In 1986, the Court for the first time agreed that mapping of districts is subject to court challenge if discrimination against *identifiable political groups* can be proved. The definition of such groups, however, was not entirely clear from the Court's opinion.[3] In the current case, it is whites arguing that they are being discriminated against.[4] (See "Constitutional Doubt Is Thrown on Bizarre-Shaped Districts," box, p. 22.)

How important is redistricting? Former U.S. representative (R-Ill.) and recent secretary of labor Lynn Martin, argues: "We're talking about changing the face of America. That's how important this is." [5]

Following the 1992 elections, Democrats controlled the state legislatures in twenty-five states, Republicans in nine states. Split control occurred in fifteen states. (Nebraska has a one-house, nonpartisan legislature.) But party numbers do not always add up to party control since several state legislatures can be run by informal, bipartisan coalitions. These coalitions may be the result of deep divisions in the majority party over the choice of house speaker. Other coalitions can be due to divisions over ideology or specific issues. Still others occur when the minority party grows in strength and seeks to redress what it sees as an abridgment of its rights by joining in a coalition with dissidents from the majority party in seeking new leadership.[6]

A unique problem of party control occurred in the Indiana house, where a 50-50 member party tie led to a dual leadership system of "speakers *du jour*" or "stereo speakers," which resulted in a difficult 1989 legislative session. One solution adopted by the legislature was to increase the membership in the House from 100 to 101 to preclude the possibility of a tie in the future.[7] But the problem was resolved when, near the end of the 1989 session, one Democratic member switched his party affiliation to Republican. In 1993, the Michigan House selected co-speakers when the 1992 elections produced a 55-55 split in seats. While most expected the agreement to last throughout the full session, "neither leader said they would stop looking for a defector." [8]

Legislative Reforms

These reapportionment decisions coincided with a general revival of state government during the mid- to late 1960s. The revival came at a time when the states sorely needed a new, more positive image. Television news programs pictured southern governors blocking school doorways to keep minority students out. Numerous publications described the apparent failures, unrepresentativeness, and corruption of state governments.[9] It took national legislation such as the Civil Rights Act of 1964 and the Voting Rights Act of 1965 and U.S. Supreme Court decisions to force state governments to fulfill their responsibilities to those they represented.

In the 1970s and 1980s, state after state passed laws that drastically reformed state legislatures and improved their public image. The following examples are representative of the kinds of laws passed:

- Tighter deadlines and improved scheduling procedures for considering legislation
- Automated bill status and statute retrieval systems
- Computerized systems for the state budget process
- Relaxation of constitutional restrictions on what issues legislators can consider

- More flexible and rewarding systems of legislative compensation
- Greater staff capability in bill drafting, legal services, budgeting, and postaudit and program evaluation
- Longer sessions, and the replacement of biennial sessions with annual ones
- Longer terms for legislators, and individual offices for each legislator
- Expanded personal staffs

Changes are now afoot as voters in many states have made their state legislatures the target of the initiative process. Reform now is aimed at restricting rather than enhancing legislatures. As noted in the introduction to Part II, by 1993 some seventeen states had adopted term limits on their elected officials, with some taking special aim at state legislators. Further, the 1990 term limits initiative in California "also cut the legislature's operating budget by 38 percent. Layoffs of staff began soon after, and California's staff has been cut substantially." [10] Budget problems in other states as well may lead to even more cuts in legislative staff.

Why are voters targeting their legislatures? One reason might be the continuing decline in public esteem of state elected officials. In a 1985 national poll, only 16 percent of the respondents rated the honesty and ethical standards of state political officeholders as high or very high—although this was better than in 1977 when only 11 percent did so. At least state officials were rated three times better than car salesmen, who were at the bottom of the list at 5 percent.[11] A recent study compiled the results of state polls that asked citizens their views on the overall performance of their state legislatures. The results indicating the legislature was doing a fair or poor job outnumbered those saying it was doing a good or excellent job.[12] Comparing these results with a multistate study in the late 1960s, which asked a similar question, it is clear that citizens' views of legislative performance have declined over the past two decades.[13]

Another reason for a decline in citizens' views of how well legislatures operate is the increasing number of states in which scandals have been found. The roster of states with such problems continues to grow and includes Arizona, California, New York, South Carolina, Tennessee, Texas, and West Virginia.[14] Alan Ehrenhalt suggests that the trend toward negative campaigning may also be a factor. The negativity of campaign rhetoric often leaves voters with the feeling that they are selecting the least of two evils when they make their decision.[15]

But some observers argue that a major cause for the decline in public support has a budgetary policy base to it. In the 1980s, the economy grew and state revenues outpaced state expenditures. It was easy to make decisions with an ever-increasing pot of money available. New or additional taxes were not needed to provide more for citizens. Beginning in the late 1980s and continuing into the 1990s, however, the states and their elected leaders began facing hard times as the economy faltered nationally and, in some states, catastrophically. The decision calculus changed dramatically as legislators and governors were forced to raise taxes even as they cut back on state services.[16]

In the 1990s, budgetary issues have taken precedence over all other issues. Legislators are facing decisions that are almost impossible to make even in nonelection years. While the size of state budget deficits seems small when measured against that of the national government, some of these deficits are so great that basic changes in what state governments do and how they pay for it are being made. For example, the California deficit is so great that even if they dismantled all educational programs beyond the high school level, the deficit would still be in the billions!

Separation of Powers

State legislatures do not operate in a vacuum. In most instances they are uneasy partners with other actors in state government. Other parts of state government, not just the legislatures, were reformed in response to the "indictment" of the states in the 1960s. Gubernatorial powers were strengthened to make governors the chief executives of the states in fact, rather than just in theory. However, these reforms did little to reduce the natural conflict between the executive and legislative branches that is built into state constitutions.

The U.S. Constitution and state constitutions share a fundamental principle: separation of powers. Consider, for example, this article from the Colorado Constitution that clearly separates legislative, executive, and judicial authority:

> Article III. Distribution of Powers. The powers of the government of this state are divided into three distinct departments, the legislative, executive and judicial; and no person or collection of persons charged with the exercise of powers properly belonging to one of these departments shall exercise any power properly belonging to either of the others, except as in this constitution expressly directed or permitted.

The principle of separation of powers is expressly adopted in the constitutions of thirty-eight states. Twenty-nine of these states include some exceptions to a strict interpretation of the principle. (The last clause of Article III above is an example of such an exception.) Nine states require strict separation with no exceptions allowed. But twelve state constitutions do not include any separation of powers provisions.[17]

Executive Branch Appointments. Appointments are perhaps the area of greatest tension between the executive and legislative branches of state government. Legislatures often have a constitutionally mandated power to confirm gubernatorial appointments. They can cause the governor problems with this authority, as Republican governor George Deukmejian of California found out in 1988 when he tried to appoint Republican U.S. representative Dan Lungren as state treasurer. In the Democratically controlled legislature, the House approved the appointment by a 43-32 vote, but the Senate voted against the appointment 19-21. This split vote raised an interesting constitutional question: Deukmejian argued that a nomination is confirmed unless rejected by both houses, but the legislative counsel argued that either house could veto an appointee. The state's attorney general, John Van de Kamp, a Democrat, agreed with the legislative counsel. Part of the politics of this situation was Lungren's ambition to run for governor in 1990 and the Democrats' view that Lungren's appointment would strengthen his future candidacy.[18] Lungren did not run for the governorship but Van de Kamp did and lost in the Democratic primary.

In some states, legislatures have the statutory or constitutional authority to make appointments to boards and commissions; they even can appoint their own members to these positions. Only four states strictly ban legislators from serving on boards and commissions. Eleven states allow legislators to serve on advisory bodies only. However, twenty states permit legislators to sit on boards and commissions that exercise management responsibilities.[19] This "legislative intrusion" into the executive branch has been challenged successfully in Kentucky, Mississippi, and North Carolina.

Legislative Veto. A second area of tension lies in the increasing use of the legislative veto—a procedure permitting state legislatures (and the U.S. Congress) "to review proposed executive branch regulations or actions and to block or modify those with which they disagree." [20] In lieu of legislative veto legislation, some states have enacted laws regarding review of administrative rule-making procedures.

In the early 1980s there was a rapid rise in the use of the legislative veto—up to forty-one states by mid-1982. However, the tide then turned against this legislative bid to gain increased control over the executive branch. Courts, both state and federal, invalidated the legislative veto as an unconstitutional violation of the separation of powers principle.[21] And voters in several states rejected their legislature's use of a legislative veto.[22] As we enter the 1990s, two state high courts—Idaho and Wisconsin—have reopened this power for their legislatures, albeit with some restrictions.[23]

The State Budget

With all of the action focused on the state budget, it is no surprise that power politics is also involved. In some states, governors and legislative leaders are locked in a struggle over who will control the state's finances. Because of uncertainty over projecting next year's revenues, the need to cut back on expenditures, or even whether or not to raise taxes, budgets are being adopted much later than in the past—some well into the budget year. Governors want increased power and flexibility over budget making, while legislators find themselves forced to make difficult decisions with little time for deliberation.

Further, when governors and legislatures argue over the budget, delays in providing funds for programs and local governments occur. This leads to the embarrassing situation of the governor and legislature fighting budget battles in broad daylight with a seeming "inability to make even the most basic decisions on time." [24] This has been the story in California between Republican governor Pete Wilson and the Democratic legislature, in Connecticut with independent governor Lowell Weicker and the Democratic state legislature, and in New York with Mario Cuomo and the split control legislature there.[25]

Part V explores different aspects of state legislatures. Rob Gurwitt of *Governing* addresses the changes occurring in the state legislatures. Tom Loftus, former speaker of the Wisconsin House, discusses the ethics problems facing legislators. And Robb Douglas in *State Government News* revisits one of the most unique reforms that has been suggested for state legislatures: a move to the unicameral legislative structure.

Notes

1. The term "gerrymander" originated in 1812, the year the Massachusetts legislature carved a district out of Essex County that historian John Fiske said had a "dragonlike contour." When the painter Gilbert Stuart saw the misshapen district, he penciled in a head, wings, and claws and exclaimed: "That will do for a salamander!"—to which editor Benjamin Russell replied: "Better say a Gerrymander"—after Elbridge Gerry, the governor of Massachusetts. Congressional Quarterly's *Guide to U.S. Elections*, 2d ed. (Washington, D.C.: Congressional Quarterly, 1985), 691.
2. See Kimball W. Brace and Doug Chapin, "Shades of Redistricting," *State Government News* 34:12 (December 1991): 6-9.
3. Quoted in Tom Watson, "Drawing the Line(s) in 1990: A High-Stakes Game to Control the Legislatures," *Governing* 1:8 (May 1988): 20-21.
4. Holly Idelson, "Supreme Court Considers Racially Conscious Map," *Congressional Quarterly Weekly Report*, April 24, 1993, 1034-35.
5. Watson, "Drawing the Line(s)," 20.
6. Malcolm E. Jewell, "The Durability of Leadership," *State Legislatures* 15:10 (November/December 1989): 11, 21.
7. James Grass, "Legislative Deadlock Makes for Full House," *USA Today*, April 19, 1989, 6A.
8. "Michigan: Co-Speakers of the House," *The Hotline*, January 15, 1993, 15.
9. See, for example, Frank Trippet, *The States—*

United They Fell (New York: World Publishing, 1967).
10. Alan Rosenthal, "The Legislative Institution—in Transition and at Risk," in *The State of the States,* 2d ed., ed. Carl E. Van Horn (Washington, D.C.: CQ Press, 1993), 127.
11. "An Erosion of Ethics?" *Public Opinion* 9:4 (November-December 1986): 21.
12. Patrick Cotter, "Legislatures and Public Opinion," *The Journal of State Government* 59:1 (Spring 1986): 47-50. A 1992 survey in Michigan indicated that fewer than 10 percent of the respondents had a great deal of trust in the information they received from state legislators regarding a proposed hazardous waste site. See *State Policy Reports* 10:17 (1992): 6.
13. Merle Black, David M. Kovenock, and William C. Reynolds, *Political Attitudes in the Nation and the States* (Chapel Hill, N.C.: Institute for Research in Social Science, 1974), 186.
14. To learn more about this problem, see "Evaluating State Legislatures," *State Policy Reports* 9:4 (January 1991): 8-13; Rob Gurwitt, "Deadly Stings and Wounded Legislatures," *Governing* 4:9 (June 1991): 26-31; and Jeffrey L. Katz, "Sipping from the Cup of Corruption," *Governing* 5:2 (November 1991): 27-28.
15. Alan Ehrenhalt, "An Embattled Institution," *Governing* 5:4 (January 1992): 28.
16. Rosenthal, "The Legislative Institution," and Thad Beyle, *Governors and Hard Times* (Washington, D.C.: CQ Press, 1992).
17. Jody George and Lacy Maddox, "Separation of Powers Provisions in State Constitutions," in *Boards, Commissions, and Councils in the Executive Branch of North Carolina State Government* (Raleigh, N.C.: North Carolina Center for Public Policy Research, 1984), 51.
18. "Politics: Split Vote Leaves Rep. Lungren Dangling," *Congressional Quarterly Weekly Report*, February 27, 1988, 549.
19. "Legislators Serving on Boards and Commissions," *State Legislative Report* (Denver: National Conference of State Legislatures, 1983), as reported in George and Maddox, "Separation of Powers Provisions," 52.
20. Walter J. Oleszek, *Congressional Procedures and the Policy Process*, 3d ed. (Washington, D.C.: CQ Press, 1988), 297.
21. The U.S. Supreme Court case was *Immigra-*

tion and Naturalization Service v. Jagdish Rai Chadha (1983).

22. New Jersey in 1985, Alaska and Michigan in 1986, Nevada in 1988.

23. "Idaho Court Says Legislature May Veto Administrative Rules," *State Legislatures* 16:6 (July 1990): 14; and "Wisconsin Finds No Separation of Power Violation in Statute Authorizing Legislative Committee to Suspend Administrative Rule," *State Constitutional Law Bulletin* 5:6 (March 1992): 1-2.

24. Linda Wagar, "Power Play," *State Government News* 35:7 (July 1992): 9.

25. Ibid. For an extensive discussion of the situations in California and Connecticut, see Richard W. Gable, "Pete Wilson: A Centrist in Trouble," and Russell D. Murphy, "Lowell P. Weicker, Jr., a Maverick in the 'Land of Steady Habits,' " in Beyle, *Governors and Hard Times,* 43-59 and 61-75.

Legislatures: The Faces of Change

by Rob Gurwitt

There was never any question that change was coming to the state legislatures in 1993. A brand-new set of district maps, an unusual number of senior members choosing to retire, an angry and vindictive-sounding electorate—just about all the ingredients seemed to be present for at least a small-scale political revolution.

And long before the election actually took place, there was a conventional wisdom as to what that revolution would include. It would feature massive turnover and big crops of freshmen all over the country, large new blocs of women and minorities, and a stronger Republican presence fueled by the hundreds of new suburban districts carved into place through redistricting. It would also reflect the citizen activism that was springing up in reaction to the careerist turn legislatures had been taking.

Well, it isn't turning out to be that simple. Now that the new legislatures are gathering, it is clear that there have been shifts of a depth and intricacy that nobody predicted even in an election year that saw "change" glibly tossed about as a mantra.

Some 30 percent of the legislators taking their seats [in 1993] are new. That figure is fairly striking by the standards of the last few legislative sessions. In 1990, for example, the turnover was barely 20 percent. But if you compare 1992 to other redistricting years, nothing all that revolutionary happened. In 1982, the last time redistricting took place, 32 percent of the legislative seats in the country turned over. A decade before that, it was 38 percent.

When it comes to women and minorities, there is no question that something significant has taken place. There are 125 more women, 27 more Hispanics and 65 more African Americans among the nation's legislators than there were a year ago. The political effect, however, is largely concentrated in a few places—in Mississippi, for example, where fully a quarter of the new black seats are located and where blacks now make up about a quarter of the House of Representatives.

But nothing demonstrates the subtlety of change in America's legislatures better than the story of the Republicans, the Democrats and suburbia.

A year ago, it was easy to predict that suburban power would grow in the legislatures: Census figures that placed nearly half the country's population in the suburbs pretty

Rob Gurwitt is a staff writer for *Governing*. This article is reprinted from *Governing* 6:5 (February 1993): 29-32.

much guaranteed that reapportionment would shift seats in their direction. And given the voting patterns of suburban America over the past few decades, it was reasonable to go on and predict that the suburban seats newly created for the 1990s would be a bastion of GOP strength.

Some places have lived up to that forecast. Republicans now control the Illinois Senate, for example, largely because of their lock on the Chicago suburbs. The Georgia House will be remade in the next few years by new Republican legislators from the outer suburbs ringing Atlanta.

In California and Washington State, however, suburban power is having exactly the opposite effect. Democrats are in firm control of those legislatures precisely *because* they did so well in the suburbs in 1992. The nuances of suburban politics, in other words, are turning out to be far more interesting than many people expected.

Washington State was a debacle for the Republican Party: Democrats took over the Senate, strengthened their hold on the House and won the governorship. The GOP apparatus, largely under the control of militant conservatives and the Christian Right, was virtually useless during the campaign, and in fact may have done the party some harm: The state GOP platform, drawn up under heavy fundamentalist influence, condemned the teaching of witchcraft in schools and at one point in its drafting included language decrying the practice of yoga. It could not have been orchestrated any better to frighten the affluent, socially liberal Seattle suburbanites who are the new power in state politics. "It got so much attention, I began to suspect this was a plot to do Republicans in once and for all," says Linda Matson, a former business lobbyist with ties to the GOP.

Just as important, Democrats offered a crop of suburban candidates who seemed to provide a legislative model for the rhetoric of change Bill Clinton was trumpeting on a national level. "They are strong believers that government can and should make a difference, but are moderate on the notion of how government should do that," says House Majority Leader Lorraine Hein. "They look first at efficiency and streamlining government—that was a steady theme throughout the campaign—and mix it with a desire to be quite realistic in approaching problems."

Much the same story played itself out on a larger field in California, where Democrats have essentially the same strength in Sacramento as they did last year—they lost a seat in the Senate, but gained two in the Assembly—despite a redistricting plan that when it was first unveiled had Republicans openly chortling about their prospects for taking over at least one chamber.

Here, too, Democrats fielded a set of suburban candidates who tended to be politically moderate and to fit comfortably into their middle-class constituencies. Those candidates, combined with economic stagnation and ideological squabbling in Republican ranks, led to an election in which Democrats won many of the new suburban seats that were supposed to be the basis of the GOP bonanza in the 1990s in the nation's biggest state. Democrats won not only in the socially liberal suburban territory around the Bay Area, but in unexpected places, such as the suburbs of San Diego County, that under the state's normal political calculus would have gone Republican.

For all those disappointments, however, there are states where things are going according to Republican plan, states that offer some hint of a GOP comeback over the course of the decade. Georgia is perhaps the best example.

Atlanta's booming suburbs—and for the first time, some suburban districts in other parts of the state—have boosted Republican strength in the Georgia House by 17 seats, the

largest numerical gain by either party anywhere in the country in 1992. While the 52
Republican seats in the 180-seat chamber
would scarcely rate notice in a northern legislature, in Georgia they mark a political water-
shed. For the first time, Republican legislators
have the numbers to make an impact on the
course of legislation.

That may be understating it. As the
legislature opens for business, there is specula-
tion of all sorts: about suburban Republicans
ganging up with conservative rural Democrats
against inner-city Atlanta; about Republicans
and liberal urbanites joining to promote a
reform agenda; about Republicans aiding
Democrats from suburbia and the smaller
cities who believe the old-line rural leadership
doesn't have their interests in mind. "Let's be
honest," says Johnny Isakson, a former House
Republican leader who is now in the state
Senate. "Until people have an opportunity to
perform under the light, you never can be sure
what substantial change there will be. But
there is one inevitability: The Republican vote
in the House can combine with one of three or
four caucuses to form a majority."

But the Southern legislature changed
most by redistricting is surely Mississippi's,
where the presence of 32 black representatives
and 10 black state senators has already made
for a new balance of power.

Soon after the November election, several
members of the legislature's black caucus introduced their own budget—an unheard-of
maneuver. The measure would boost spending
on AIDS and for the state's historically black
colleges, and includes funds to raise teachers'
pay. "We're signaling that they can't just ram
through a budget like they have in the past,"
says Ed Blackmon, a Canton attorney who has
become the informal leader of the caucus.

Just how important a factor the black
caucus will be is still uncertain. The caucus
has itself been badly divided in the past year,

especially over redistricting. Just as important,
many of the new black legislators arrive in
Jackson with considerable backgrounds as
lawyers, school administrators and state or
local officials. It is by no means certain that
they will be willing to follow Blackmon's lead
or act as a bloc at anyone's insistence.

Still, the black caucus seems destined in
the long run to have a dramatic effect on
partisan politics in Mississippi—and serve either as a model or a warning for other states.
The reason is that Democratic success in much
of the South has come to rest on the party's
ability to put together biracial coalitions that
join African Americans and liberal whites with
conservative whites from rural districts. The
more the Democratic Party falls into two distinct legislative factions, one black and one
white, the harder it will be for the party to
bring those factions together in an election.
"Then," says political scientist Charles Bullock
of the University of Georgia, "you just reinforce
the tendency of whites to vote Republican."

Indeed, Republicans can look with some
satisfaction on long-term prospects throughout
the South. A decade ago, despite Ronald Reagan's popularity both in Dixie and at the
national level, they held just 17 percent of the
Southern legislative seats; this year they hold
29 percent. They are tied with Democrats in
the Florida Senate and made more than respectable progress in 1992 in South Carolina,
Texas and Georgia. Clearly, argues Karl
Kurtz of the National Conference of State
Legislatures, the Democratic stranglehold on
Southern legislative power has been broken.

But that news comes within a larger
context that Republicans cannot help but find
troubling. Democrats have now held between
57 and 63 percent of the country's legislative
seats for virtually all of the past three decades.
[In 1993], despite a net GOP gain of about 40
seats among the nearly 7,500 in the 50 states,
the overall Democratic share is still at about

I'll Match Your Nine Lobbyists and Raise You Twelve

. . . In city councils and county commissions and state legislatures everywhere, the era of one-man power lobbying, conducted at lunch and on the golf course, is drawing to a close. The era of swarm lobbying has begun.

Alan Rosenthal, a Rutgers University political scientist, provides some remarkable examples of this change in his insightful new book, *The Third House: Lobbyists and Lobbying in the States.* One thing he shows is that Florida may in fact be the swarm lobbying capital of America. A couple of years ago, the major car rental companies fought it out in the Florida legislature over the rental surcharge known as the collision damage waiver. For complex reasons, Hertz and Avis wanted it legally abolished. Alamo, based in Florida, wanted to keep it. After a battle that involved 50 lobbyists, 18 of them working for Alamo alone, Alamo won.

But if Florida represents the state of the art, it is not by much. When Texaco fought Pennzoil in the Texas legislature, 25 independent "contract" lobbyists found themselves gainfully employed by one of the two sides. "It was almost an insult not to be hired," one of them said. In some high-stakes contests, rich corporations and interest groups are doing with lobbyists what the St. Louis Cardinals used to do with shortstops—signing up more than they need, just so the opposition can't get them. Dayton-Hudson did that in promoting a bill in the Minnesota legislature aimed at protecting itself from a hostile takeover. At one point, there were 15 lobbyists on the Dayton-Hudson team—a virtual monopoly of the people who had any credentials on the subject.

It is no mystery why this is happening in so many diverse places at the same time. Power has been dispersed. Legislative institutions throughout the country are opening up their decision-making process to even the most junior members. On many of them, there isn't really a "man to see" anymore. If you want to win, you are well advised to see them all. And that can take a lot of bodies.

"It used to be," Alan Rosenthal says, "that if you could get to the legislative leader, you had it. But as power gets more fragmented, you have to deal with every which one. You've got to work every member."

Source: Alan Ehrenhalt, *Governing* 6:4 (January 1993): 7-8.

---

59 percent. Democrats are holding roughly even nationally despite significant losses in the South. And there is a reason for that: States in the North that used to be competitive or even tilt Republican at the legislative level have turned so heavily Democratic that it is hard to envision the GOP controlling them any time in the foreseeable future.

Republicans now control both legislative chambers in nine states—up from six in 1992—but Democrats hold both chambers in 25 states. Even more striking, Republicans control state government entirely—that is, both the governorship and the legislature—in only three states, Arizona, Utah and New Hampshire, while Democrats do so in 16. Crucial legislative bodies—the California Assembly and Senate, the New York Assembly, the Illinois House—seem to have all but permanent Democratic majorities.

It is no coincidence that those last three all have full-time legislatures that meet year-round and have come to attract politicians who treat legislating as a profession. Republicans have

Leadership in the Colorado General . . .

. . . Colorado has a system of institutionally strong leaders. In the General Assembly the single most powerful position is that of House speaker. Elected by the majority caucus, the speaker is the undisputed leader of the party and is authorized by chamber rules to appoint all majority party committee members and all committee chairmen and to assign bills to committees. In addition, the speaker may alter the size of committees (within limits set by the rules) and grant such important exceptions to House rules as waiver of bill deadlines and bill introduction limits.

Other top House posts include the majority and minority leaders. The majority leader is a close associate of the speaker and is influential both in floor proceedings and in the workings of the majority party. The minority leader can be influential, too, in publicly countering majority party positions and maneuvers and in lining up minority party members on vetoes, veto threats and the like. Colorado has had a Republican legislature and Democratic governor for all but two of the past 20 years.

The leadership arrangement in the Senate is similar, except that the Senate president, who is elected by the majority caucus, shares power more broadly with the majority leader. But as in the House, leadership decides committee and committee chairmen assignments, determines where bills go, and controls the implementation of chamber rules. During the 1980s, seven legislators held the positions of speaker or majority or minority leader in the House, and eight did so in the Senate. Of the seven in the House, four were among the 22 with over eight years of service. In the Senate, the longtimers numbered four of the eight. Had the term limit been in place a decade earlier, the major positions of leadership would have been in different hands in more than half of the instances (8 of 15). From another perspective, of the 130 House members who either quit at or before serving eight years or who were still in office with fewer than eight years of service, only three held one of the key leadership seats. In the Senate, just four of the 54 shorttimers held key leadership positions. Clearly, then, it is the longtimers, those who would have been eliminated by term limitation, who have disproportionately held the levers of power in the recent past.

Even more interesting, and perhaps more important, are the particular individuals who comprised the group of 17 Senate and 22 House longtimers. Arguably the most powerful member of the General Assembly in recent decades was Speaker Carl "Bev" Bledsoe. An eastern plains rancher with a close-to-the-vest style and a reported affinity for Machiavelli's *Prince*, he served in the House for 20 years, 10 of them (the full decade of the 1980s) as speaker. Bledsoe took full advantage of the speaker's powers, especially in committee assignments, bill referrals and rules waivers. He knew how to construct committees with collective predispositions that fit comfortably with his own, and he knew how to use these committees to pass, kill or modify policy proposals.

For most of his tenure, Bledsoe kept a like-minded protégé on the powerful six-member Joint Budget Committee, as JBC chairman in alternate years, and as chairman of the House Appropriations Committee each year. Bledsoe, now a Statehouse lobbyist, became a legend of sorts; liberals and much of the Colorado press detested his policies and tactics, while conservatives and farm-ranch interests cherished his support

lost ground in the big states largely because, as a party suspicious of government in general, they have found it difficult to generate candidates willing to make the careerist commitment.

The political climate of 1992 appeared to offer them some good news, in the form of citizen resentment against careerism and prolonged incumbency all over the country. Term-limit proposals were on the ballot in 14 states in November, and passed in all 14. By

... Assembly and Term Limitation

and protection.

Joining Bledsoe as majority leader for six of his 10 years as speaker was Ron Strahle, another now-retired 20-year veteran. Strahle, a quick-minded attorney, knew the House rules well and knew how to use them. In addition to his years as majority leader, he served as chairman of the House Judiciary Committee for several years, and for two years he served as speaker. Strahle, too, wielded significant influence. He was followed as House majority leader for the other four years of the 1980s by Chris Paulson, who retired in 1990 after 10 years of service.

Thus, for the entire decade of the 1980s, the two most powerful positions in the House majority party leadership, and indeed in the House itself, were held by lawmakers who would not have been there had the term limits been in place a decade earlier.

The situation with the House minority party was a bit different. Four different representatives held that position in the 1980s and just one, the current leader, served more than eight years. The three who did not included Frederico Pena, who later became Denver's first Hispanic mayor, David Skaggs, who went on to the U.S. House (and wrote dozens of bad checks), and Larry Trujillo, who became a Colorado state senator and minority leader in that chamber. The one longtimer, Ruth Wright, an able and articulate attorney, is as influential as a leader can be when heading a caucus that has been out of power for nearly two decades and that changes leadership frequently.

A similar picture emerges from the Senate. A 1974 amendment to Colorado's Constitution replaced the lieutenant governor as the chief presiding officer of the Senate with an elected Senate president. Since then, just two people have served in that powerful position and both of them, Republicans Fred Anderson and Ted Strickland, now have (Strickland) or had (Anderson) lengthy tenure. Anderson served in the Senate for 16 years and Strickland for 24, albeit with one two-year break when he was appointed to serve out a partial term as lieutenant governor and then failed in a bid to become governor. Anderson, who is now a very successful Statehouse lobbyist, served as Senate president for eight years and developed what were then known as "Anderson's rules," so-named because of his firm control of the chamber.

Also in the Senate, one of the two members who served as majority leader during the 1980s had surpassed eight years of service (16 years), as had one of four Democrats who served as minority leader.

With an eight-year limit, then, the Colorado General Assembly would have been without the influence of a powerful speaker, the Senate's first two presidents, an especially effective majority leader, and several other long-tenure leaders. There is, of course, no way to tell whether others, equally unique or of comparable influence, might have been there instead. . . .

Source: John A. Straayer, "Possible Consequences of Legislative Term Limitations," *Comparative State Politics* 13:3 (June 1992): 1-15. Reprinted with permission from *Comparative State Politics.*

the end of the decade, term limits will be a fact of life in legislatures throughout much of the country, including, most prominently, California.

That may eventually serve to reduce the Republican disadvantage, but in the short run the 1992 election presents a very different lesson. The fact is, despite the anti-careerist sentiment and despite the popularity of term limits, more than 70 percent of incumbents have been returned to office, a higher percentage than in the past two redistricting years, when no such discontent appeared to exist. The implication is that the long-run trend toward professionalism is more powerful than the current frustrations of the electorate.

And that point is borne out by the results from 1992 in several smaller states, states where the tradition is amateur-style citizen politics but where it is professionalism that shaped the legislatures now taking office.

In Vermont, for example, Democrats picked up 16 House seats to win control of that body for the first time in the state's history. It was a victory that far outshone the GOP gain of one seat to break a tie in the Senate.

At first glance, it might seem that the Democrats' success was a natural development. Once viscerally Republican—despite an occasional Democratic governor—Vermont has for years been losing its GOP cast. But the result has not, in fact, been a Democratic or even a liberal state. Rather, says University of Vermont political scientist Frank Bryan, it is a state that is almost impossible to label, one in which the most predictable quality is unpredictability. Under those circumstances, the ability to recruit strong candidates and support them in campaigns is making an ever-greater difference, even in a state whose politicians tend to cringe at the mere mention of the word "professional."

Democrats took the Vermont House in 1992 largely because Speaker Ralph Wright spent the last several years recruiting, coaching and helping to fund Democratic candidates, setting up campaign seminars and appointing a small coterie of Democratic House members to keep close watch over the individual campaigns of the party's nominees.

"All races in Vermont tend to be individual," says Representative Barbara Grimes, one of the Democratic "coaches." "It's how long a candidate has been in the community, how public they are, their social and business connections. It's becoming clear that you have to have quality candidates, not just sponge. And the process we put our candidates through made them better."

If there is a consolation for Republicans, it is that they can play this game too, if they are willing to take the trouble. In Kansas [in 1992], Republican leaders in both houses of the legislature took an active recruitment role, basically for the first time, and enjoyed results comparable to what the Democrats achieved in Vermont. The GOP took back control of the Kansas House, which it had lost for only the second time this century in 1990, and built up a lopsided majority in the Senate.

Kansas Republican leaders started early by making sure that their incumbents were planning to work hard for reelection. "The message was, 'Either run a tough race or don't bother running,' " says Steve Brown, the state GOP's executive director. The result was that a fair number of senior legislators, particularly in the Senate, retired—no real loss for the party in a year when incumbency held its share of disadvantages. Republicans then recruited a set of generally younger, eager candidates, and dispatched staff to help them write speeches, produce brochures and advertising, and track their campaigns.

Much of that was new territory for Kansas Republicans. "In the past, the Democrats have been aggressive and organized, while Republicans have been stoic and statesman-like," says Jeff Wagaman, chief of staff to Senate President Paul "Bud" Burke. "This time, we decided to match them blow for blow. The old days when you put your name on the ballot and put up some billboards are gone in Kansas. Now it's tracking, it's polling data, it's complicated campaigns that track media. It's almost scary how this is evolving—we're a part-time legislature, but running for office is becoming a near full-time job."

Legislative Ethics:
The Rules of the Game

by Tom Loftus

"I'm not a saint, but I'm not a mortal sinner." With that pithy statement, big-time Wisconsin lobbyist Gary Goyke sought to put a more innocent spin on his activities that became the center of a 1989 ethics scandal in the Wisconsin Legislature.

Goyke was a former seminarian who ran for the Legislature and later was elected and distinguished himself as a post-Watergate reformer who fought for openness in government. He was defeated in 1982 when reapportionment dealt him a bad hand. He turned, like many former legislators, to lobbying.

He was a natural. Soon he was known as "Goyke Inc." and his stable of clients grew to include the who's who of those with their hands out. He had the world by the tail until a disgruntled employee, in an act of self protection, gave copies of office documents to a free-lance reporter.

It seems Goyke routinely reimbursed employees for campaign contributions given at his directions. In an August 1988 interview with criminal investigators from the Wisconsin Department of Justice, former Goyke employee, Gail Shimon, recalled a comment made to her by a fellow employee: "Lucky you weren't here. I was the only one around and had to write a check for Gary."

That was laundering. And, under the law in Wisconsin, laundering campaign contributions is a felony.

I came to the Wisconsin Legislature in 1976 with a class of reformers determined to restore the confidence in government shaken by Watergate and the Vietnam War. When the dust settled, Wisconsin had on the books: public financing of campaigns, restrictions on political action committee contributions, election-day voter registration, a tough-as-nails ethics law, and model open-records and open-meetings laws.

When I left the Legislature at the end of 1990, Wisconsin had an even tougher ethics code—a lobbyist now can't even buy a politician a cup of coffee—and the Dane County district attorney had just closed the books on the last of the legislators who had been caught in the only modern day scandal in Wisconsin worthy of the name.

One state senator was forced from office and spent time in jail. Eleven other legislators paid fines for violations. Goyke pleaded guilty

Tom Loftus is former speaker of the Wisconsin Assembly and is a visiting professor at Rutgers University. This article is reprinted with permission from *Spectrum: The Journal of State Government* 66:1 (Winter 1993): 27-30.

to a felony for laundering contributions in a deal with the district attorney that allowed him to continue lobbying.

What is the lesson?

You need more than tough, understandable ethics and lobbying laws. Three more things are needed, like the legs of a three-legged stool.

First, legislative leaders must understand the law and conduct themselves inside its boundaries and set an example. Leaders must not be expected to police their colleagues. This has to be done by an independent group. However, leaders set the ethical tone of the institution.

Second, prosecutors must apply the law consistently. To deter lawmakers from succumbing to daily temptations by lobbyists, there must be an understandable example set by the prosecutor when a violation occurs.

Third, fear of the consequences is the most important deterrent to unethical behavior; and fear of the press is paramount. The thud of the newspaper at the doorstep should make a politician's heart beat a little faster. A watchful, picky, even vengeful—but consistent—muckraking newspaper is better than legal strictures that try to anticipate every human foible and temptation.

There are several simple tenets for good legislative ethics and for workable ethics laws.

Legislators shouldn't ask for favors and lobbyists shouldn't offer them. And, disclosure is key. If you are in the legislature, the public should know who you owe, what you own and how you make your money. Legislators work for the people.

Goyke was right in implying the standard expected cannot be saintly behavior. Ethical behavior is not saintly behavior, but it is more than good table manners. I believe in strong ethics laws and strict rules to govern lobbyists.

Ethical behavior is more than not doing things that are illegal. Politicians often think if something is not illegal, it is right. So the stricter the laws, the better.

Perhaps ethical behavior is the way legislators would act in their mothers' presence. This may be an unworkable enforcement mechanism, but it's not too little to expect.

Strong ethics laws reflect high expectations. The ethics of a legislature will reflect the expectations of a state's political culture. Tough laws raise expectations and change the political culture for the better.

I recently testified before the Kentucky Legislature's Task Force on Governmental Ethics, which was set up after a rather base and unimaginative scandal, and I told them: "Do something. It doesn't have to be Wisconsin's law. It's not the details of the law; it's whether you understand that there is a problem and you pass it willingly, hoping it will help, so the people see it as sincere and not a condescending gesture. So they know you get it. Because, now they think you don't get it."

The downside of strong ethics laws are mostly based in myth. Tough ethics laws will not prevent good people from running for office. Financial disclosure laws are not a hardship on officeholders (lawyer-legislators in Wisconsin have to publicly list their clients). And if legislators pay for their own dinner, they will not be struck down by the god of knives and forks.

There is more required than strong ethics laws. If there is fear of nothing more than a minor penalty, some in the legislature willingly skate on thin legal ice because they know it is shallow below. Furthermore, punishment at the polls for ethical transgressions rarely happens.

If newspapers simply complain about the legislature, like drunks on adjoining bar stools, and reporters mistake this for the work it takes to make politicians believe someone is looking over their shoulder, they have failed. Things work best if legislators think twice about crossing the ethical line because there is a

When It Just Looks Bad

Most legislators and their staff agree that avoiding the appearance of impropriety is important. The difficulty is in determining what behavior is perceived as improper, according to a report by the Josephson Institute of Ethics.

The California-based institute conducted a series of national surveys last year to find out whether legislators, staff and journalists agree on the propriety of certain acts.

According to the results, more than 90 percent of journalists, legislators and staff members agreed that "when matters of self-interest are involved, public officials should not engage in conduct that creates appearances of impropriety regardless of their personal beliefs in its propriety."

However, views on what is improper varied. For example, 78 percent of legislators and staff said it would be improper to offer legislation that would benefit an industry in which a lawmaker has a direct financial interest. Slightly more journalists agreed that it would be improper.

But only 63 percent of legislators and staff said it would be improper to introduce legislation that would benefit a major campaign contributor. A total of 81 percent of journalists opposed the idea.

In addition, California legislators and their staffs generally were stricter in their responses than legislators and staffs in other states.

• Seventy-three percent of those surveyed in California said it was wrong for legislators to serve as paid consultants to companies affected by legislation before their committees. A total of 41 percent of legislators in other states said such activity was improper, and 74 percent of journalists found such behavior objectionable.

• Sixty-eight percent of California legislators said it was wrong for the president pro tem of the Senate to be an attorney who regularly represents clients on matters before the state Department of Taxation, compared with 34 percent of other states' legislators and 64 percent of journalists.

The report attributed the disparity to differences in the views of a full-time legislature and a part-time legislature.

Part-time lawmakers in many of the other states have other interests, which make it more difficult to control conflicts of interest and appearances of impropriety.

The four anonymous surveys had a margin of error of 4.5 percent.

Source: State Government News 35:3 (March 1992): 33. Reprinted with permission.

realistic chance mischief will end up on the front page.

The role of the prosecutors and the press gets little attention but means so much to an ethical "atmosphere" in a legislature. If prosecutors and reporters fail as watchdogs, they become part of the problem.

Not one of the misdeeds in Wisconsin was uncovered by the capital press. Reporters had become unsuspecting, thinking Wisconsin's reputation for clean government did not need tending. Like lazy gardeners, they let weeds take root, and were surprised at stunted growth.

The Goyke story broke in a coffee-table magazine that bought it from a free-lancer. At the time, capital reporter Stan Milan said, "Now there's going to be a lot more looking. There's going to be some scrutiny."

This did not happen. Instead the press, awakened from its nap, crucified the unrepentant.

Political Protocol
Part II

As a legislator, you are the speaker at a breakfast meeting of local officials interested in what's happening at the state level. One mayor, the host, later hands you an envelope with $250 and expresses the group's appreciation for your time and expertise so early in the morning. Should you accept?

One of the jobs of a legislator is dealing with constituents and educating the public. Legislators do not merit extra compensation for doing their jobs. A number of states prohibit legislators from accepting honoraria awarded to them in their capacity as public officials. All states should have such a prohibition. However, when a legislator is invited to speak on an outside occupation, an honorarium may be acceptable. Thus, a banker-legislator may address a group on banking practices, and an engineer-legislator on engineering, and so forth.

I appreciate how difficult it is to turn money down, but abstinence makes life simpler. Assume that you were to take the envelope from the mayor. Should you count the money in front of the mayor or should you excuse yourself and count it in the rest room? Assuming it's all there, do you feel obligated to kick back any of the $250 or do you just take the money and run? One moral dilemma leads to another. Just refuse the envelope. You can hope, after all, that somehow the $250 makes its way to your re-election campaign account.

Source: Alan Rosenthal, State Government News 35:8 (August 1992): 38. By permission.

Tom Hauke, assembly majority leader during the recent ethical unpleasantness, was accused of spending a weekend at a resort on Lake Michigan on Goyke's tab. Hauke said he was there as the guest of a representative of the local commercial fishermen and assumed they paid his bill. He was surprised to learn that Goyke, who lobbied for the fishing industry, had paid. He fought the charge.

He took on the press and the prosecutors in a most impolite way. Although his crime was relatively minor, he became the center of news coverage and vilification.

This was too bad, because it distracted from the real ooze that had seeped from the rot that had been uncovered. Swept aside by prosecutors were more cases of laundering, instances of cash demanded and delivered, and a wink at one lawmaker for a serious misdeed and a conviction of another on the same charge. To top it off, the lobbyists involved were allowed to continue to ply their trade.

Even though they didn't have a case against him, the prosecutors let Hauke twist in the wind (although on a rope partly from his own weaving). The press willingly hung Hauke without a trial because, unlike the others, he did not go quietly.

During this long and bloody bout between the press and Hauke (his hometown paper called for his resignation), the prosecutors kept secret that Goyke had vigorously denied that Hauke knew who paid. Since Goyke had spilled his guts, fingered others and admitted to more serious violations, prosecutors had no reason to doubt him.

Hauke paid his fine when, after several appeals, a judge reinterpreted the law's original intent and said that the fact Goyke paid, even if Hauke didn't know, was a violation.

I agree with the ruling. If you are a legislator, it's your responsibility to find out who is paying the tab. I believe "no cup of coffee" laws are workable. Everybody knows the rules and, furthermore, it's hard to figure out just where on the menu corruption begins.

It's much better than Minnesota's law that allows a lobbyist to spend a certain amount entertaining a legislator. This provision has been turned into a stipend by some lawmakers.

Leaders who set an example, penalties uniformly applied and capital press muckrakers will keep legislators on their best behavior. "No cup of coffee" laws are workable, but laws alone will not make saints out of mere mortals.

Going Nebraska's Way

by Robb Douglas

Nebraska's unicameral legislature has remained a curiosity in American political life for more than half a century. But politicians and analysts are taking another look at the system, promoting it as a streamlined way of dealing with 21st century issues.

California Senate Majority Leader Barry Keene has championed the idea of a one-house legislature as part of a major constitutional overhaul in the nation's biggest state. "Divided government is a guarantee of stalemate," Keene says. "The problem is worsened by divisions between the two houses of the legislative branch."

A conference committee of the California Assembly is considering a proposal that would create a Constitutional Revision Commission charged with recommending structural changes in the state government. But the budget impasse has put the constitutional debate on the back burner.

In January [1992], Iowa representatives Darrell Hanson and Rod Halvorson proposed a plan to consolidate that state's two legislative houses into one. Hanson and Halvorson argued that a unicameral system would be cheaper and would bring greater accountability to legislative decision-making. However, their proposal failed to get out of committee.

There have been efforts in other states to change to a unicameral system, but none have succeeded. In Maine, for example, a legislative proposal to change to a one-house legislature has been postponed indefinitely.

Nebraskans continue to tout the advantages of their solution. "I am proud of the fact that this state is the only one to recognize the obvious virtues of such a legislative system," says U.S. Rep. Peter Hoagland.

Advocates of a one-house system believe the simplified structure of a unicameral legislature brings government more directly to the people. In a two-house system, a lobbyist may only need to influence a small number of people on a conference committee. In a one-house system, conference committees don't exist, forcing lobbyists to make their case before a broader group of representatives.

U.S. Rep. Doug Bereuter of Nebraska argues that the legislative process in a unicameral system is "inherently more open and visible to the public because it contains no conference report."

Robb Douglas worked for The Council of State Governments' office in Washington, D.C. This article is reprinted from State Government News 35:12 (December 1992): 14-15. ©1993 The Council of State Governments.

How a Bill Becomes State Law

This graphic shows the most typical way in which proposed legislation is enacted into law in the states. Bills must be passed by both houses of the state legislature in identical form before they can be sent to the governor to be signed or vetoed. Of course, the legislative process differs slightly from state to state.

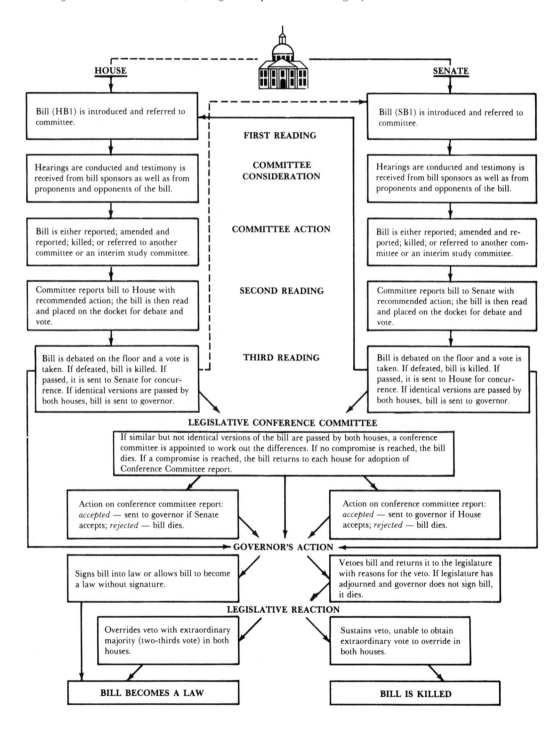

According to supporters, a unicameral body makes legislators more accountable to constituents. Elected officials cannot advocate a position in one chamber while encouraging colleagues in the other to do the opposite. The unicameral legislature also offers greater responsibility to individual legislators and increased cooperation between the executive and legislative branches of government, backers claim.

Advocates of the two-house legislature disagree. They claim a one-house body can be more easily swayed because lobbyists need to persuade fewer people.

Bereuter conceded that one-house bodies may not restrain the impact of lobbying, pointing out that in a one-house legislature there is only one set of leadership to influence.

Two-house proponents also contend that a unicameral system does not always allow for careful consideration of a bill before it becomes law. In a two-house system, one house might enact a law under the sway of emotion, only to have cooler heads prevail in the other.

Supporters of the two-house legislature believe a one-house system violates American constitutional principles because it does not allow for the tradition of checks and balances in government. They point out that the two-house system gives each and every citizen at least two people in the state legislature who will represent their interests.

Even Nebraska did not always have a unicameral legislature. The state's first constitution prescribed a bicameral system, and it was not until 1934, after several abortive attempts, that voters adopted the change.

One reason the switch finally passed was the leadership of U.S. Sen. George Norris, who spearheaded the movement. Norris believed a one-house system would be more effective. He also contended that the two-house system created a barrier between representatives and their constituents.

Concerns about government spending helped sway voters to adopt the change. The nation was struggling to survive the Great Depression, and the prospect of spending less on the Legislature in Lincoln appealed to the state's citizens.

Today, proponents continue to argue that the unicameral legislature is less costly. The figures don't fully support this argument, however. The Nebraska Legislature operates on a $10.5 million budget, or $6.65 per inhabitant, while neighboring Iowa spends $17 million, or $6.12 per inhabitant, on its two-house Legislature. And, while Nebraska ranks 39th in absolute spending among the 50 states, it ranks 23rd in per capita spending on the legislative branch and 17th in percentage of government funds spent on the legislature.

Another component of Norris' successful campaign in 1934 was to make the Nebraska Legislature nonpartisan. Supporters of this innovation believe it makes elected representatives more accountable to constituents, who can cast their votes based on individual qualifications and not party alignment.

State Sen. George Coordsen believes the system works as advertised. Nebraska legislators feel free to vote according to what is in the best interest of their districts without having to toe the party line. "There is no control of the process by outside party officials who may have a different agenda from the immediate needs of the state," Coordsen says.

Nonetheless, the non-partisan aspect of the Legislature has evoked more debate among Nebraskans in recent years than its unicameral structure. Republicans and Democrats have argued that a partisan system would allow the governor to coordinate programs and legislative agendas with members of the Legislature. The parties also could broaden political participation by providing money and resources to candidates who might not otherwise have a chance to seek office, they say.

Despite the debate, Nebraska remains the only state to have a unicameral, nonpartisan legislature. Faced with budget reductions and increasingly complex demands, California and other states are looking for new ideas and new solutions. Whether they decide to go Nebraska's way remains to be seen.

VI.   GOVERNORS AND THE EXECUTIVE BRANCH

As the head of state politics and government and the elected representative of the people, governors must perform a wide variety of duties. They greet visitors, travel to other states and even other countries to lure new businesses to their states, rush to the scene of disasters to demonstrate concern, prepare annual and biennial agendas for government activity, and, on occasion, discuss important issues with the president. From state to state the record varies on how well these and other gubernatorial responsibilities are fulfilled. Some governors are reelected to another term, others are excluded from service, and still others are elected to higher office.

Since its weak beginnings after the overthrow of colonial rule, the American governorship has grown in power and influence. The extensive reforms of the past two decades are becoming evident throughout the executive branches of the fifty states. As Larry Sabato reported a decade ago, "Within the last 20 years, there has been a virtual explosion of reform in state government. In most of the states, as a result, the governor is now truly the master of his own house, not just the father figure." [1] Many of the powers that were restricted have been expanded, and governors now have new powers at their command, such as the ability to reach the people directly through the media and to serve as the key state official in the intergovernmental system of grants and programs.

Moreover, the caliber of the individuals who serve as governors has changed in recent years. Most states have been able to say "goodbye to good-time Charlie" and hello to "a thoroughly trained, well regarded, and capable new breed of state chief executive." [2] This does not mean that all governors have spotless records. There have been several cases of governors and former governors who have run afoul of the law and spent time in prison. [3] One governor, Evan Mecham (R-Ariz., 1987-88), was impeached by the state House, convicted by the state Senate, and removed from office. In April 1993, Governor Guy Hunt (R-Ala.) was convicted "of diverting $200,000 in inaugural funds for personal use" and was automatically removed from office. [4] And as of this writing, Governor David Walters (D-Okla.) is facing a grand jury investigation of alleged irregularities in his raising of campaign funds. [5]

Governors Edwin Edwards (D-La., 1972-80, 1984-88, 1992-) and Bill Sheffield (D-Alaska, 1983-87) had well-publicized escapes from legal and ethical problems in the mid-1980s, but were turned out of office when the voters did what the authorities could not do. In 1991, Edwards was reelected to the office despite his less than glorious departure at the hands of the voters four years previously. More recently, former governor Arch Moore (R-W.Va., 1969-77, 1985-89) agreed to plead guilty to charges of extortion, mail fraud, tax fraud, and obstruction of justice, crimes that he committed during his last two races for governor and during his last term in office. [6]

These governors' activities, other gubernatorial missteps, and what he decried as one of the weakest groups of newly elected governors in 1986 led one careful "governor-watcher" to wonder if the trend toward having better governors may be ebbing in the states. [7] In the 1990s it is not clear whether the governors are better or not. But one thing is very clear, the governors of every state are facing fiscal problems of a magnitude not felt before in the states. [8] Regardless of their skills at politics and governing, as they address these fiscal problems by cutting programs and raising taxes the voters are repaying them with low approval ratings of their performance.[9]

But with the shift in program and fiscal responsibility from the federal government to the states, governors and other state leaders have been put into the spotlight. They are the ones who now must address the domestic side of our policy agenda. Governors have to take the lead in making sure state budgets are balanced at a time when revenues are falling (along with federal government assistance) and the needs of the citizens of the states are increasing.

Leaving recent gubernatorial ethical and legal missteps aside, it is important to realize that governors as a group are tackling the problems of the states in often painful, but very necessary ways. They have developed answers to budgetary and program problems not by rapidly increasing the amounts the states borrow, as does the federal government, but by making difficult decisions on where to cut back existing programs, and when and where to increase revenues by raising taxes. These governors names are constantly in the press, and they are very controversial for what they are having to do. Pete Wilson (R-Calif.), Lowell Weicker (I-Conn.), Lawton Chiles (D-Fla.), Bill Weld (R-Mass.), Jim Florio (D-N.J.), Mario Cuomo (D-N.Y.), and Ann Richards (D-Texas) are just a few.

When national political figures decry their low performance ratings amongst the public, they should look to the states and see what happens to the state politicians who have had to make such difficult decisions. For example, a national poll taken in late June reported that respondents gave new President Bill Clinton a 46 percent approval rating.[10] In twenty-four states reporting polls taken between February 7 and June 16, respondents gave their governors an average approval rating of just 44 percent.[11] Individual ratings ranged from a high of 73 percent for Tommy Thompson (R-Wis.) to a low of 15 percent for

Pete Wilson (R-Calif.). It is not only hard times for the states, but for governors too.

Governors and the State Ambition Ladder

An interesting aspect of the governorship is its place on the "ambition ladder" that eager politicians climb to attain higher and higher levels of success. Clearly, the governorship is the top political office in the states, though there have been instances where the true political leader was a U.S. senator. For example, in Louisiana in the 1930s Huey Long moved his power base from the governor's chair to the U.S. Senate, and in Virginia U.S. senator Harry Byrd ran the famous "Byrd Machine" for several decades earlier in this century.[12] On the whole, though, few offices hold as much promise of political power as does the governorship.

Governors may be all the more powerful if their party also controls the state legislature, though if it holds too many legislative seats, ideological and personal splits in the party can arise and diminish the governor's ability to control. Only twenty states presently have a political makeup in which one party has control of both the governorship and the state legislature—sixteen controlled by Democrats and four by Republicans. More states have a political power split than a political power concentration that could enhance the governor's position.

With both potential and actual political power available, it is no surprise that the governorship is a coveted position at the apex on most states' political ambition ladders. Certain pre-gubernatorial positions are particularly valuable while climbing the ladder: state legislative office, other statewide elective office, law enforcement work, and local elective office. More recently, those holding congressional or U.S. senatorial office are shifting toward the governorship, as are some individuals who have had no previous elective position at all.

Those who succeeded in becoming governor tended to use a "state-based" career ladder: the legislature and other state elective positions. Moving up from a local position, usually as mayor of a large city, has not been built into this ladder, although recent results suggest this might be changing in some state political systems. While moving from a federal position—representative, senator, or cabinet member—has not been part of this ladder in the past, using the U.S. House of Representatives as a launching pad to the governorship appears to be developing, as evidenced in the most recent elections in Delaware, New Jersey, South Carolina, and Washington State.[13] Even members and former members of the U.S. Senate have looked at this track.[14] Still, capturing the governorship from a position outside state politics appears to be difficult. However, there have been a growing number of successful candidates for governor who have not used a "state-based" or other ladder—they just started at the top and won.[15]

But what is the next step after the governorship? Is it a higher elective office? Three of our four most recent presidents were governors—Jimmy Carter (D-Ga., 1971-75), Ronald Reagan (R-Calif., 1967-75), and Bill Clinton (D-Ark., 1979-81, 1983-92)—and sixteen former governors are serving as U.S. senators.[16] But these are the exceptions rather than the rule. Most governors do not attain higher elective office.

Most former governors enter the private sector, usually to develop a lucrative law practice. These governors must give up what former governor Lamar Alexander (R-Tenn., 1979-87) called "the very best job in the U.S.A."[17] Ronald Reagan indicated that "being governor was the best training school for this job [of being president]."[18] Is there life after being governor? The National Governors' Association (NGA) asked some former governors what had happened to them since leaving office. Yes, there was life, but the quality of that new life can be determined only by the individual. By planning early for the transition, NGA suggests, the governors "can also help ease their own adjustment to the 'good life.' "[19]

Campaigning for Governor

Being elected governor is not as easy as it once was. One reason is the new style of campaigning that has led candidates to create their own organizations instead of relying solely on their political party. Opinion polls, political consultants, advertisements tailored to specific audiences in the major media markets, direct mailings, telephone banks, and air travel are extremely expensive, and full-time fundraisers often are needed to help gubernatorial candidates wage winning campaigns. Without the party to alert the faithful and bring in the straight-ticket votes, candidates must create what Sabato calls their own "instant organization" or "party substitute."[20]

This way of building a campaign organization is obviously expensive, and indeed the cost of running for governor has escalated greatly in recent years. But to be competitive, a candidate must raise considerable funds for his or her campaign. For those with private wealth, or access to wealth, this hurdle can be overcome more easily than for those without such resources. For these latter, conducting a campaign for the governorship requires continuous fundraising, or the campaign will be impaired.

Tied to the increase in cost of campaigns is inflation. Like everything else, the cost of politics rises when inflation erodes the dollar. If the 1991 dollar is used as the base point, the dollar was worth thirty-one cents in 1972 and seventy-one cents in 1982.[21]

In addition, gubernatorial races are more

competitive. Awareness of the importance of state government and of the key role of the governor in state politics has increased the number of candidates for the office. In the fifty-three separate gubernatorial elections between 1989 and 1992, there were 412 candidates seeking their party's nomination for governor, for an average of 7.8 candidates per election. Of these candidates, 220 were strong enough to receive more than 10 percent of the party primary or convention vote. In 1990, nineteen candidates sought the governorship in California, sixteen in Nevada, fifteen in Texas, and twelve each in Hawaii and Minnesota. Clearly, there is no shortage of people who wish to become governor of their state.

Finally, there has been a decline in the number of opportunities to be elected governor. All but three states allow governors to serve four-year terms and only two limit a governor to just one term.[22] In addition, the power of incumbency gives a sitting governor a considerable advantage in any reelection campaign. The result is that fewer new governors are being elected in the states. Between 1900 and 1910 there was an average of 3.3 newly elected governors in each state; in the 1980s, the average across the fifty states was 1.1 new governors elected per state.[23]

One Among Many

The governor is not the only official in the executive branch of state government who is elected statewide. The states elect more than 500 officials, including forty-three attorneys general, forty-two lieutenant governors, thirty-eight treasurers, and thirty-six secretaries of state. There are even five land commissioners, five secretaries of labor, and one commissioner of mines elected by the voters of some states. Eleven states elect their boards of education, and fifteen elect their superintendents of public instruction. The legislatures appoint some state officials, mainly in the postaudit function,

and the lieutenant governors in a few states have some appointive power. This means that governors have little or no power over some parts of state government, except their own power of persuasion or the power they can create through the budget.

Fragmentation of executive branch leadership complicates the politics between the actors involved. In the early 1980s, for example, the governors and the lieutenant governors of California, Missouri, Nebraska, and New Mexico were pitted against each other over the issue of who is in charge of state government when the governor is out of state. Can the lieutenant governor make appointments to office or the bench (patronage)? Call a special session of the legislature? Issue pardons? And who receives the governor's salary while he or she is absent? More recently, some governors have had difficulties with other elected officials: in Virginia, the governor and lieutenant governor fought over the budget surplus and taxes; in Idaho, the governor and the attorney general have been squabbling over regulating the amount of timber exported from the state; in Georgia, the fight was between the governor and the attorney general, with the two officials battling over the state's open meetings law and personnel matters; and in North Carolina, the governor and attorney general fought over the governor's right to contract leases and appoint certain officials.[24]

Executive branch fragmentation has other consequences. Perhaps most importantly, it restricts what governors can accomplish in high priority areas such as education. A gubernatorial candidate may pledge to improve primary and secondary education, but, once elected, have difficulty fulfilling this goal because other elected officials with responsibility in the education policy area may have different views on what should be done.

Recent federal court decisions have begun to restrict a chief executive's ability to remove or fire government employees, an action often needed to open up positions for appointing the executive's own team. In the 1976 *Elrod v. Burns* decision, the U.S. Supreme Court held that "patronage firings" violate the First Amendment's protection of an individual's freedom of political belief and political association.[25] In the 1980 *Branti v. Finkel* decision, the Court reaffirmed its position but did indicate "if the employee's private political beliefs would interfere with the discharge of his public duties, the First Amendment rights may be required to yield to the state's vital interest in maintaining governmental effectiveness and efficiency." [26] In its 1983 *Connick v. Myers* decision, the Court again affirmed its position but held that "the First Amendment does not protect from dismissal public employees who complain about their working conditions or their supervisor." [27] All three cases concerned local government situations but, by extension, affect governors as well.

In 1990, the Supreme Court decided narrowly in *Rutan et al. v. Republican Party of Illinois* that state and local government violates an individual's "First Amendment rights when they refuse to hire, promote or transfer . . . [an employee] on the basis of their political affiliation or party activity." [28] This case, which focused on the patronage process of the Illinois governor's office, highlights a basic tension in these situations. There is a tension between the right of employees to be protected for their political beliefs and the need of an executive to put into place individuals who will seek to achieve the goals for which that executive was elected.

The most significant restriction on a governor's ability to be governor is the relationship that he or she has with state legislators. There are many types of advice and counsel that governors give each other on this relationship; consider these comments by incumbents to newly elected governors in 1982:

Don't necessarily judge your success by your legislative score card. . . . Avoid threatening to veto a bill. You just relieve the legislature of responsibility for sound legislation. . . . A governor successful in managing the selection of legislative leadership gains a Pyrrhic victory. . . . It's too easy to dismiss one or two legislators because there are so many. You do so at your own peril. . . . Legislators will complain about your spending too much time with the staff, but what they really mean is you don't spend enough time with them. . . . If someone urges your support on a bill by saying it's a "merely" bill, sew your pockets shut; there are no "merely" bills. . . . Legislators will learn that press coverage comes from opposition to the governor.[29]

Part VI provides a close-up view of the governorship as we move through the 1990s. Alan Ehrenhalt of *Governing* explores the question of what happens when a "real" governor becomes president. Kathleen Sylvester of *Governing* looks at the changes Governor William Weld is trying to bring about in Massachusetts. David Osborne in *Governing* talks about his concept of "reinventing government" while still remembering politics. And H. George Frederickson in *Governing* raises a few cautionary remarks about new ways of approaching government.

Notes

1. Larry Sabato, *Goodbye to Good-time Charlie: The American Governorship Transformed,* 2d ed. (Washington, D.C.: CQ Press, 1983), 57.
2. Ibid., xi.
3. Otto Kerner (D-Ill., 1961-68), Spiro Agnew (R-Md., 1967-69), Marvin Mandel (D-Md., 1969-77), David Hall (D-Okla., 1971-75), and Ray Blanton (D-Tenn., 1975-79).
4. "Alabama Gov. Hunt Guilty; Office Now Folsom's," *Congressional Quarterly Weekly Report,* April 24, 1993, 1035.
5. "Oklahoma: Two More Indictments in Gov. Walter's Probe," *The Hotline,* April 23, 1993, 14-15.

6. "Former Governor of West Virginia to Plead Guilty," [Raleigh] *News and Observer,* April 13, 1990, 8A.

7. Query by Larry Sabato at the "State of the States" Symposium, Eagleton Institute, Rutgers University, New Brunswick, N.J., December 18, 1987.

8. For a discussion of these problems in ten states, see Thad L. Beyle, ed., *Governors and Hard Times* (Washington, D.C.: CQ Press, 1992).

9. Ibid., 11-13.

10. "CNN/USA Today/Gallup: On the Road Back to Net Positive?" *The Hotline* (July 2, 1993), 18.

11. Thad Beyle, "Approval Ratings of Current Governors, 1993" (July 5, 1993).

12. V. O. Key, Jr., *Southern Politics in State and Nation* (New York: Knopf, 1949), 19-35, 156-182.

13. James Florio (D-N.J.) in 1989; Carroll Campbell (R-S.C.) in 1990; and Thomas Carper (D-Del.) and Mike Lowry (D-Wash.) in 1992.

14. Lawton Chiles (D-Fla.), Lowell P. Weicker (I-Conn.), and Pete Wilson (R-Calif.) in 1990.

15. Recent examples include Fife Symington (R-Ariz.), William Weld (R-Mass.), Ben Nelson (D-Neb.), and David Walters (D-Okla.) in 1990; Kirk Fordice (R-Miss.) in 1991; and Steve Merrill (R-N.H.) and Mike Leavitt (R-Utah) in 1992.

16. The U.S. senators are: Dale Bumpers (D-Ark., 1971-75); David Pryor (D-Ark., 1975-79); Bob Graham (D-Fla., 1979-86); Wendell H. Ford (D-Ky., 1971-74); Christopher S. Bond (R-Mo., 1973-77, 1981-85); Jim Exon, (D-Neb., 1971-79); Bob Kerrey (D-Neb., 1983-87); Richard H. Bryan (D-Nev., 1983-87); David L. Boren (D-Okla., 1975-79); Mark O. Hatfield (R-Ore., 1959-67); John H. Chafee (R-R.I., 1963-69); Strom Thurmond (R-S.C., 1947-51); Ernest F. Hollings (D-S.C., 1959-63); Charles S. Robb (D-Va., 1982-86); John D. "Jay" Rockefeller IV (D-W.Va., 1977-85); and Judd Gregg (R-N.H., 1989-93).

17. Lamar Alexander, *Steps Along the Way: A Governor's Scrapbook* (Nashville: Thomas Nelson, 1986), 9.

18. "Inquiry: Being Governor Is Best Training for Presidency," *USA Today,* September 11, 1987, 11A.

19. "Is There Life after Being Governor? Yes, A Good One," *Governors' Weekly Bulletin,* August 8, 1986, 1-2.

20. Larry Sabato, "Gubernatorial Politics and the New Campaign Technology," *State Government* 53 (Summer 1980): 149.

21. These figures are based on the Consumer Price Index Annual Average figures from the Bureau of Labor Statistics, U.S. Department of Labor, *Consumer Price Index Detailed Report* (Washington, D.C.: Government Printing Office, October 1991), 7.

22. Those states with two-year terms are New Hampshire, Rhode Island, and Vermont; those restricting their governors to only one term are Kentucky and Virginia.

23. Thad L. Beyle, "Term Limits in the State Executive Branch," in *Limiting Legislative Terms,* ed. Gerald Benjamin and Michael J. Malbin (Washington, D.C.: CQ Press, 1992), 164.

24. "People: Some Governors Get No Respect," *Governing* 1:2 (November 1987): 67.

25. Elder Witt, "Patronage Firings," *Congressional Quarterly Weekly Report,* July 3, 1976, 1726.

26. Elder Witt, "Supreme Court Deals Blow to Public Employee Firings for Solely Political Reasons," *Congressional Quarterly Weekly Report,* April 5, 1980, 899-900.

27. Elder Witt, "Employee Rights," *Congressional Quarterly Weekly Report,* April 6, 1983, 791-792.

28. Cheri Collis, "Cleaning Up the Spoils System," *State Government News* 33:9 (September 1990): 6.

29. Thad L. Beyle and Robert Huefner, "Quips and Quotes from Old Governors to New," *Public Administration Review* 43:3 (May-June 1983): 268-269.

What If a *Real* Governor Became President?

by Alan Ehrenhalt

Anybody who's been a governor in the last decade has had one good reason after another to be mad at Washington: presidents who seemed to enjoy cutting back programs the states depended on; a Congress that ignored the budget-balancing rules every state has to live by; a Supreme Court that thought federalism went out with the Federalists. For any governor who takes his job seriously, Washington has been enemy territory.

But what if a governor became president? A *real* governor—not somebody who happened to pass through the statehouse on his way to national office, but one who had spent a good part of his life struggling to make state government work. Somebody who knew what it felt like to get hit on the head with an incomprehensible $100 million mandate. Would *that* make a difference?

Well, we are about to find out. Bill Clinton has been a governor for 12 years, far longer than anyone who has ever been elected to the presidency. Fifteen presidents were governors at one time or another, but most of them for just two years, or four at the most. The only one who ran a state for more than five years was Ronald Reagan. And even Reagan's admirers never accused him of harboring a fascination with the minutiae of state government. He was, from the beginning, a national political figure; Sacramento was a means to an end.

Clinton is different. No matter how ambitious he may have been, the governorship of Arkansas wasn't just a vehicle for him—it was the only job he had ever held for any significant length of time. Bill Clinton has been a governor nearly half his adult life.

That in itself doesn't prove a thing. No president is going to see government from the perspective of the states; the view from the White House is radically different. It would be foolish to expect Clinton to look at things the same way he did from his office in Little Rock. But it would be just as foolish to assume that his perspective on American government and the federal system won't be affected by the 12 years he spent in that office, coping with one piece of federal mischief after another.

The one that must have been hardest to forget came at the very beginning. In 1980, in the middle of Clinton's first two-year term, President Carter admitted into the United States some 120,000 refugees from Fidel Cas-

Alan Ehrenhalt is a staff writer for *Governing*. This article is reprinted from *Governing* 6: 3 (December 1992): 6-7.

President-Elect Played Major NGA Role

Arkansas Gov. Bill Clinton, elected U.S. president [in November 1992], has played a substantial role in NGA [National Governors Association]. As NGA chairman from August 1986 to August 1987, he oversaw efforts on his year-long initiative "Making America Work: Productive People, Productive Policies."

It focused on developing strategies for local and regional economic development and for bringing down the barriers that hinder productivity and individual achievement.

Gov. Clinton was a leader in a successful NGA effort to enact national welfare reform legislation and a new child care bill. He also was instrumental in developing the national education goals at the President's education summit with governors in 1989.

Source: Governors' Bulletin 26:23 (November 9, 1992): 1.

tro's Cuba; many of them were sent to the Fort Chaffee army camp, in Sebastian County on the western edge of Clinton's state. These unruly refugees, many of them with criminal records, made Arkansas voters nervous from the start. Clinton asked the Carter administration to beef up security at the camp, but they didn't do it. He got them to promise not to send any more refugees to Fort Chaffee, but they reneged on the promise. Clinton lost his reelection bid that fall by 32,000 votes, and the mess at Fort Chaffee was one of the main reasons. The whole episode was enough to make a defeated one-term governor wonder whether any administration in Washington— even a "friendly" one from the same political party—could ever be trusted to help a gover-

nor with his problems.

By the time Clinton won the office back two years later, the Fort Chaffee problem was history. But a much more serious one had replaced it: the loss of millions of dollars in federal funds that Arkansas had come to depend on but that the Reagan administration had eliminated from the budget.

As Diane Blair points out in her excellent book, *Arkansas Politics and Government,* the state has always been more dependent than most on federal help. In 1984, for every tax dollar Arkansas sent to Washington, it got $1.27 back in federal programs. But by then, as Clinton was completing his second term, the federal aid squeeze of the 1980s had already had its effects. Revenue sharing to the states was gone, and money from dozens of categorical programs was disappearing as well. All the major gubernatorial initiatives of the 1980s that Clinton boasted of in his presidential campaign—in education, health, economic development—came against the background of a federal government that was steadily cutting back in its financial commitment to a backward state that used to be one of its most eager clients.

Meanwhile, Washington was asking Arkansas to spend more of its own money every year on Medicaid, on corrections, on mandates and requirements of a bewildering number and variety. That's not to say the federal government was treating Arkansas any different from the way it treated other states. It wasn't. The shriveling of federal largess was a fact of life for any governor in the '80s. But it can't help being part of the mindset of a politician preparing after 12 years to make the move from one end of the federal system to the other.

It isn't just a governor's attitude toward Washington that provides a clue to his future presidency. There is also the question of his relationship with his own state legislature.

Unlike someone who comes to the White House from Congress, a governor has a track record at doing something all presidents must do—stroking, punishing and cajoling a legislative body.

That was certainly true in the case of Jimmy Carter, the last southern governor who made the journey Clinton will make [in January 1993]. Carter, who served only one term in the Georgia Senate and had few friends there, was principled, stubborn and aloof in dealing with the legislature during his four gubernatorial years. He won passage of one major item on his legislative agenda: a consolidation of hundreds of unwieldy state boards, agencies and commissions into a smaller number of departments. But he never dominated the institution, never reined in the power brokers who had run it for years before he arrived. By and large, he went his way and they went theirs.

Carter's relations with Congress were very much the same. He was not close to the membership, did relatively little personal lobbying, avoided strong-arm tactics in pushing the members where they did not want to go. And, after a brief honeymoon, his influence dwindled to the point where he became largely an irrelevance. Congress went about its business essentially without him.

Clinton's story in Arkansas was entirely different from Carter's in Georgia. Arkansas had a tradition of entrenched legislative power, but by the time Clinton arrived in 1979, the tradition was largely broken. His two predecessors in the 1970s, Dale Bumpers and David Pryor, had figured out how to control the legislative process, and Clinton simply took off from there. Returned to office in 1982 after a term out of power, he pressured the legislature publicly and privately through a long special session until it raised the sales tax from 3 cents to 4 cents to pay for his new education program. Then he made the education program the focus of his next campaign for reelection.

In 1991, as he prepared to run for president, Clinton was still applying the pressure, badgering one more package of education tax increases out of the legislature at a time when most states were trying to evade new taxes even amid dire emergency. In Arkansas, the legislators caved in rather quietly.

There is room for legitimate disagreement about how much Clinton's education reforms have accomplished in Arkansas and about whether the money was aimed at the right targets. But there isn't much doubt about the way Clinton handles a legislative body: He uses a full-court press. If he needs to make a deal with a member to gain his support, he makes it. If he has to compromise, he compromises. But he doesn't leave them alone.

"I'm a very active, hands-on person," Clinton told Ted Koppel in Little Rock the night after he defeated George Bush. "It's my style. It's the way I've governed here. It's the kind of president I expect to be."

That the experiences of a gubernatorial career help shape a president's outlook and style should come as no surprise. The tantalizing question is whether they are the sort of experiences that make for a good president.

There is evidence enough on either side of the question. Jimmy Carter's combination of personal aloofness and lack of familiarity with Washington turned out to be lethal. Perhaps if he had spent a few terms in Congress and knew more of the members, his legislative relations might not have been such a disaster.

John Kennedy had served 14 years in Congress and knew all about Washington. But he had never had to manage a legislative body—he had never held an executive position of any sort in his entire life. And that showed, too. For all the grace and eloquence that define Kennedy's reputation in history, biographies of him make it clear that he was thoroughly buffaloed by his opponents in Congress. At the time of his assassination, he had all but given up trying to influence it in most major areas of domestic policy.

Franklin Roosevelt didn't really have that long a political résumé when he became president in 1933: two years in a state Senate, a pair of two-year terms as governor. But he turned out to be terrific at almost every important phase of the job—manipulating Congress, appealing to the people, motivating those who worked for him. In the end, there is no substitute for greatness.

Whether they are great or mediocre, though, all presidents are the product of their own personal range of experiences in American government, at a particular time and in a particular place. In Bill Clinton's case, those are almost exclusively the experiences of a southern governor in the 1980s. For better or worse, they are the prologue to the next four years.

The Weld Experiment

by Kathleen Sylvester

Shortly after William F. Weld took office as governor of Massachusetts, it came time to submit state contracts with public employees to the legislature as part of his budget. He refused.

The contracts had been negotiated by the preceding Dukakis administration, and, as a matter of course, Weld was expected to honor them. But Weld understood that if he delayed, the contracts would become void and the state would not have to give its employees a pay raise. He also understood the political implications of his move: It would alienate virtually every unionized public employee in the state. That was all right with him. "They are not my people," he told one legislator. "They are not my constituents."

Forty-six-year-old William Weld, an affable, self-confident trust-fund millionaire and the first Republican to govern Massachusetts in nearly 20 years, is a man who always seems to know who his people are. He doesn't care about pleasing everyone. He doesn't care much for the whole idea of consensus. At a time when his counterparts all over America are struggling hard not to offend any major interest group—and generally failing—he is succeeding in Massachusetts with a hard calculation of just which ones he needs and which

ones he can afford to do without. And he is quite happy to admit it. "If we are going to do things in a different way," he says, "maybe we can't have everybody on board. Maybe we can't have consensus government."

All this makes Weld, a year and a half into his term, by many estimates the most interesting new governor in America. To his admirers, though, he is more than that: He is the instrument of revolution—a conservative bold enough to tame big government in a way other conservatives have been too timid to do. National groups on the Republican right have already begun to talk about him as a leading presidential contender for 1996.

Within Massachusetts, there is no question that a great deal has changed since Weld succeeded Democrat Michael S. Dukakis. Taxes have been cut in the depth of a recession. There have been massive reductions in the scope of social welfare programs. Prison health care and mental health services are being privatized.

Still, it is something less than a revolution. There has been no fundamental restruc-

Kathleen Sylvester is a staff writer for *Governing*. This article is reprinted from *Governing* 5:9 (June 1992): 36-40.

turing of state government in Massachusetts, and Weld seems less than passionate about promoting one. This new governor with an ambitious agenda for change still manages to make time for regular squash games on busy weekday afternoons. Indeed, for a revolutionary, he seems remarkably nonchalant about the whole process of government. "I've spent my time putting ideas and programs and initiatives on the table," he says matter-of-factly. "Some have made it; some haven't." The failures do not seem to trouble him.

The truth is that William Weld, taking over at a time of enormous resentment against Michael Dukakis and liberal Democratic government in general, has achieved remarkable political success without any great investment of zeal. Whether his administration achieves more than that—whether there is a Weld revolution in any meaningful sense—may ultimately turn on just how long he stays interested in the job.

Whether it turns out to be a revolution or merely a diversion, William Weld brings to his experiment in Massachusetts a well-honed set of operating principles and beliefs.

The essence of them is that he wants less government. While the boilerplate description is that Weld is a conservative on economic issues and a liberal on social issues, the truth is simpler than that: He is a libertarian. He doesn't like government intervening in the marketplace, and he doesn't like it intervening in the lives and decisions of individuals. Weld says that should surprise no one, that he was talking a libertarian line even before 1980, when he decided that U.S. Representative Philip Crane was the closest thing to a libertarian in the Republican presidential field and managed Crane's Massachusetts campaign.

In fact, the governor says, his libertarian roots go back to the 1960s, when he majored in classics at Harvard and studied economics at Oxford. Watching politicians prescribe government as the solution to every problem, he says, made him spend years "rattling the newspapers and saying this is crazy and upside down and cockeyed and backwards."

"I've thought for decades that the Lyndon Johnson Great Society was crazy," he insists. "It seemed to me that it was being all things to all people and being very paternalistic, but I never had a chance to put my thoughts into practice until this job."

For an intellectual with interests in classics and economic theory, however, Weld has rarely been far from politics in his adult life. With a law degree from Harvard, he began his career in private practice, but interrupted it to run unsuccessfully for state attorney general in 1978. He enlisted in the Crane campaign two years later. When Crane dropped out, Weld supported Reagan and was rewarded with an appointment as U.S. attorney for Massachusetts. He quickly made a reputation as a corruption fighter by indicting and convicting scores of veteran Massachusetts political figures, then moved on to Washington in 1985 to head the criminal division of the U.S. Justice Department. Weld returned three years later to private practice in Boston—an obvious Republican contender for statewide office.

Weld's hard line against crime and taxes, and his conspicuous support for gay rights, legalized abortion and environmental concerns, seemed to fit the mood of the Massachusetts electorate fairly well. Still, he was an underdog throughout the 1990 fall campaign. In the end, only a string of impolitic remarks by the Democratic nominee, Boston University President John Silber, allowed Weld and running mate Paul Celluci to slip through with 50.2 percent of the vote.

"If you studied what Massachusetts voters wanted in January 1990," says University of Massachusetts professor and political observer Ralph Whitehead, "they would have

The GOP: Pockets of Power in Big Places

Republicans still hold five very large prizes in state politics—the governorships of California, Illinois, Ohio, Michigan and Massachusetts. The people who hold those prizes are having to adjust to a very different year in 1993, a year in which they will be under increased scrutiny as national leaders but will be working without the benefit of a GOP White House willing to make friendly appointments and listen to their complaints.

Some of these big-state Republican governors start the year in much better shape than others. John Engler in Michigan has the benefit of Republican control in the Senate and a tie in the House, and can plausibly claim that things are moving in his direction in state politics as a whole. Not only has population shifted away from the Detroit area into smaller cities and towns where Republicans have always been strong, but Detroit suburbs that were once solidly Democratic have become partisan battlegrounds.

"The state is becoming dramatically more conservative in terms of what the public expects of state government," says Craig Ruff, president of Public Sector Consultants, a think tank in Lansing. "We are now a poor state, and that has transformed politics. Economic anxiety has bred political conservatism."

Jim Edgar might not want to make that claim in Illinois, but he too can point to some encouraging legislative numbers. Republicans are still badly outnumbered in the state House, but the Senate is Republican for the first time in a decade, thanks in large part to a suburban Chicago vote that withstood the statewide Clinton landslide. The common assumption is that Edgar, who has favored relatively austere budgets during his two years in office, is more likely to see spending plans he recognizes get passed in the year ahead. Issues such as transportation funding and economic development are likely to be treated with a more suburban twist than they were last year.

George Voinovich of Ohio has a situation somewhat like Edgar's, with the momentum shifting slightly in his favor. As in the past two years, he has a Republican Senate to work with, and the House, which was Democratic by a relatively healthy 61-38 margin in 1992, has now changed to 53-47. Voinovich did not find it easy getting a hearing for his legislative ideas from House Democrats in the old lineup, however, and that may not change much despite the new numbers.

William F. Weld of Massachusetts remains fairly popular as he enters his third year governing a massively Democratic state, but he also faces a problem he did not confront up to now: Democratic legislative majorities whose size—31 of 40 seats in the Senate and 124 of 160 in the House—may be large enough to override his vetoes. The legislature appears ready to roll back some of the enactments with which Weld is most closely identified, such as privatization of state government functions. In the current climate, it may not be easy for him to build the reputation as a chief executive that a prospective national GOP leader needs.

Of the five GOP governors, however, the one whose lot seems least enviable is Pete Wilson of California. The state's economy, which has shown no signs of picking up steam even as the rest of the country displays modest improvement, has turned dealing with the budget into an annual exercise in name-calling. Nor is it at all clear that Wilson will get much help from his own party's legislators, especially in the Assembly. Never an especially cohesive bunch, Assembly Republicans returned to Sacramento this year with a more conservative cast—several districts that might have sent moderate Republicans chose Democrats rather than the conservative Republican nominees. And there is a new leader: Wilson ally Bill Jones stepped down right after the elections, and was replaced by Jim Bruite, who comes from the party's conservative wing.

Source: Rob Gurwitt, *Governing* 6:5 (February 1993): 31.

picked an innovative 45-year-old high-tech entrepreneur who was fairly liberal on social and cultural issues." Weld was not a high-tech entrepreneur, but he fit the other elements well enough. Never mind, says Whitehead, that Weld was "a fairly traditional Brahmin figure—wealthy, aloof and cavalier. People began to cast him in the role they wanted in order to rise to their expectations." And Weld began to cast himself in that mold as well.

In search of a framework for his ideas, Weld quickly embraced the new notion of "entrepreneurial government." In an inaugural address laden with the rhetoric of change, he promised "to make history as well as headlines by reinventing the way state government functions."

Weld promised taxpayers "a fair and measurable return" on their investments. Since that speech, Weld has come back often to this theme of measurable results: "Instead of asking ourselves how many teachers we employ or how many street cleaners we send out," he argues, "we should ask how much our children are learning and how clean are the streets."

As Weld's notion of entrepreneurial government has evolved, however, it has become nearly synonymous with privatization. The basic question to ask, he says, is "Why is government performing this service? Could somebody else do it better?"

In the Weld administration, the answer to the second question is usually yes. Weld closed five of 34 state hospitals after a commission determined that the facilities were operating at 18 percent capacity. Their patients are now being served by the private sector. When four more hospitals are closed, the state predicts it will save $60 million a year in operating costs and another $144 million in capital costs. Health care for prison inmates has been privatized, with a projected savings of $8 million a year. And the management of four state-run skating rinks was put out to bid [in 1991], a

deal expected to reduce the state's losses on the rinks. Weld would like to go further: He would like to dissolve the Massachusetts Turnpike Authority and sell the highway.

Where he cannot privatize, Weld is simply spending less. In order to balance the state budget and provide the tax relief he promised, Weld has made enormous cuts in state spending, most noticeably in social welfare programs, which were among the most generous in the country. Last year, he cut 15,000 of 39,000 people from the general relief rolls— the program of last resort for the poor. This year, he has proposed cutting 9,000 more off these emergency aid rolls and reducing the $338 monthly payments for the rest by 10 percent.

Funding for higher education has been cut drastically. About 5,300 state employees have been fired; there have been furloughs and deferred pay raises for the rest. And despite passage of a ballot measure directing the state to increase aid to cities and towns by $1 billion, Weld initially cut that aid by $230 million. Over and over, he has been able to use the same refrain: "There is no money to pay for it."

Indeed, Weld does not want there to be enough money to pay for much of what Massachusetts was doing under his Democratic predecessor. "Reducing the money available for the beast," he suggests, portraying state government as the beast, "is one sure way to limit spending.... When the money is there, a legislature, any legislature, is going to figure out a way to spend it."

There is no question that Weld inherited a fiscal mess in January 1991. A $2 billion deficit was looming, and the state's bond rating was heading for the junk pile. Dukakis' much-proclaimed "Massachusetts miracle" had gone up in smoke. But the multitude of state programs spawned in the era of prosperity were entrenched in government. After 16 years of

Democratic dominance, says political consultant Barry Kaplovitz, "there was no culture of self-criticism in Massachusetts. It was a one-party state, and the party couldn't say no." Weld was the antidote.

Taming the Democratic legislature proved remarkably easy. In its first year, the Weld administration delivered a balanced $13.6 billion budget—the first on-time state budget in six years. Helped by the urgency of the fiscal crisis and armed with the threat of a sustainable veto in the state Senate, he even delivered his promised cut in the income tax—from 6.25 percent to 5.95 percent. "It was a stunning string of political successes—a bipartisan lovefest," says James Braude, head of the Taxpayers' Equity Alliance.

Part of that success was simply that William Weld was not Michael Dukakis. While Dukakis was viewed even by members of his own party as rigid and frequently inaccessible, Weld has proved to be a refreshing and welcome change. During the long nights of that first budget debate, when tensions were high, the governor called Democrats on the House floor and invited them down to his office for a beer or a soda. Dukakis, all agree, never would have done that.

John Moffitt, who has run both of Weld's political campaigns and now serves as his chief secretary, suggests that one of Weld's most important personal weapons is his thick skin and refusal to take criticism personally. "It may seem like a small thing," says Moffitt, "but he doesn't have all the hangups of most politicians. He's not trying to prove something."

The question for many Weld-watchers is how much a leader who has nothing to prove can ultimately achieve. Even those who are comfortable with the lack of passion in William Weld—who say it makes him more flexible, more approachable, even more likable as a politician—suggest that without passion, he may succeed politically but still fail to make any lasting change in the way state government functions.

"It is not at all clear to me," says Ralph Whitehead, "that Weld is interested in restructuring the public sector in Massachusetts. It is an enormously difficult job, and he is Reaganesque in his point of view. It's dirty, blue-collar work, and he'd rather be on the squash court."

By Weld's own definition of the ultimate goal of his revolution—less government but also a reformed, streamlined, harder-working government—the second goal is still far away. "He just shrank government," complains consultant Kaplovitz, who has worked for both Democrats and Republicans. "Weld cut down the size, but the faulty habits of mind and the stupid ways of doing things are still embedded. The waste is still there; the bad planning and implementation are still there."

Even supporters of Weld's conservative fiscal policies worry that his top-down approach to reforming government will have only limited success. Thomas Finneran, the conservative Democratic chairman of the House Ways and Means Committee, suggests that most of Weld's initiatives, such as plans to sell off state assets, lack the "rigorous cost-benefit analysis they require. The actual implementation of some of these ideas takes lot more thought and detail and analysis than a three-paragraph campaign statement."

On the Democratic left, the concern is not so much that Weld is failing to restructure government but that he experiments with it casually and thinks about it as a game—without much concern for the losers. At one point, he joked that his plan to sell off state properties was similar to playing Monopoly. That sent chills down the spines of those who don't think state government should be treated as a game at all.

Deborah Weinstein, who runs the Massachusetts Human Services Coalition, complains that the Weld administration makes changes in poor people's programs and then tells the advocates: "We're going to try this, so let us know what disastrous results occur."

She points to the state's current attempt to restructure the Medicaid system. Massachusetts is converting to a managed care system—assigning Medicaid recipients to private physicians or health maintenance organizations. Advocates argue that because it emphasizes prevention and health maintenance, it should result in better care for patients and lower costs to the state.

And it may. At the moment, however, this effort bears all the earmarks of slapdash experiment that Weld's critics charge him with.

By the end of [July 1992], more than 400,000 Medicaid clients [were] to be switched over to the new system. As of early May, however, the state had not signed up enough doctors to handle the transition, and results of a pilot program indicated that only 30 percent of the clients were responding to the letters informing them of the change. In the administration's eagerness to try out a new idea, critics say, problems are being ignored.

Weld is characteristically unmoved by the complaints. "You can come up with an anecdotal case to argue against any position," he says, "but that's not persuasive to me. Of course, if the anecdotal evidence mounts up and you've got people dying on the grates, that's different. But I haven't been confronted with that evidence yet."

Peter Forman, the Republican leader of the Massachusetts House, says Weld has "a thinking out loud" approach that is a gutsy way to run state government, but concedes that it is "a little difficult for Republican party leaders to have trial balloons going up all the time. . . . If we have to vote on one of his trial balloons, we're stuck."

When a trial balloon causes a problem—as did Weld's plan to raise the pay of his cabinet secretaries by $20,000 while state employees were being furloughed—the governor usually backs down. "With a lot of other people, that approach would blow up in their face," says Forman. "But nothing blows up in his face. He just sort of brushes it off and says maybe it was a stupid idea and tries something else."

Robert Haynes, secretary-treasurer of the state's AFL-CIO, refers to Weld's approach as "government by see-if-it-sticks. He's been very successful at throwing stuff up in the air and hoping it sticks to the ceiling. If it doesn't, that's OK. He just goes on to the next foray."

As often as not, however, politics has something to do with those decisions to move on to the next foray. As willing as he may be to have large segments of the Massachusetts populace angry at him, he is sensitive about offending any significant chunk of the middle class. When Weld tried to exclude some elderly with annual incomes over about $15,000 from Medicaid assistance for nursing home care, there was a howl of protest from the middle-class children who might have been forced to take over the care for those parents. The governor reversed his position. "He always knows who his constituents are," says Representative Richard Moore, a Democrat.

But there is one constituency even more important to Weld than the middle-class voter: business. One of the governor's major goals is to send a message that the commonwealth is friendly to business and job creation. To that end, he is working aggressively at deregulation on an industry-by-industry basis. "Sometimes the best thing that government can do," says the libertarian governor, "is to get out of the way."

And he wants to cut taxes again. Weld has proposed a new $200 million tax package that includes a capital gains tax cut and credits for job creation and expansion. He also wants to reduce income taxes again—from 5.95 percent to 5.75 percent. There is widely held skepticism about whether the state can afford the cuts and whether they would spur any real economic growth. But Weld has moved himself into a position of political advantage by putting legislators in the position of saying no to cutting taxes.

Weld acknowledges that he may not get the tax cuts. But that does not seem to worry him too much, either. If that happens, he says cheerfully, "it's not fatal from a public policy point of view."

On one important issue, however, Weld's consistent pro-business posture has set up a crucial test of his leadership.

That issue is education. During the 1990 campaign, Weld was critical of waste and abuse in the state's school system—the high-priced consultants, the politicization of local school committees. "It was quite a superficial attack," the governor admits now, conceding that he didn't know as much about education as his opponent.

In the past year, however, Weld has embraced education reform, largely because of political pressure from the business community. A broad-based coalition called the Massachusetts Business Alliance for Education Reform is supporting a plan for fundamental change that includes school-based management, abolition of teacher tenure, a choice program for the public schools and receivership for the worst schools.

Jack Rennie, president of an aerospace firm called Pacer Industries and head of the alliance, says it was because the plan came from the business community that Weld listened, gradually coming around to the argument that good schools are critical to the state's future work force and its economy. But meaningful implementation of the plan will probably require a change in the state's property tax laws. The business community told Weld very plainly, says Rennie, that they are willing to pay more taxes "if that's what it takes to fund meaningful education reform in the state."

The business community supports the revision of Proposition 2 1/2, the state's decade-old tax limitation law, so that the local support of school funding could rise each year by the rate of inflation, rather than the current limit of 2.5 percent. If the law is not revised and local contributions necessarily fall short, Rennie and other business leaders believe the plan will be compromised.

Here, Weld's desire to be an education reformer runs up against his libertarian abhorrence of taxes—not to mention his campaign promises. "He agreed with the plan," says Mark Roosevelt, chairman of the Education Committee in the Massachusetts House, but when it came to the structural financing to pay for it, "he wouldn't countenance any of the things that would do it. That's the frustrating underbelly of the Weld administration."

As far as Roosevelt and many of the liberal Democrats are concerned, the problem is not just Weld's supply-side ideology, but his lack of passion and commitment in general. "We have communities that have laid off 40 percent of their teachers, where there are class sizes of 67," says Roosevelt, "but I have never once been with him in which he has said something impassioned or purposeful—that what we're seeking to do here in education is right and necessary to our future." Roosevelt says Weld's view is pragmatic: "He says, 'OK, it seems like we've got to do this, so let's figure out how we do it.' It's always a very cold, political approach."

To remain popular in Massachusetts and the focus of national attention, William Weld may not need to accomplish much in the way of changing education or restructuring Massachusetts government. At a time when citizens are disillusioned with government, voters may not insist that it be reformed. They may be

131

simply grateful to pay less for it. By that standard, Weld is already a success. He has done nothing to offend his core constituency, and he has achieved some general approval for bringing stability to the state's economy.

Weld probably could win a second term in 1994 without shaking up Massachusetts government much more than he already has. Or he could move into national politics. Or he could simply declare victory at that point and return relatively unscarred to a comfortable private life.

Alternatively, he might determine to stay in office for eight years and try to implement a real revolution. "It would be better if it was eight in terms of making sure you don't sputter out," he says. "The problem is I've never held a job more than four years."

Reinventing Government Means Remembering Politics

by David Osborne

Government and business are very different animals. Hence public and private management are very different disciplines. The biggest difference can be summed up in one word: politics.

Private-sector managers must navigate the waters of internal politics, of course. But in government, managers live within a sea of politics. Businesses live within markets: Their risks and rewards, their incentives, their bottom lines are all dictated primarily by the market. In government, these things are dictated by the political process.

This difference is nowhere more glaring than in the state of Florida today. No governor is doing more to revolutionize public management than Lawton Chiles. Yet few governors have lower approval ratings than Chiles does.

When he took office [in January 1991], Chiles launched a full-court press to reinvent Florida's government. He has already racked up half a dozen impressive victories.

Chiles helped pass an Education Accountability Act, which gives the schools far more flexibility to spend their state funds as they see fit, in return for performance measurement, rewards for success and penalties for failure. He pushed through a "productivity enhancement" initiative that required 5 per-

cent budget cuts from most state agencies, but returned one-fourth of that money to agencies that dreamed up plans to improve their productivity.

Chiles convinced the legislature to sunset the state's old civil service system, called Career Service. A new version will reduce the number of job classifications; allow broad, market-based salary ranges; give managers more freedom to hire and fire; and end the practice of using seniority rules to allow one employee to "bump" another when layoffs are necessary.

Meanwhile, Chiles convinced the legislature to free two divisions from both Career Service and line-item budget restrictions immediately, so they could experiment with new approaches. The results have been nothing less than spectacular. [In 1992] the legislature extended the experiment to the entire Labor Department, with 5,000 employees, and the mammoth Department of Health and Rehabilitative Services, with 41,000.

Finally, Chiles sold the legislature on a major decentralization of HRS—which will gradually shift its operations to 15 boards

David Osborne is a staff writer for *Governing*. This article is reprinted from *Governing* 5:10 (July 1992): 86.

around the state and use performance contracts and other market mechanisms to engage many different service providers. HRS even won the freedom to declare "innovation zones," in which it can suspend the rules for two years for those who come up with better ways to accomplish their missions.

In the world of state government, these are revolutionary changes. When I describe them to officials in other states, they are agog. When I add that Governor Chiles' approval rating is in the mid-20s, they go into shock.

What's the problem? Are the reforms that unpopular? Not at all. In fact, to the extent the public knows about them, Chiles' reforms are quite popular. The governor's failings lie in the realm of communication: He has flunked the test of *politics*.

First, the governor raised expectations far too high. He made it sound as if he would "reinvent" and "rightsize" state government overnight. More important, he promised that he would not raise taxes until he had fundamentally improved government's performance.

Second, Chiles focused primarily on reforms that were invisible to the average voter. He played inside baseball. To most voters, civil service, decentralization and budget flexibility are abstractions. Schools, crime and roads are real.

Third, Chiles announced—after barely a year in office and no widely perceived improvement in state government—that it was time to raise taxes.

All of this severely damaged his political standing. But his greatest error was actually an error of omission. He never barnstormed the state to communicate a compelling, cohesive vision of where he wanted to go—and how that would change life for the people of Florida. As a result, the average citizen, who pays little attention to government, had no idea what the new administration was trying to do.

This is the ultimate lesson of the Chiles regime so far. The first duty of every elected leader who wants to make fundamental change is to articulate a vision—to "beat the drums and light the candles," in the words of former St. Paul Mayor George Latimer.

Unless voters understand where the leader wants to go, they will be confused by change. The inevitable shouting that accompanies fundamental reform, particularly during hard times, will sound not like a battle between the forces of light and the forces of darkness, but simply like noise. It will distract and discourage—and the leader who prompted it will appear more embattled than inspired.

If you want to reinvent government, in other words, you must first master the politics of change.

Painting Bull's-Eyes
Around Bullet Holes

by H. George Frederickson

These are hard times for state and local government. Consultants, journalists and professors are crisscrossing the land selling books and giving speeches about how to make things better. Mostly they are describing and prescribing the governmental innovations of the 1980s. As we say about consultants who come from afar, they paint bull's-eyes around bullet holes.

What is wrong, we are told, is bureaucracy—bureaucratic bloat, bureaucratic thinking, bureaucratic paradigms, bureaucratic systems. Bureaucracy is a very useful word for consultants, journalists and professors. No one, of course, is for it. What we need, we are told, is to break through bureaucracy; what we need is entrepreneurial government.

The principles of entrepreneurial government include empowered "customers," competition, markets, reducing regulations, charging fees and making money, decentralization and privatization. The twin notions of taking on bureaucracy and promising better government for less money are especially beguiling for those wishing to be mayors, governors, legislators and even president.

There is no question that many governments, especially at the state and local level, have been and are innovative. Financial crisis has been the mother of innovation. State and local crises include the sharp reduction in support from the national government, the continuation of many national government mandates, and the insistence of the courts that jails and prisons avoid cruel and unusual punishment and that the schools be equally funded. A combination of increased taxes, charging fees and instituting lotteries, deferring maintenance on infrastructure, setting up single-purpose special districts, some increase in contracting out and privatization, and extraordinary managerial pluck, guile and hustle has so far gotten state and local governments through these crises.

This may be a description of some of the more interesting governmental innovations in our recent past. But is it a good prescription for our state and local government future?

First, promises of better government for less money are simplistic and misleading, regardless of the "principles" upon which they are based. In government, as in business, over the long run you get what you pay for.

H. George Frederickson is the Edwin O. Stene Professor of Public Administration at the University of Kansas. This article is reprinted from *Governing* 6:1 (October 1992): 13.

Governing Arizona

Arizona's problems are so unique that they may not have any national significance. The state was the most recent to impeach a governor and the only one that couldn't resolve who would be the governor without a special election. That governor (R) has serious legal problems from past involvements in the savings and loan industry and lower approval ratings than the low approval ratings being logged by other governors. Twenty legislators have already indicated they are not running again, up from a previous record of 18 set in 1972.

The governor's theme of bringing business management to government led to a business-oriented task force to deal with issues like improved management, better organization, and cost cutting. This standard approach for newly-elected governors, particularly Republicans, has produced some non-standard results. Project SLIM (State Long-Term Improved Management) is itself expensive—a $1.5 million contract with Coopers & Lybrand for consulting help and a $4.5 million appropriation request for FY 1993. Most such exercises rely on loaned business and/or state executives and small budgets, often contributed by business. Exceptions, like a recent Connecticut effort, spend more but only for one-time consultant reports on specific topics.

A prominent utility executive resigned his post as chairman of the steering committee. Another key member soon followed. Legislators, particularly in the Senate (D-led), may not fund Project SLIM, at least not at the levels the governor wants.

The legislature has problems of its own, including gigantic ideological gulfs between its extreme members, well-publicized corruption, *and* all the other election-year problems associated with divided partisan control in a year of tight finances. More than average effort is devoted to debating reversals of past decisions, such as a mandatory insurance law and a "Drano tax." Two redistricting plans have been adopted. The legislature is suing the governor over veto power issues. Proposed tax cuts are being seriously discussed more or less independently of spending plans.

Newspaper editorials may not be a good place to get impressions, but the *Arizona Republic*'s comments on April 19 merit some attention:

> Would it be asking too much for the Arizona Legislature, which since early January has been simultaneously procrastinating on essentials and squabbling about trifles—would it be asking too much for this garrulous assembly to get on with the real business of the state, adopt a budget and get out of town?
>
> Its lackadaisical work habits last year led to a 160-day regular session—a record—and four special sessions. This year's Legislature already has established a record for special sessions—it is working on its eighth—and easily could exceed last year's 160-day marathon. This is an inexcusable waste of time and money.

Source: State Policy Reports 10:12 (June 1992): 18-19.

Second, governments are not markets. The vaunted market has brought American workers lower net wages over the last 20 years, hostile takeovers, huge debt based on junk bonds, short time horizons, asset selloff, greenmail, strategic bankruptcy and the movement of manufacturing to countries with very low wages. It would be better to stop trying to make governments function like markets and try to make them function like governments.

Third, citizens are not the customers. They are the owners. Customers choose between products presented in the market; citi-

1993 Occupants of Statehouses

Listed below are the governors and the governors-elect of the 50 states, and the year in which the next election for each office will be held.

Alabama—Jim Folsom Jr. (D) 1994
Alaska—Walter J. Hickel (I) 1994
Arizona—Fife Symington (R) 1994
Arkansas—Jim Guy Tucker (D) 1994
California—Pete Wilson (R) 1994
Colorado—Roy Romer (D) 1994
Connecticut—Lowell P. Weicker Jr. (I) 1994
Delaware—Thomas R. Carper (D) 1996
Florida—Lawton Chiles (D) 1994
Georgia—Zell Miller (D) 1994
Hawaii—John Waihee III (D) 1994
Idaho—Cecil D. Andrus (D) 1994
Illinois—Jim Edgar (R) 1994
Indiana—Evan Bayh (D) 1996
Iowa—Terry E. Branstad (R) 1994
Kansas—Joan Finney (D) 1994
Kentucky—Brereton Jones (D) 1995
Louisiana—Edwin W. Edwards (D) 1995
Maine—John R. McKernan Jr. (R) 1994
Maryland—William Donald Schaefer (D) 1994
Massachusetts—William F. Weld (R) 1994
Michigan—John Engler (R) 1994
Minnesota—Arne Carlson (R) 1994
Mississippi—Kirk Fordice (R) 1995
Missouri—Mel Carnahan (D) 1996
Montana—Marc Marcicot (R) 1996

Nebraska—Ben Nelson (D) 1994
Nevada—Bob Miller (D) 1994
New Hampshire—Steve Merrill (R) 1994
New Jersey—James J. Florio (D) 1993
New Mexico—Bruce King (D) 1994
New York—Mario M. Cuomo (D) 1994
North Carolina—James B. Hunt Jr. (D) 1996
North Dakota—Edward T. Schafer (R) 1996
Ohio—George V. Voinovich (R) 1994
Oklahoma—David Walters (D) 1994
Oregon—Barbara Roberts (D) 1994
Pennsylvania—Robert P. Casey (D) 1994[1]
Rhode Island—Bruce Sundlun (D) 1994
South Carolina—Carroll A. Campbell Jr. (R) 1994
South Dakota—Walter Miller (R) 1994
Tennessee—Ned McWherter (D) 1994
Texas—Ann W. Richards (D) 1994
Utah—Mike Leavitt (R) 1996
Vermont—Howard Dean (D) 1994
Virginia—L. Douglas Wilder (D) 1993
Washington—Mike Lowry (D) 1996
West Virginia—Gaston Caperton (D) 1996
Wisconsin—Tommy G. Thompson (R) 1994
Wyoming—Mike Sullivan (D) 1994

[1]As of mid-July 1993, Mark Single (D) was acting governor while Gov. Casey recovered from transplant surgery.

Source: Congressional Quarterly Weekly Report, November 7, 1992, 3599. Updated June 1993.

zens decide what is so important that the government will do it at public expense. In the best of governments, the citizens and their representatives define the greater good and employ qualified civil servants—bureaucrats—to implement that good. The idea of the American as a customer of government significantly diminishes both the concept and the potential of the noble concept of citizen.

Fourth, it is incorrect to assume that either those who work for government or the system of government work are the primary problems. The problems are power and politics, not bureaucracy. Government agencies and programs are established by law and are funded by legislatures. Behind every agency and program is a significant interest group, often several of them. Bureaucrats and bureaucracies generally make as much sense out of government programs as is possible.

Fifth, downsizing, rightsizing, cutback management and the other means of reducing the size and costs of government, when combined with deregulation, have significantly diminished the capacities of some units of government to function effectively. This particular combination provided the incubator for both the HUD and S&L scandals.

If concepts such as entrepreneurial government and breaking through bureaucracy are not the prescription for better government in the 1990s, what is? If the past is any guide, we are leaving the era of hyper-individualism and recreational greed and are entering an era of greater concern for the general interest. We need political leadership which will articulate the concerns of this new era, leadership that can build the public commitment to deal with the significant problems of the day—health care, education, infrastructure, race relations, poverty, housing and so forth.

This political leadership will need to see these issues as common or governmental, and not attempt to define them as bureaucratic, managerial or primarily amenable to business solutions. Nor will this leadership be able to assume that governments can manage these problems without resources; this leadership will need to be honest about costs. And, as always, competent and qualified civil servants will need both the resources and the latitude to get the job done.

In short, state and local government must be more rather than less governmental. These are the bullet holes which will be made by the genuinely effective governments of the 1990s.

VII. STATE
BUREAUCRACIES AND
ADMINISTRATION

Departments and agencies within each state carry out the laws passed by the legislature and approved by the governor. These departments vary in size and in responsiveness to executive control. Transportation, human services, corrections, education, and health usually are large departments with sizable budgets and staffs. These "big ticket" agencies perform services quite visible to the public, and governors and legislators alike pay close attention to them. Governors appoint the heads of these agencies with great care, and the legislatures often must confirm the appointments.

Many parts of the state bureaucracy, however, appear to be remarkably immune to the vagaries of legislative and gubernatorial politics. The key to successful bureaucratic politics is to keep a low profile. Governors come and go, legislators come and go, but some agencies keep on doing what they have always done with minimum intrusion from outside. State government encompasses so many agencies and activities that it is virtually impossible for the governor and the legislature to keep track of them all.

Between a Rock and a Hard Place?

State bureaucrats—this is not a derogatory term—often are torn by competing values: economy and efficiency on the one hand and political expediency on the other. In the world of politics, points often are scored for achieving an electorally advantageous goal rather than for saving money or doing a job efficiently.

Another problem is accountability. To whom are state employees accountable? To the governor, the legislature or particular legislators, the interest served by the agency, the public at large, themselves? The numerous lines of accountability give those in the state bureaucracy the opportunity to play one group against another and thereby do what they want.

In recent years important changes have been made that have improved the caliber of the states' work forces. The standards for hiring, promotion, and retention have been raised. Educational requirements are more exacting. In-service training has been upgraded. State employees who report wrongdoing in state government—"whistleblowers"—are better protected against retaliation. And more employees are covered by civil service and merit systems, which has reduced the number of patronage positions. Moreover, minorities now have better opportunities for employment and advancement within state government.

Another related development has been the growing political influence of state employee organizations. State employee groups and state employee labor unions have become stronger in almost all of the states. Like other interests, they lobby their own concerns and proposals before the governor and the state legislature— and with increasing effectiveness. What do they want for their efforts? Higher wages, better health and retirement benefits, and more recognition of their professional status. When it comes to preparing the budget, the most influential parties often are those who carry out the intent of the budget—namely, state employees.

Finally, we must note the dynamic growth of state governments over the last several decades. Since 1950 the number of state government employees has increased by 300 percent; only the increases in primary and secondary education employment were greater. While there was a consistent 'core' of about forty administrative agencies in most of the states in the late 1950s, this had grown to over seventy-five by the mid-1980s.[1] So both the number of people working for state government and the number of agencies in which they work increased greatly.

However, in the last few years the fiscal woes of the states have changed dramatically these dynamics. Growth has stalled with precipitous declines in many states' revenues. Cutbacks in state work forces, not growth, seem to be the guiding philosophy for governors and legislators seeking to balance state budgets. Further, this trend has affected state power structures. The strength of state employees has been reduced as governors and legislators look for new ways to cut back on the size of state governments and their budgets. The goals of seeking higher wages, better health and retirement benefits, and recognition of professional status within state bureaucracies have given way to trying to protect programs, agencies, and jobs, and trying to hold the level of salaries and benefits at current levels. Hard times have cut very sharply into state bureaucracies.

Organizational Problems

How are state agencies organized? Some would argue they aren't. Governors trying to "run" state government or citizens trying to find out where to get help often are baffled by the apparent organizational chaos of the many departments and agencies. Periodically, the states reorganize their executive branch departments. This usually is done either to improve economy and efficiency, to clear up the lines of accountability so that the governor is the chief executive in fact as well as in theory, or to gain control over some agencies that are perceived as out of control—usually the control of the governor or of the legislature.

Not surprisingly, reorganization often is resisted by the agencies themselves and by groups with vested interests in the way things are. Those who know how the system works prefer the status quo and are extremely reluctant to learn new ways. And when the goal is to give the governor more power and influence, the agencies fight hard: they are far from

willing to lose or share their power. Organizational battles are so difficult to mount and win that many governors and legislatures avoid them, believing victory is not worth the political costs.

Republican governors have been particularly attracted to setting up economy and efficiency commissions to survey state government programs, organizations, and policies in an effort to find ways to save the taxpayers money. These commissions, which usually are made up of members of the business community and supported by an out-of-state consulting firm specializing in such studies, review a state's budget, governmental organization, and programs. The commission issues a well-publicized final report pointing out waste in state government and indicates 300-400 suggested changes as to how the state could save millions of dollars.

Some of the suggested changes make sense; others do not. They usually include some reorganization and consolidation of agencies, turning over some of what the agencies do to the private sector (privatization), eliminating some programs, charging or increasing user fees for some services, or transferring a program to another level of government.[2] One observer concludes that such studies have "been largely discredited" and may be more "a political than an administrative tool."[3] Even reorganizations have been criticized as doing more to spawn confusion "about program goals and work responsibilities" and sparking "political brushfires" that keep "managers from getting back to those basic issues of responsibility and accountability."[4]

Major executive branch reorganization efforts have occurred in twenty-two states since the 1960s. The goals usually articulated in these efforts were "modernization and streamlining of the executive branch machinery, efficiency, economy, responsiveness, and gubernatorial control."[5] Reorganizations are not apolitical events; they involve a battle for power among the branches of government. Aside from the built-in resistance that state bureaucrats have to such changes, legislators often oppose them as well because reorganizations usually increase the power of the governor over the executive branch at the expense of the legislature. For example, the number of independent boards, commissions, and agencies usually declines precipitously, such as in Georgia, where the number of such units dropped from 300 to 22, or in Louisiana, where the drop was from 300 to 19.[6] Furthermore, the few bodies that survive the reorganizations are often headed by a single gubernatorial appointee rather than by a multiperson board, which means more control for the governor and less access for the legislature. The most recent example of success in this occurred in 1989, when West Virginia governor Gaston Caperton gained legislative approval for consolidating 150 executive boards and agencies into seven departments.[7]

Rather than seek major reorganization of the bureaucratic structure, state leaders may attempt partial reform when there is a pressing need to consolidate overlapping and confusing jurisdictions, or when they wish to tackle a particular problem facing the state by eliminating organizational barriers. This has been especially important in economic development, in the environmental area, and in the actual administration of state government.

Since the mid-1970s, thirty-six states have followed Colorado's lead and adopted some form of sunset legislation—legislation that calls for the automatic termination of an agency, board, or commission unless the legislature reauthorizes or reestablishes it. Licensing and regulatory agencies are the agencies most often governed by sunset laws. However, six states have since repealed their sunset laws, and six other states have allowed their laws to lapse into inactivity.[8] Many states also have

passed "open government" laws to give the media and interested citizens better access to the activities and records of state government.

Management and Personnel Changes

Where the states have made the most headway is in adopting new management techniques. Budgets no longer are worked out in the back rooms of statehouses by employees wearing green eye shades; they are part of a larger policy-management process headed by the governor.[9] The recent fiscal downturns experienced in the states have forced governors to take an even firmer grasp of the process. Nearly all governors must operate under a balanced budget requirement. If there are any mid-year problems or revenue shortfalls, the governor needs to know about it immediately so he or she can take appropriate remedial action.

Changes in state government administration and personnel have been made but not without considerable furor. Controversies over affirmative action (Should minorities have a leg up in hiring and promotions?) and comparable worth (Should men and women be paid equally for dissimilar jobs of similar skill levels?) are bedeviling state legislators and administrators. A March 1987 U.S. Supreme Court decision, *Johnson v. Transportation Agency, Santa Clara County, Calif.,* supporting the promotion of a woman over a slightly more qualified man in a local government personnel situation, indicates judicial branch support for affirmative action principles. Another Supreme Court decision, *City of Richmond v. Croson* (1989), declared unconstitutional another state and local government affirmative action effort called set-asides, in which a fixed portion of public works funds are reserved for minority-owned companies. Using the legal concept of strict scrutiny, the Court argued any such program must meet a compelling state interest to be used. The concept of strict scrutiny historically has been difficult to specify legally, especially in the area of racial discrimination.[10]

Politically, it makes sense to open up jobs for women and other minorities; they are becoming more active in politics and their support often is needed to win elections. Hence, it is no surprise that the number of women in state-level cabinet positions increased by 114 percent between 1981 and 1989. In a 1989 survey of the forty states with a cabinet structure of government, women held 150 of the 703 cabinet-level positions, or 21 percent.[11] The director of administration in Louisiana said she still sees evidence of male chauvinism in state government but felt "the good ol' boy network is aging and it is likely I will live to see their replacements."[12]

A recent study of state government agency heads suggests that women in state government are circumventing the so-called "glass ceiling" or administrative lid rather than trying to break through it. They are doing this by moving into expanded state government activities, such as consumer affairs and arts agencies, by involvement in governmental and political activism, and by reaching parity with men in terms of education, experience, and professionalism. "The administrative ballpark or ball game [has been] substantially enlarged. The park's gotten bigger."[13]

After the 1992 elections, women held 72 of the 324 available positions in state executive branches (22.2 percent). This compares to twenty-nine women holding such jobs in 1977.[14] Women also held 1,517 of the 7,424 state legislative seats (20.4 percent) after the 1992 elections.[15] This represents more than a quadrupling of the number of women who served in 1969.[16] "Ten years ago, no state legislature was even one-third women; the top ten states from ten years ago would be below today's national average."[17] According to one observer of the state government scene: "We're going to have to move beyond the good ol' boy network to include in the profoundest way the good ol' girls and the good ol' minorities."[18]

There have been considerable changes in the type of personnel working at the administrative level in state governments. According to Deil Wright, who has studied state administrators since 1964, the 1988 cadre of administrators differed from their 1964 counterparts in the following ways: there were fewer males (83 percent in 1988 vs. 98 percent in 1964); fewer whites (91 percent vs. 98 percent); they were younger (median age of 43 vs. 53); and better educated (only 2 percent had a high school education or less vs. 15 percent, and those with graduate or professional degrees rose from 40 percent to 57 percent over the period).[19]

Ethics

How government officials, elected or appointed, behave while in office is increasingly a topic of concern at the state level. We generally recognize a corrupt act—or do we? Handing cash to a public official to influence a decision would seem to be a corrupt act. But what about a public utility political action committee that contributes funds to incumbent legislators' campaigns so that legislators might look more favorably on revising the utility rate structure? Is that a corrupt act? Or is that politics?

Like beauty, corruption and ethical misbehavior often are in the eye of the beholder. Some states are trying to clarify this issue by establishing ethics codes, standards, and commissions. Recently, several states have established inspectors general offices to probe into allegations of wrongdoing in state government. In some instances, the inspectors general have the authority to "identify programs or departments that *might be vulnerable* to corruption. . . ."[20] Some observers suggest that these steps, along with measures to open up electoral and governmental processes and to develop accountability measures, "have ... been at least as significant as the other reforms" occurring in the states over the past few decades.[21]

While there are several state governments with a history of ethical and corruption problems, few can match the recent situation in West Virginia. Consider the following events, which occurred in about one year's time: the popular, recently reelected state treasurer A. James Manchin was impeached and resigned in July 1989 after auditors found losses of nearly $300 million in the state's Consolidated Investment Fund; state attorney general Charlie Brown resigned one month later after being accused of perjury during a custody hearing involving his ex-wife and daughter, and a grand jury that was investigating the perjury charges also subpoenaed Brown's campaign finance records from 1984 through 1988; three state senators were forced to resign, two over charges of taking money in return for votes, the other over a felony income tax charge; up to fifty other state and local officials were under investigation for alleged wrongdoing; and in April 1990, former governor Arch Moore (R, 1969-77, 1985-89) pleaded guilty to federal charges of extortion, mail fraud, tax fraud, and obstruction of justice.[22]

Most recently, other states' elected officials have found themselves on the wrong side of an ethical question. The treasurers of Oklahoma, Nebraska, and Wisconsin, and the attorney general of Arkansas all were caught for various misdeeds while in office and lost their jobs as the voters did not send them back to office.[23] The Louisiana insurance commissioner and a former New Jersey deputy attorney general were both convicted of felonies while in office, and the Tennessee secretary of state committed suicide after his name surfaced in a corruption case.[24]

In April 1993, Alabama governor Guy Hunt (R) was convicted of breaking the state ethics law by diverting 1987 inaugural funds for his own use. The judge told the jury that Alabama law does not allow using political funds for personal use. Upon conviction of the felony, Hunt was immediately removed from office and replaced by Lieutenant Governor Jim Folsom Jr. (D).[25] Former Rhode Island governor Edward DiPrete (R, 1985-91) was fined for "steering state contracts to two political cronies" and neglecting to file his conflict-of-interest statement.[26]

Part VII explores some of these and other controversies concerning state bureaucracies. Charles Mahtesian from *Governing* discusses why state bureaucracies never seem to shrink. Jonathan Walters from *Governing* looks at what should and should not be considered when civil service reform is on the agenda. And Steven Gold in *State Government News* lays out the adversarial nature of budgetary politics in the states.

Notes

1. Deil S. Wright, Jae-Won Yoo, and Jennifer Cohen, "The Evolving Profile of State Administrators," *Journal of State Government* 64:1 (January-March 1991): 30-31.
2. Tim Funk, "Efficiency Study Commissions: Is an Old Idea a Bad Idea?" *North Carolina Insight* 11:4 (August 1989): 42-43, 46-50.
3. James K. Conant, "Reorganization and the Bottom Line," *Public Administration Review* 46:1 (January/February 1986): 48.
4. Les Garner, "Managing Change Through Organization Structure," *Journal of State Government* 60:4 (July/August 1987): 194.
5. James K. Conant, "In the Shadow of Wilson and Brownlow: Executive Branch Reorganization in the States, 1965 to 1987," *Public Administration Review* 48:5 (September/October 1988): 895.
6. Ibid., 902.
7. Elder Witt, "A Governor Seeks Less Government," *Governing* 2:9 (June 1989): 66.
8. Richard C. Kearney, "Sunset: A Survey and

Analysis of the State Experience," *Public Administration Review* 50:1 (January/February 1990): 66.

9. See James J. Gosling, "Patterns of Stability and Change in Gubernatorial Policy Agendas," *State and Local Government Review* 23:1 (Winter 1991): 3-12; and Robert D. Lee, Jr., "Developments in State Budgeting: Trends of Two Decades," *Public Administration Review* 51:3 (May/June 1991): 254-262.

10. Linda Greenhouse, "Ruling Ends Part of Affirmative Action Debate," *New York Times News Service*, reprinted in [Raleigh] *News and Observer*, January 25, 1989, 2A.

11. National Women's Political Caucus, "More Women Hold Top State Positions," *USA/Today*, February 27, 1989, 6A.

12. Mireille Grangenois Gates, "More Women Join State Cabinets," *USA/Today*, October 24, 1986, 3A.

13. Study by Deil S. Wright and Angela M. Bullard, reported in Liz Lucas, "Women Winning State Posts," *Chapel Hill* (North Carolina) *News*, May 7, 1993 7, 12.

14. Center for the American Woman and Politics, "Fact Sheet: Women in Elective Office 1991, 1993" Eagleton Institute of Politics, Rutgers University, March 1991, May 1993.

15. Study by the Center for the American Woman and Politics, "Fact Sheet," May 1993.

16. Center for the American Woman and Politics, "Fact Sheet," March 1991.

17. Study by the Center for the American Woman and Politics, reported in *The Hotline,* November 19, 1992, 13.

18. Comment by Jesse L. White, Jr., former executive director of the Southern Growth Policies Board and a public policy consultant in "On the Record," *Governing* 4:8 (May 1991): 18.

19. Wright, Yoo, Cohen, 32.

20. Cheri Collis, "State Inspectors General: The Watchdog over State Agencies," *State Government News* 33:4 (April 1990): 13.

21. Fran Burke and George C. S. Benson, "Written Rules: State Ethics Codes, Commissions, and Conflicts," *Journal of State Government* 62:5 (September/October 1989): 198.

22. No one has put together the whole story yet, but some of the pieces can be found in: "In Briefs: West Virginia," *Comparative State Politics Newsletter* 10:2 (April 1989); "West Virginia Woes," *State Policy Reports* 7:17 (September 1989): 30; "West Virginia Problems," *State Policy Reports* 7:24 (December 1989): 9; LaDonna Sloan, "In Briefs: West Virginia," *Comparative State Politics* 10:6 (December 1989): 37; and "West Virginia Problems," *State Policy Reports* 8:8 (April 1990): 24.

23. "Final Election Results: Oklahoma," *USA/Today*, November 8, 1990, 9A; "Zeuske Ousts Smith as State Treasurer," *Milwaukee Journal*, November 7, 1990, B5; and Amy E. Young, "In the States," *Common Cause Magazine* 17:3 (May/June 1991): 41.

24. Larry Tye, "A Tide of State Corruption Sweeps from Coast to Coast," *Boston Globe*, March 25, 1991, 1, 16.

25. "Alabama: Guilty Verdict Ushers in 'Time of Sorrow,'" *The Hotline*, April 23, 1993, 13.

26. Amy E. Young, "In the States—Rhode Island Issues an SOS," *Common Cause Magazine* 18:1 (January/March 1992): 29.

Why the Sun Rarely Sets on State Bureaucracy

by Charles Mahtesian

[In 1991], just as it does in every odd-numbered year, the Texas Sunset Advisory Commission took a long, hard look at the state's bureaucracy. It reviewed the performance of 30 agencies, boards and commissions, factoring in usefulness, efficiency and public benefit. Finally it concluded that Texas could live without a Good Neighbor Commission. But it voted to prolong the existence of the Cosmetology Commission and the state Board of Barber Examiners.

This sort of process isn't exactly what proponents of "sunset" laws had in mind in 1976 when the nation's first sunset review act was passed in Colorado. Their idea was to create a process by which all agencies of state government—big and small alike—would be made more accountable and responsive. But a close look at the history of sunset shows that the sun only goes down on the bureaucratic small fry—those without a mobilized or politically connected constituency. And the big agencies tend to escape scrutiny altogether.

What sunset laws do is schedule a periodic date of nominal termination for all agencies included under them. The affected agencies—which vary from state to state—then undergo a review by legislative committee or, as in Texas, by an independent commission.

Then the legislature votes to terminate or else to reverse the decision and give the agency a new lease on life.

By the early 1980s, the good-government appeal of Colorado's sunset legislation program had convinced 36 other states to create their own versions. And for a number of states, the early results were very encouraging. In its first year of review in 1979, Arkansas terminated 15 agencies, councils and commissions that its reviewers judged no longer necessary. That same year, Texas terminated nine agencies and combined several others, for an estimated savings of about $7.1 million.

During the 1980s, however, some states began to experience problems. Legislators and staff—particularly those in part-time legislatures—were overwhelmed by the excessive time demands that a detailed review required. Others questioned the cost-effectiveness of the whole enterprise. In all cases, heavy lobbying pressure thwarted efforts to rein in or eliminate larger and more politically sensitive agencies. Beginning with North Carolina in 1981, 12 states suspended their sunset programs or

Charles Mahtesian is a staff writer for *Governing*. This article is reprinted from *Governing* 5:9 (June 1992): 24-25.

Table 1   The Growing Bureaucracy

Ten largest states	Year	Population	Full-time equivalent employees	Employees per 10,000
California	1970	20,007,000	195,000	98
	1980	23,668,000	249,000	105
	1990	29,760,000	325,000	109
New York	1970	18,268,000	185,000	101
	1980	17,558,000	215,000	122
	1990	17,990,000	285,000	158
Texas	1970	11,236,000	112,000	100
	1980	14,229,000	169,000	119
	1990	16,987,000	223,000	131
Florida	1970	6,848,000	72,000	105
	1980	9,746,000	105,000	108
	1990	12,938,000	160,000	124
Pennsylvania	1970	11,813,000	118,000	100
	1980	11,864,000	127,000	107
	1990	11,882,000	127,000	107
Illinois	1970	11,128,000	106,000	95
	1980	11,427,000	124,000	109
	1990	11,431,000	145,000	127
Ohio	1970	10,664,000	85,000	80
	1980	10,798,000	115,000	107
	1990	10,847,000	139,000	128
Michigan	1970	8,890,000	91,000	102
	1980	9,262,000	126,000	136
	1990	9,295,000	144,000	155
New Jersey	1970	7,193,000	58,000	81
	1980	7,365,000	87,000	118
	1990	7,730,000	112,000	145
North Carolina	1970	5,098,000	62,000	122
	1980	5,882,000	87,000	148
	1990	6,629,000	107,000	161

Source: Jonathan Walters, "The Shrink-Proof Bureaucracy," *Governing* 5:6 (March 1992): 35.

repealed them altogether. "People lost faith that these things were ever going to sunset," says Bob Geolas, research director for the National Center for State Laws and Regulations.

Still, a majority chose to retain the review process, responding to criticism of the sunset process by altering their statutes. For Vermont, that meant extending the review cycle for each agency from six years to 12. In Kansas, legislators streamlined the process by removing a number of agencies from its coverage.

Of those states that retained sunset, some have reported modest cost savings over the years since then. But one lesson nearly every state has learned is that, as the experience in Texas shows, certain entities are untouchable. "You could get [terminate] one that's very small and has a limited number of people supporting it," says Bill Wells, director of the Texas Sunset Advisory Commission. "The mid-range agencies you are not going to eliminate." One senator resigned from the Texas commission in 1986, frustrated by the inability to control larger agencies. He termed the sunset process "pet food for lobbyists."

The list of agencies Texas has reviewed and reauthorized since beginning its sunset process in 1979 reflects this problem. The commission has considered 197 agencies and voted to abolish 26—but most of the 26 have been of little consequence or cost to the state. The sunset process has focused its sights on such agencies as the Texas Navy Inc., the Pink Bollworm Commission, the Stonewall Jackson Memorial Board and the Texas Historical Resources Development Council.

Meanwhile, two politically powerful agencies, the Alcohol Beverage Commission and the Department of Public Safety, have won postponement from sunset review even though they are supposed to be covered under the Texas Sunset Act. And although critics have pointed for years to the excessive number of occupational licensing boards in Texas, only two such boards—the Board of Tuberculosis Nurse Examiners and the Board of Examiners in Social Psychotherapy—have ever been eliminated through sunset. It's a matter of "just not wanting oversight," insists Susie Woodford, executive director of Texas Common Cause. "They want to continue the good ol' boy way of running business."

In Texas, there are the closest of ties among the Alcohol Beverage Commission, the multibillion-dollar liquor industry and the legislature. Financial disclosure records indicate, for example, that one lobbyist, a former assistant director at the Texas ABC, spent more than $30,000 in 1990 and 1991 entertaining legislators. The first time the ABC was up for review, in 1987, the legislature simply passed a bill moving the date to 1991. Later that year, another bill extended the lease for two more years. "They are, thank God, finally going to be reviewed in 1993," says Woodford.

Other states usually follow the same path—avoiding the politically sensitive work of evaluating important agencies and spending their time going after regulatory bodies for groups like hearing aid dealers, masseurs and masseuses, arborists, soil classifiers and watchmakers.

But even seemingly innocuous groups like these do not let their occupational licensing boards go down without a fight. In fact, some of the most tenacious lobbying efforts come from these quarters. "You can have very reasonable recommendations about ending a program, but if you've got 50,000 barbers and cosmetologists writing letters and wanting a piece of paper for their wall, it's probably not going to happen," says Brad Mallon, director of Policy and Research for the Colorado Department of Regulatory Agencies. He notes that barbers and cosmetologists have thwarted three efforts so far to kill the Board of Barbers and Cosmetologists.

The barbers and cosmetologists argue, of course, that a licensing board provides a credible method of certification that instills public confidence and helps screen fly-by-night operators. Critics respond that any benefit to the public from weeding out an occasional incompetent practitioner is less significant than the unnecessary obstacles that licensing can place in the path of those who want to enter the field. The harder it is to become a barber—or

149

a masseur or a watchmaker—the fewer of them there are in a state, and the more they may be able to charge customers as a result. "All the policies in statute put money in somebody's pocket and take it out of somebody else's pocket," says Bill Wells, of the sunset commission in Texas, "So every statute has a constituency."

Mallon argues, however, that elimination of agencies should not be the primary goal of the sunset process. States that believed so had unrealistic expectations. "The beauty of sunset," he says, "is not so much that you can get rid of something. The beauty is the chance to take an objective look at an agency and make needed changes." The original sponsor of sunset legislation, Colorado state Representative Jerry Kopel, agrees. "We have made enormous modifications to the agencies that are still around," he insists, "that would not have been done without sunset."

In Colorado, for example, the regulation of motor clubs and cemeteries used to be handled by the state Insurance Division. The sunset commission recommended transferring this job to the Division of Financial Services, and that move proved to be a success. A 1986 study of 28 sunset states, undertaken by the South Carolina State Reorganization Commission, revealed that useful changes were made in many states in a similar way. The changes ranged from the merger and combination of agencies to increased public participation in government. In 16 states, agencies' disciplinary and investigatory functions were increased. Tennessee reported that of the 200 agencies reviewed under its sunset process, about 50 percent were modified.

It is hard to gauge whether sunset has saved much money. Some states dropped it in the 1980s because the cost of the reviews proved to be high compared to the amount of money that ultimately was saved. In Vermont, researchers concluded, "the laws have certainly improved, but many in the legislature believe sunset is a waste of money." Alaska reported that it is "impossible to evaluate on a dollar-and-cents basis."

But proponents believe the focus on money is short-sighted. Bill Wells says the return in Texas has amounted to about $20 for every dollar spent by the commission. He estimates that over the 13-year span of sunset in Texas, even without taking on many of the big-budget agencies, the state has saved about $200 million. Much of that is money that defunct agencies would have spent had they not been sunsetted.

Meanwhile, some states, including Florida and Texas, have moved beyond sunset to the concept of a "sunrise" requirement. If it is difficult to put an unnecessary agency out of business, they have found, it may be possible to keep it from being launched in the first place. Florida and Texas initiated sunrise after discovering that new agencies were sprouting faster than old agencies were sunsetting, resulting in a net gain of bureaucracy. At least 14 states now use some form of commission or committee to pass judgment on prospective new agencies of state government before the legislature has formally created them.

"It isn't enough just to do the sunset," says Colorado's Jerry Kopel. "Every year you're going to have seven to nine attempts by groups to be licensed. It's tough for legislators to say no." A sunrise process, Kopel argues, is a way to help legislators vote against the creation of new licensing boards and other agencies that serve no public need.

But whether the sun is rising or setting, two requirements remain: Those involved in the process need to be tough enough to handle a barrage of lobbying, and they need to be willing to lose their share of battles. "I think the main thing that disheartens me," says Bill Wells of Texas, "is that states don't think the principle is worth fighting for—since you're probably going to get beat 80 percent of the time."

How *Not* to Reform Civil Service

by Jonathan Walters

Last December [1991], Florida announced that it was going to stride brashly into the promised land of civil service reform. The state, Governor Lawton Chiles announced, would be "sunsetting" its civil service system.

That got people's attention.

The inspiration for the effort was couched mostly in terms of governmental efficiency, although occasionally Chiles would fall back on a more traditional politician's position: State employees needed a kick in the pants. Chiles wasn't as hard on government workers as his predecessor, Bob Martinez—who had compared state employees to "lard bricks"— but Chiles continued the familiar rhetoric, at one point asking, "What are we about here? Are we just providing jobs for people?"

Whatever the inspiration, it was time to unleash Florida from the strictures of civil service. Florida's civil service system was officially sunsetted on June 30, 1992.

Except it wasn't, really. In fact, Florida continues to operate under the same personnel system it had before civil service's much ballyhooed trip into the twilight.

Confused? Welcome to the hot-air, hyped-up world of over-reaching civil service reform. It is a world that is getting more attention lately as governors across the country

take a look at personnel systems as an avenue to solving all government woes. State executives would do well to study Florida before doing anything precipitous themselves, but not for reasons Governor Chiles would like. Florida's hard-learned lesson: If you try for a revolution, you could end up with an oversold, uncoordinated, misdirected and ultimately fumbled drive at reform. Something else to keep in mind: Big-splash civil service reform efforts don't save money. They cost money.

Ultimately, what Florida needs—what quite a few states and localities need—is probably a little bit of civil service reform at a time, reform offered up in politically, economically and administratively manageable doses. Some jurisdictions are going at it that way; others, however, seem hopelessly enamored of the big splash. In the real world of civil service reform, the tortoises are winning the race.

Civil Service: The two words conjure up images of gross overstaffing, government inflexibility, warrens full of dyspeptic shirkers and featherbedding bureaucrats who have become expert at manipulating Byzantine sys-

Jonathan Walters is a staff writer for *Governing*. This article is reprinted from *Governing* 6:2 (November 1992): 30-34.

Black Monday

... On Oct. 5 [1992] ... New Jersey's Supreme Court—the ultimate referee in a brutal fight over budget cuts—lifted a temporary restraining order that had been obtained by the unions. In doing so, the high court, in effect, gave almost 1,500 state workers their walking papers. For most, the walk led right onto the unemployment line in a state where more than 9 percent of the total workforce, public and private sectors combined, was already looking for a job.

"Black Monday," as this episode has come to be called within the bowels of the bureaucracy, was the capstone on four months of contention and confusion over how to cope with an ever-widening deficit in the state's nearly $15 billion budget. In addition to a sizeable number of intramural political riffs within the back rooms of the Statehouse, the furor also revealed a range of serious gaps and shortcomings in a Civil Service system that had undergone "reform" just six years ago.

For one thing, the layoffs—which accounted for only $50 million in savings out of $1.1 billion in Republican-sponsored cuts—sent thousands of workers ping-ponging into new jobs. Rules and contract provisions governing seniority and so-called "bumping" rights turned middle managers with little computer training into budget analysts, budget analysts into social workers, and social workers into unemployment compensation applicants. Other state employees found their seniority didn't count at all. ...

Source: Mark J. Magyar, "The Bureaucratic Whirlpool: Why New Jersey's 'Uncivil' Service System Needs Massive Reform," *New Jersey Reporter* 22:4 (November/December 1992): 30-34.

tems to their full career advantage. Try to fire a slacker, goes the popular wisdom, and he envelopes himself in an impenetrable cocoon of red tape and paper until his nemesis gives up and goes away.

To be fair about it, the rap isn't without some merit. At a conference of the National Association of State Personnel Executives in August [1992], top personnel officers from all over the country complained about the testing, hiring, pay and promotion rules they must live by that don't give them the flexibility they need to find, hire and keep more good people in government. And when one presenter at the conference asked if performance was one of the criteria—other than seniority—that could be used when agencies were considering whom to lay off in a downsizing, only a smattering of hands in the crowd went up.

Many states and many localities still operate on a policy of "last hired, first fired," regardless of whether the newer person is doing a better job than the veteran. More amazing still, the "rule of three," by which managers are allowed to choose only from the three top-scoring candidates on civil service tests, still constricts many state and local hiring systems, even in the face of overwhelming evidence that such tests don't tell employers anything close to the whole story about a job candidate. And in many states and localities, the central personnel office is still the funnel through which all hiring and other personnel actions have to pass.

To be equally fair about it, though, neither all civil servants nor all civil service systems can be painted with the same brush. There are about 14 million state and local government employees, most of whom are doing good work, many of them under trying circumstance There are hundreds of state and local civil service systems. Some are horribly inefficient and inflexible. But many now operate with an efficiency and flexibility equal to that found in the best-run large corporations.

On top of that, some of the classic criticisms of civil service simply don't ring true, say experienced public-sector managers. While firing a public employee can be a laborious process, the paper case that public-sector managers have to make to get rid of someone is actually not much different in the private sector. Carolyn Ban, an associate professor at the Rockefeller College of Public Affairs and Policy who has studied personnel systems nationwide, has interviewed managers with experience in both sectors who say it is *easier* to fire someone in government.

Nor does deference to seniority have to be a mandatory feature of civil service. Several systems now use it only as a tie-breaker when considering equally qualified candidates, while some don't weigh it at all, ever. As for the role of civil service in confounding downsizing, New York State has what is widely regarded as the most constricted, calcified and complicated civil service system in the country, and employees there have been laid off by the thousands. Downsizing tends to be an issue of political will, not system flexibility.

But the most important point to be made about civil service is that there are two very good reasons why it exists. The first is the public's demand that the process of staffing government be as clean and politics-free as possible. It is a demand that state and federal legal systems have sustained time and again. The second reason why civil service exists is that it ensures some security, continuity and constancy at key levels of government even as administrations change. Such constancy is key to the success of any long-term, complex enterprise; overhauling broad layers of personnel

with each new administration is bad for business, not to mention morale.

Which is why Florida's claim that it was "sunsetting" civil service was so misleading. Call it well-intentioned political dramatics. Call it hype. Call it wishful thinking. No state *could* sunset its civil service system. Besides being politically, logistically and legally impossible—programs funded by the federal government require it, and it is constitutionally mandated in many states—sunsetting a civil service system would make it very hard to staff a government.

What the Florida legislature actually did was to amend the existing civil service statute to say, in essence, that the state ought to reform its civil service system and that those reforms should be effected at the rule-making level. Those changes would be shaped mostly by the recommendations of the state's Civil Service Reform Commission, set up shortly after Chiles took office in 1991. The commission, made up of gubernatorial and legislative appointees, had been hard at work on a long list of technical fixes to civil service rules, prior to the legislative action authorizing reform.

The evidence now is that the commission loaded the reform effort so heavily that it is in the process of sinking. In all, the commission has made nearly 100 recommendations in 10 general areas of personnel management. A lot of them are good suggestions and arguably long overdue. But implementing them all quickly or in a coordinated fashion is unrealistic. On top of all that, the commission recommends that Florida implement Total Quality Management statewide. That in itself would be extremely difficult to achieve without a significant investment in time and money.

Tom Herndon, Chiles' chief of staff, disagrees that the effort was overly ambitious. "It's tempting to say that it's too big an agenda, and let's take this one step at a time, but so often you have interaction between all

Political Protocol
Part III

You are indignant over a state policy initiative and decide to write a letter to the editor of the local newspaper. The topic has nothing to do with your state job. Should you use your state title or mention your state job?

No. Your position and affiliation are not relevant to the topic. (They may not even be relevant to your job, but that's an entirely different can of worms.) Nor should you write on state letterhead, even if you black out the name and address of the agency that employs you. Letterhead should be reserved for official communications, and your letter to the editor is unofficial. You are writing as a citizen; you have the right to do so.

"Citizen legislators," as the designation suggests, lead dual lives. They have work on the outside, as well as in public office, and are up to their ears in political activity as well. They must always be conscious of whether they are in the legislative role or their private occupational role.

I, too, face problems of identification. By virtue of my Ph.D., I am entitled to identify myself as "doctor" in professional life. I never do; well, hardly ever. The truth is I use the title when making airline reservations. I've been told that it somehow helps in booking, and fortunately, I've never been called on to treat a passenger who has taken ill on the plane.

Source: Alan Rosenthal, *State Government News* 35:10 (October 1992): 34. ©1993 The Council of State Governments. Reprinted with permission from *State Government News*.

shape if the state's economy was in much better shape, and he is no doubt right about that.

Over-ambitious or not, however, some argue further that the Florida effort misses the whole point. They say that the state should actually be looking at extending civil service protection to higher-level managers and not just at reforms affecting lower-level people. Currently, 2,400 of Florida's top managers function with no civil service protection at all. If leadership is one of the public-sector manpower issues of the 1990s, argue advocates of increasing protection, then states should be looking for ways to build constancy and continuity into that leadership by making it less vulnerable to political change.

The Florida reform effort missed the boat in one other key area, an area that Tom Herndon agrees is still a huge problem: The state doesn't pay its people well, and even the best-intended civil service reform isn't going to make people happier if they are underpaid.

Underpaid is an understatement for some Florida state employees. More than 10 percent of them qualify for food stamps. Estimates for how far some Florida workers lag in pay behind the state's *local government* workers range from 10 percent to 30 percent. State employees have not gotten raises in two years, and the raises they received in the three previous years failed even to keep up with inflation.

Nowhere have those points been driven home harder than in the two departments that Florida is said to have "set free" of civil service rules as an experiment concurrent to the overall reform effort. Here again, the rhetoric is ruled by hyperbole: While it's true that the Department of Revenue and the Division of Workers' Compensation in the Department of Labor were allowed more flexibility to hire, train and pay people, the departments were by no means exempted from civil service.

these little things, you can't really move ahead on one without the other." Herndon also thinks the effort would be in much better

In the revenue department, a relative handful of low-level employees received bonuses for increasing their output (a measurement of typing keystrokes, mostly). Staff making $12,000 a year were able to make an extra $1,000 to $1,500—hardly a formula for across-the-board employee satisfaction. Meanwhile, a number of experienced managers were dumped in favor of Chiles' people, and training money that was supposed to accompany the revenue department's reform efforts was pulled, restored, pulled again and finally grudgingly restored.

The effort was not a total failure. Herndon, who was head of the revenue department when the program was first implemented, is given high marks for boosting departmental morale. But observers of the experiment credit Herndon's management style, not any new system flexibility, with whatever gains were made there. And it is perhaps a measurement of the Chiles administration's current commitment to civil service reform that Herndon has left the revenue department to become Chiles' chief of staff and Frank Scruggs, head of the labor department, has left for the private sector.

To Barton Wechsler, an associate professor at Florida State University's School of Public Administration and Policy, the unimpressive results of the experiment with the two agencies highlight the biggest myth about civil service reform in Florida, and the one on which it could ultimately founder: that civil service reform will quickly turn governments into lean, efficient, tax-increase-spurning machines. If anything, reform as outlined by Florida's Civil Service Reform Commission—including its well-intentioned and ambitious plans for training—would cost the state two or three times the supposed $200 million to $300 million that reform would save.

What is it that has led so many public officials in Florida to put so much time and

energy into what is fundamentally an off-the-mark, overblown effort? Frank Sherwood, a colleague of Wechsler's at the University of Florida, thinks he knows: a fascination with both the substance and the rhetoric of "reinventing government," as embodied in the widely read and provocative book of that title published earlier this year.

David Osborne, co-author of *Reinventing Government* ... has been a close adviser to Governor Chiles. In the book, Osborne and Ted Gaebler describe civil service as one of government's great evils. Indeed, the Florida Civil Service Reform Commission's executive summary resonates with language that could just as well have come straight from the book. A sample: "Civil service reform is designed to reduce waste, increase productivity and enhance human resources. As a result, agencies will be empowered; managers, supervisors and employees will receive the training needed to deliver services efficiently and effectively; performance evaluation will be improved and linked to the reward system; and employees will be involved in improving the quality of service delivery. Through civil service reform, state government will be able to do more with less, eliminate waste and increase productivity, and meet the needs of Florida's taxpayers."

No one would argue with those goals. But in the face of that kind of rhetoric, what politician in his right mind is going to suggest that what Florida really needs is to pay its people better? Or that Florida's fundamental economic problems can't possibly be solved through civil service reform, no matter how sweeping?

For his part, Osborne argues that Florida's effort is still developing and that it's way too early to write its obituary. He also argues that piecemeal reform might work in a state where "the politics is rational," but not in a state, like Florida, where it is a contact sport. In such states, he says, it is critical to get the public on the side of reform. To get the public's interest and backing, reform has to be sweeping. Chiles' failing, Osborne believes, is not that he has been too ambitious but that he hasn't sold the reforms to the public.

Another governor is about to test Osborne's theory. Massachusetts' William F. Weld seems bent on a plan of sweeping civil service reform, despite concerns about its political feasibility. Weld's staff, like Osborne, believes the battle will pivot on Weld's ability to rally public support.

The thrust of Weld's plan: Eliminate civil service protection for all state employees and give managers more power to hire, promote, move and fire people. Within that large framework, Weld has made some long-overdue recommendations for streamlining the state's personnel system. They include giving agencies more discretion in hiring, moving away from multiple-choice exams as a way to screen candidates, and creating a central job bank for all open government positions. The trouble is, those good ideas could sink along with the whole plan, because of Weld's insistence on a complete overhaul of the system. The political resistance to the plan will be fierce. In the first place, say opponents to the Weld plan, eliminating civil service protection for state employees smacks of a return to the spoils system. And, more to the point, Massachusetts is a collective bargaining state with very powerful public employee unions. They are not going to sit still for a wholesale stripping of civil service protections or for giving managers more power.

Despite the certainty of a bloody fight, Weld's people are determined to reinvent, full speed ahead. "We're going to get whacked," admits Lisa Blout, assistant secretary for strategic planning in the administration and finance department. But a little change would not satisfy the urge to remake government from top to bottom. "Life is too short," says

Blout. "[Elective] terms are too short. You just can't operate that way."

Other states would argue that you *can* operate that way and that you had better, or all you are reinventing is failure. A number of state and local civil service systems have undergone gradual reform in ways that address many of the classic complaints about civil service. They have done so with little conflict. The states of California, Minnesota and Virginia and the cities of Baltimore, Dallas, Indianapolis and San Diego, for example, have decentralized their hiring systems and have dumped the rule of three. All but Baltimore and Dallas have also moved away from written tests to evaluate job candidates.

Iowa offers a good example of how incremental reform can work. That state has for several years been dealing with many of the classic criticisms of civil service. It has been handling them one by one. Most recently, it tackled the problem of burgeoning layers of middle management. Last session, the legislature passed a bill that calls for halving the layers of management in all agencies and for increasing the ratio of staff to supervisors by 50 percent. Complementing that effort, the state personnel office has allowed some departments to experiment with new pay grades for technical and front-line staff so they don't have to be promoted into managerial positions in order to get raises for doing good work or taking on increased responsibility. "No one has raised the issue of sunsetting civil service," says William Snyder, legislative liaison for the state personnel department. "We have talked mainly in terms of making the system more responsive to agencies." A number of states and localities have even successfully addressed such delicate political issues as veterans' preference, either offering it only on a limited basis or not at all.

For those public officials who are bored by that kind of incremental, detailed and focused reform, there is reasonable opportunity, yet, for a little reinvention. Two areas of reform offer some middle ground between an Iowa-level dose of change and a Florida-style administrative and political Hail-Mary pass. Both get at many of the classic complaints about the confining nature of civil service.

The first is the concept of "broad-banding" of occupational classes and pay grades. The second is a general rethinking of the role of central personnel offices and whether certain functions should be pushed down to individual agencies, leaving central offices to act more as personnel consultants than as the gate through which all personnel decisions must pass.

Broad-banding refers to the creation of a set of occupational "families" in place of the current and often complex multilayered system of job classification and compensation. The job classification inflation that many states have seen is very often the result of managers creating a new job title to ensure that a candidate really fits the job that is open. It has also been the traditional way of getting a valued employee more money or a better title. The effect of such title or class inflation is a system that has hundreds or even thousands of classes for only one or a handful of employees. Civil service systems end up so clogged and complex that shifting manpower according to new priorities becomes a nightmare.

By broad-banding, proponents argue, the system becomes more flexible, especially in the areas of shifting manpower and compensation. What broad-banding does not protect against, argue its critics, is mismatching of candidates and specific-skill, highly technical jobs. But that could be remedied by allowing managers more say in whom they interview for those jobs, a policy that is in effect now in dozens of jurisdictions.

By way of a model, a recent study done for the federal government by the National Academy of Public Administration recommends grouping the 459 current federal occupational series into 10 occupational families covering a wide variety of skill levels and types and levels of responsibility. It's not the only solution, says Barbara S. Wamsley, who directed the classification study for the academy, but it does deal with many of the traditional criticisms of the inflexibility of civil service systems.

The debate over decentralization of personnel systems, meanwhile, is similar to the debate that has occurred in the past decade over information technology agencies: Should a centralized office run the whole show, maintaining tight control over one function, requiring all other agencies to come to it for services? Or should it exist more as a consultant to other agencies, advising on specific departmental needs? In the case of personnel, the agency could offer advice on matters of staffing, pay, job classifications (including how to broadband) and other general personnel management issues. Agencies could also consult in specific management areas, such as implementation of TQM.

Decentralization of some functions has obvious advantages. It has the potential to speed up hiring. It also allows agencies more say in who works for them and how they are treated after they are hired.

A number of states have already decentralized the hiring function, allowing agencies to write their own job descriptions and do their own hiring. Virginia and California have extremely decentralized systems, where the central personnel offices provide general guidelines for personnel policies but leave particulars up to the agencies themselves.

While California's decentralized system works well for the most part, there are some drawbacks to moving responsibility and authority out to individual agencies, according to Gloria Harmon, executive officer of the California Personnel Board. For one thing, there is no longer any central listing of state job openings. And some worry that such Balkanization of agencies will mean less interagency movement of staff, especially of good people who want to stay in government but try new things.

Still other personnel executives argue that decentralized systems will only lead to expensive redundancy in personnel staffing and operations. Hilda E. Ford, secretary of Maryland's Department of Personnel, says the idea of letting all of Maryland's agencies loose to do their own hiring and firing gives her nightmares, and not just on the efficiency side. As the veteran of multimillion-dollar discrimination lawsuits, she wants to keep a close eye on whom the state is hiring.

But clearly some loosening of the personnel strings is in order. On the cost side, it was, ironically, budget constraints that led California to a decentralized personnel system, says Harmon. As the central personnel office's budget got cut, it had to turn more responsibility over to agencies. And arguably, after things are decentralized, central agencies could continue to facilitate interagency transfers, monitor agencies for compliance with equal opportunity laws and act as clearinghouses for information on job openings government-wide.

Whatever states do, though, to make their personnel systems work better, they need to be realistic about how much they can change at one time. Efforts like Florida's may get a lot of press but end up yielding little reform. California, notes Harmon, is already doing a lot of what Florida and Massachusetts aspire to. Change happened quietly and over time. "Our system has been modified dramatically over the years. But it has been incremental civil service reform." When asked if civil service reform is an issue in her state, Harmon replies matter-of-factly, "You just don't hear that much about it."

The Budget Shootout

by Steven D. Gold

Why were there so many heroes at the Alamo?

Because there was no back door.

This is not just a sick joke. It gets to the heart of the fiscal predicament facing the states in the 1990s, says John Shannon, former executive director of the U.S. Advisory Commission on Intergovernmental Relations.

Shannon draws a sharp contrast between the tough decisions made by governors and state legislators and the lack of fiscal discipline at the national level. When Pete Wilson of California and Lowell Weicker of Connecticut were U.S. Senators, he says, they were just like their colleagues. But when they moved into the governor's chair, they were transformed into decisive chief executives who boldly led their states down new paths.

But how far should the Alamo analogy be pushed? Are governors and legislators in a trap with no way out, just waiting to be massacred by state fiscal problems?

Well, they are in a trap. But there are ways to escape.

The trap is the state budget. Many states have structural deficits, with tax revenues falling persistently short of what's needed to maintain services and comply with federal mandates. The recession has made the fiscal situation much worse, but states would be fiscally stressed even if the economy were growing.

There are six major factors that add up to a hostile state fiscal environment in the 1990s:

- The economy.
- Demographics.
- Federal policy.
- The courts.
- Cost increases from other sources.
- A taxpayer revolt.

Economic growth is the main determinant of state fiscal conditions. If the economy grows strongly and steadily, it generates automatic revenue increases that can go a long way in compensating for other budget problems.

If the economy is weak, state finances suffer. That is why New England has had the nation's most acute fiscal crisis; its economy has been in a virtual depression the past few years.

A weak economy hurts both sides of state

Steven D. Gold is the director of the Center for the Study of the States at the Nelson A. Rockefeller Institute of Government in Albany, New York. This article is reprinted from *State Government News* 35:3 (March 1992): 6-10. ©1993 The Council of State Governments. Reprinted with permission from *State Government News*.

Causes of Fiscal Stress

While nearly all states will have serious budget problems in the 1990s, the nature of those problems varies. Before a state can develop a strategy for coping with a structural deficit, it needs to understand its sources. Problems can be divided into four categories:

- **The economy**

  A strong economy is a big help in avoiding fiscal stress, but the outlook for economic growth is uneven. According to projections by DRI/McGraw Hill, annual employment growth between 1991 and 1996 will vary from a high of 3.3 percent in Nevada to a low of 0.9 percent in Missouri.

- **Demographics**

  States with burgeoning populations of school-age children and low-income people are at a major disadvantage. California is an example of a state with both conditions.

- **Tax systems**

  States that rely little on income taxes or that have tax rates that are not very progressive can boost revenue growth by changing their tax structure. Income taxes in 22 states have a top rate starting at $30,000 or less, implying that they are not very progressive. Higher taxes are no panacea for state budget woes, but they can help.

- **Spending policies**

  States that refuse to touch "sacred cows" will suffer most. Sacred cows vary from state to state, but big state hospitals, prisons and college campuses (that help local economies by creating jobs), formula-driven school aid programs, and earmarked revenues for highways and other programs are examples.

Source: Steven D. Gold, *State Government News* 35:3 (March 1992): 9. ©1993 The Council of State Governments. Reprinted with permission from *State Government News*.

budgets. State tax revenue nationwide grew just 3.4 percent in the 12 months ending in June 1991, far short of what was needed to cope with the explosive growth of state spending.

At the same time, the recession increased poverty levels and hence welfare caseloads. From July 1989 to October 1991, the number of families receiving Aid to Families with Dependent Children rose by one fourth. Since AFDC recipients are automatically eligible for Medicaid, the state budget was hit twice.

The U.S. economy will grow more slowly in the 1990s than it did in the 1980s because labor force growth will be much less. The reason is demographics: Relatively few children were born immediately following the end of the post-World War II baby boom. So, even though the United States is taking in more immigrants, the labor force is destined to grow slowly in the years ahead.

Of course, other problems are plaguing the economy, such as the debt individual consumers took on in the 1980s, which is likely to restrain spending in the 1990s. For states, this means slower revenue growth even though the pressure to increase spending has intensified.

Population Dynamics

Aside from slow labor force growth, two other demographic factors spell trouble for states. They involve faster growing populations of the very young and the very old.

School age populations are growing about 1 percent annually on the average. This contrasts with a 14 percent decline in enrollment from 1973 to 1984.

Although 1 percent does not sound like much, it has a major impact on state finances because school aid is the biggest item in every state's budget. Besides, the increase is much greater in some states than in others: in California, it is close to 3 percent a year.

The other major demographic change is the increase in the number of people over age 75. The U.S. Census Bureau predicts that their numbers will grow more than 40 percent in the 1990s.

Since many people in that age group require nursing home care, this should boost Medicaid spending considerably. Surprisingly, in the 1980s the increased number of senior citizens did not add much to Medicaid enrollment because there was a big decrease in the poverty rate among the elderly. But that experience may not be repeated in this decade.

The federal government can have a tremendous impact on the health of state finances.

No. 1 is Medicaid, which is the biggest reason why the state fiscal outlook is so bleak. Medicaid spending is rising more than 20 percent a year, and big increases appear inevitable until the American health care system is substantially changed.

The U.S. Congressional Budget Office projects that state Medicaid spending will jump from $39.6 billion in 1991 to $95.1 billion in 1997, a phenomenal 140 percent increase. And the 1997 estimate is conservative because it assumes that increases will slow considerably.

A recent econometric study by Edward Gramlich, on the faculty of the University of Michigan, provided striking, though indirect,

evidence of the major role Medicaid plays in state finances.

Gramlich found that health cost inflation is powerful in explaining why the fiscal conditions of state and local governments have deteriorated so much since 1984. Although health costs affect state budgets in several areas, including state employees' health insurance, Medicaid is particularly important.

Part of the reason for the growth of Medicaid is, of course, federal mandates, which have increased eligibility and expanded benefits. Already on the books is a gradual increase in coverage for poor children. The increase eventually will guarantee Medicaid benefits to everyone under the age of 18 with a low income.

Other federal mandates enacted in 1989 and 1990 added to state costs in areas such as child care, disabled persons, transportation, the environment, education and coverage of employees by Social Security.

Martha Fabricius, of the National Association of State Budget Officers, estimated that the new mandates imposed during those two years alone will cost state and local governments $15 billion over five years.

Legal Challenges

The impact of court decisions on state budgets also is growing. For years, judges have been forcing states to spend more on prisons and mental health. For example, 41 states are under court order or consent decree to reduce overcrowding and otherwise improve prison conditions.

Recently, there has been a cascade of court decrees based on the Boren Amendment, which requires that states reimburse Medicaid providers fairly. But states have not been increasing their hospital reimbursements as dictated by the amendment.

The big unknown is the extent to which the courts will force states to revamp their

Political Problems in California

The political situation is unpredictable. The rules call for two-thirds votes to enact the budget, but even building a majority is difficult and passing legislation over the governor's veto is nearly impossible. Legislative leaders (D) blame the governor as uncooperative. The governor (R) returns the accusations in equally heated terms. Each side seems to agree on one premise, which is not widely accepted in other states—that voters must resolve the basic issues by giving them a mandate before progress can be made.

The voters aren't sending clear mandates. After the acrimonious legislative session of 1992, they returned incumbent Democrats to legislative power. But they voted no confidence in the legislature by mandating a reduction in legislative staffing and refusing to flex the rules to allow the auditor and legislative fiscal office to escape the ax. They refused to endorse solving the state's fiscal problems by raising taxes on the rich and corporations. They also refused to endorse solving them by cutting welfare payments and increasing the governor's control over the budget.

It is difficult to see how California will avoid another year of highly partisan battles and another round of initiatives that again preoccupy major interest groups with proposing and fighting sharp changes in policy, such as the welfare cuts, corporate tax increases, and universal health care measures on the November ballot this year. The governor has already indicated that he will not support renewal of temporary revenue raising measures (a sales tax increase and elimination of corporate loss carry forwards). Many legislators won't accept the cuts in education and social services required to provide a balanced budget without these revenues. The California players aren't ignorant of their own conduct and its effects. . . .

Source: State Policy Reports 10:24 (December 1992): 13, 14.

spending on schools. More than 20 states have challenges to their school finance systems in the pipeline.

When these suits are upheld—as they recently have been in Kentucky, Montana, New Jersey and Texas—they usually force states to make sweeping changes in their tax systems to equalize resources. To enhance equity, states are much more likely to raise spending in poor districts than to lower outlays in affluent areas.

State budgets also are bearing the brunt of higher spending in other areas, such as treating AIDS patients. And the drug war is expanding prison populations. Adding it all up—higher spending for health care, education and corrections in particular—there is tremendous pressure to increase state spending just to maintain the existing level of services.

If states want to improve the quality of schools or expand child care programs, they will need to spend even more. This enormous momentum behind higher spending runs directly into public resistance to higher taxes.

State and local taxes have been rising faster than taxpayers' income since 1982. From that year through 1990, state-local tax revenue increased from $10.59 per $100 of personal income to $11.46. Still, this is considerably lower than the all-time peak in 1973 when state-local tax revenue was $12.41 per $100 of personal income. But the recent trend is clearly up, and after last year's tax increases, it is higher now than it was in 1990.

One fact makes it especially difficult to raise taxes. The average family is on an economic treadmill, with little if any increase in real income in more than a decade. It is tougher to impose higher taxes under these conditions than during times when income is rising. Nevertheless, tax increases are inevitable amid pressure for higher state spending. They will, however, have to be strongly justified in voters' eyes.

How? Dedicating the revenue from tax increases to popular programs like improving schools is one approach. Referenda recently upheld large sales and income tax increases for education in Nebraska and Oklahoma, and in 1991 there was no electoral backlash against a big 1990 tax increase for schools in Kentucky.

To be politically acceptable, general tax increases also must be preceded by major efforts to make programs more efficient and to cut low-priority programs. State officials need to explain better to the public why tax increases are needed and why some alternatives are worse than a tax increase.

With huge budget gaps facing the states, it is unrealistic to expect all of the budget balancing to rely solely on either spending reductions or revenue increases.

So states are in a trap that is not of their own making. Citizens want better schools and are sending more kids to them; they want criminals to face tough prison sentences; and the federal government forces the states to devote ever growing resources to Medicaid.

Tax increases can be used to cover part of the budget gap, but tax possibilities are limited. In other words, most states have structural deficits, with the spending needed to maintain services and comply with federal mandates persistently exceeding the revenue from the tax system.

The way out of this predicament is to reform taxes, spending and policies affecting local governments. Make the tax system more productive and programs more efficient. This approach will minimize the need to reduce

services and to increase taxes to eliminate structural deficits.

A major part of tax reform is to make tax revenue more responsive to economic growth. One method of accomplishing this is to increase reliance on the personal income tax because its revenue tends to grow faster than that of other taxes. Other approaches are to make income taxes more progressive and expand the sales tax to the fast-growing service sector.

Another approach calls for ignoring the effects of inflation by allowing people to be pushed into higher tax brackets by cost-of-living raises.

Three themes can go a long way toward reforming spending: increased emphasis on accountability, targeting, and reliance on incentives.

• Accountability has many implications. The results of programs need to be carefully monitored, costs of new initiatives must be projected, and the design of some programs should be changed. For example, some state programs that aid local governments may undermine accountability and undesirably stimulate local spending. Most legislatures already require fiscal notes for spending bills, but often they are churned out with too little information to back them up.

• Public spending and tax breaks should be carefully targeted. Tax breaks should have a means test so the rich don't get a free ride. And government subsidies to the well-to-do can be cut.

Many states are already moving in this direction, for example by raising tuition at state universities. And to help those who can t afford such hikes they are increasing financial aid.

• Increased reliance should be placed on incentives, which can fundamentally change the way state and local governments are organized.

Table 1   Projected Growth of Non-farm Employment, 1991-1996

State by rank	% growth	State by rank	% growth
Nevada	3.3	Vermont	1.7
Florida	2.6	Wisconsin	1.7
Arizona	2.6	Mississippi	1.7
Texas	2.3	Oklahoma	1.6
Utah	2.2	South Carolina	1.6
Colorado	2.1	Maryland	1.6
Louisiana	2.0	New Hampshire	1.6
Kansas	2.0	Wyoming	1.6
Oregon	2.0	Tennessee	1.6
Arkansas	1.9	Alaska	1.6
California	1.9	Virginia	1.6
Minnesota	1.9	Illinois	1.6
Hawaii	1.9	West Virginia	1.5
Idaho	1.9	North Dakota	1.4
Indiana	1.9	Alabama	1.4
New Mexico	1.8	Michigan	1.4
Washington	1.8	Delaware	1.3
Montana	1.8	Maine	1.3
Nebraska	1.8	Massachusetts	1.2
North Carolina	1.8	New Jersey	1.1
Ohio	1.8	Pennsylvania	1.1
Iowa	1.8	New York	1.0
South Dakota	1.7	Connecticut	0.9
Georgia	1.7	Rhode Island	0.9
Kentucky	1.7	Missouri	0.9
		District of Columbia	0.6

Reinventing Government, a new book by David Osborne and Ted Gaebler, provides many examples of how this can be done. One of their key metaphors involves a boat on a river: Government, they say, is better at steering than rowing. In other words, government can set priorities while leaving the delivery of services to the private sector. Within government, incentives can be used to minimize bureaucratic waste.

Here is the story in a nutshell: Confronted by a massive fiscal crisis that won't go away when the recession ends, state officials need to abandon business as usual and rethink which services are essential and how to best provide them.

They also must better explain themselves to citizens. In that way, they can live to tell about their showdown at the Alamo.

VIII. STATE COURTS

The third branch of state government, the judiciary, probably is the one part of state government with which most citizens would prefer not to have any dealings. State courts handle the crimes reported in the news—drunk driving, child abuse, robbery, murder, and rape. Personal disputes, divorce cases, and other civil matters also are tried in state courts.

Despite the importance of the judiciary in state politics, it is perhaps the least visible branch. One reason is because citizens want it that way; they want the courts to be above the hurly-burly of politics. The legislature may conduct its business in a circuslike atmosphere and the governor may crisscross the state to keep an impossible schedule of appointments, but the courts must be a model of decorum, a place where the rational presentation of facts and arguments leads to truth and justice. Lately, however, serious breaches of this decorum have occurred when individuals accused of particularly heinous crimes have been attacked, even killed, in the courtroom by grieving relatives of the victims.

The Court System

The several levels of state courts each have different responsibilities. At the lowest level are trial courts, where cases are argued and juries may be called to weigh the facts presented. Intermediate appellate courts, the next level in the state judicial system, are where the decisions of the trial courts and other lower courts can be appealed. (Thirty-five states have intermediate courts.) Finally, each state has a court of last resort, usually called the Supreme Court, but in Maine it is called the Supreme Judicial Court; in West Virginia, the Supreme Court of Last Resort; and in New York, the Court of Appeals. Here, the final appeals to lower court decisions are made unless a federal question is involved,

which then means that appeal to the federal appellate courts is possible.

State court judges rule on a variety of concerns. Part of their workload is administrative (for example, the probating of wills). Another part involves conflict resolution (for example, deciding which party is correct in contested divorce settlements and property disputes). And still another area of responsibility includes the criminal prosecution and appeals process.

In a broader sense, state court judges are policy makers. It is often in court decisions, rather than in legislation or constitutional amendments, that state policies are modified or set aside. Courts are reactive institutions of government, and their decisions are limited by the nature and timing of the cases brought before them. Judges establish new norms of acceptable behavior and revise existing norms to match changing circumstances. Their interpretations of the law may or may not have the backing of the public or of the governor or state legislature. Nonetheless, what they say goes—that is, of course, unless it is overturned by another court decision or by another decision-making body. In some instances, court decisions simply are ignored because the judiciary has no bureaucracy of its own to enforce decisions.

The norm of separating partisan politics from the judiciary is part of our national and state political cultures. But judges must be selected in some manner; and inevitably, politics become a factor.

Judicial Selection

The methods used to select judges vary from state to state. Sometimes judges are appointed by the governor and confirmed by the state senate. In Connecticut, the legislature appoints judges from nominations submitted by the governor. In Texas, judges are elected as Democrats or Republicans. Other states—Montana, for example—elect judges on a nonpartisan basis.

Some states have adopted a variation of the "Missouri Plan" to remove politics from the selection process as much as possible. In this process, a nonpartisan group such as the state or district bar association screens the many candidates and recommends the top contenders to the governor, who then makes the final decision. The argument is that merit will be the foremost criterion in the screening and nomination process.

The Missouri Plan also provides that when their terms expire, judges can "run again" on their record. The voters are asked: Should Judge X be retained in office? If the voters say yes, the judge serves another term. If the voters say no, the selection process starts anew. In this way, the judiciary is accountable to the citizens of the state.

In the mid-to-late 1980s, the world of partisan elective judicial politics also was in considerable ferment. Political observers were startled in 1986 when three states—California, North Carolina, and Ohio—all had well-publicized, negative, and very expensive partisan races for their state's chief justiceship. California voters rejected liberal Democratic chief justice Rose Bird, appointed to that post by former Democratic governor Jerry Brown. The divisive campaign was centered around Bird's consistent objection to capital punishment. In North Carolina, the longstanding tradition whereby the governor appoints the longest-serving Supreme Court justice to the post of chief justice when that office is vacated was violated by Republican governor Jim Martin. Martin refused to appoint ranking Democratic supreme court justice Jim Exum and instead elevated his own newly appointed Republican supreme court justice Rhoda Billings. This led to a series of political ma-

neuvers, resulting in Exum's resignation and a subsequent successful challenge of Billings in the 1986 general election. In Ohio, Chief Justice Frank Celebrezze was defeated in a heated campaign after serving in a manner that provided for "rancorous controversy and political infighting of a sort rare for state high courts." [1] In the 1990s, partisan judicial politics has become less intense in the states.

In early 1987, a U.S. district court judge in Jackson, Mississippi, ruled that Section 2 of the Voting Rights Act of 1965 applies to judges elected at the state level. At issue was the question of whether electing judges from at-large, multimember districts dilutes minority voting strength. The impact of the decision probably will mean that state judges will be elected from single-member districts, thereby offering the possibility of greater minority representation in the state judiciaries. [2]

In December 1989, a three-judge federal appeals court upheld the concept that the Voting Rights Act applies to judicial election districts. [3] So, in those states covered by the provisions of the Voting Rights Act, any changes in judicial district lines or the addition of judges must be precleared with the U.S. Department of Justice before being implemented. [4] In April 1990, the Department of Justice threw out Georgia's system of electing judges because it was discriminatory against blacks. The problem with the system was the election of judges in broad judicial circuits by a majority vote, rather than by a plurality vote. This has the same effect as at-large elections often do: diluting the strength of minority groups. [5]

In 1988, political fights swirled around the Texas Supreme Court as nine justices came up for election. This was the first time since Reconstruction that a majority of the court faced the voters at one time. The political contest had several elements: [6]

- In 1987, two justices were criticized separately by the Texas Commission on Judicial Conduct for improper ties to lawyers;

• The state supreme court was criticized by Texaco and the national press for refusing to hear the appeal of the $10.53 billion judgment by a state court trial judge against Texaco in favor of Pennzoil;

• Some of the leading contributors of political funds to the members of the current court turned out to be Pennzoil lawyers, although Texaco lawyers also gave money to some candidates (though they were outbid $315,000 to $72,700);[7]

• The resignation of Chief Justice John Hill in January 1988 to campaign for an appointed system of judgeships was quickly followed by the resignation of senior justice Robert Campbell to campaign for continuing the electoral system for selecting judges;

• Republican governor William P. Clements, Jr., appointed Texas's first Republican supreme court chief justice of the twentieth century and two well-known Democrats, all of whom ran for election to the court as Republicans.

The 1988 Texas Supreme Court campaigns, which cost an estimated $10 million, had "the nastiest, most negative campaigning I have ever seen," one Texas legislator told North Carolina's Judicial Selection Study Commission. "If you are before a judge in Texas now, you've got to be worried if you are a Democrat and he is a Republican."[8]

Is justice for sale as some critics suggest? Giving money to political campaigns, even judicial campaigns, is legal and "that's the problem," according to a Texaco spokeswoman.[9] One Houston lawyer suggested that "it looks just as bad for a lawyer to give a lot of money to a judge as for a judge to take a lot of money from a lawyer."[10] This is all cannon fodder for those wanting to remove the judicial selection process from electoral politics.

Tides of Judicial Policy Making

A current issue in the states concerns who should take the lead in the judicial system—the federal judiciary interpreting the U.S. Constitution, or the state judiciaries interpreting the individual state constitutions. For decades, the loud cry of "states' rights" masked inaction by state courts on segregation, malapportionment, and other unconstitutional practices.

During the 1950s and 1960s, under a broad interpretation of the Constitution (especially the Fifth and Fourteenth Amendments), the U.S. Supreme Court moved to upset the states' intransigence and, in some cases, illegal activities. Led by Chief Justice Earl Warren (the governor of California from 1943 to 1953), the U.S. Supreme Court overturned state laws upholding segregation, forced state legislatures to apportion themselves on a one-man, one-vote basis following each census, expanded voting rights, legalized abortion, and broadened the rights of the accused in the state criminal justice system. The Warren Court set minimal standards for the states to follow in these areas and often reversed state court decisions that narrowly construed the rights of individuals.

In recent years, the U.S. Supreme Court has become more conservative in its decisions. It has even backed away from some of the minimal standards it set earlier. Several state courts have decided not only to uphold these minimal standards but, in a new form of judicial activism at the state level, to exceed them. Former U.S. Supreme Court justice William J. Brennan, Jr., once described this trend as "probably the most important development in constitutional jurisprudence today."[11] Ronald Collins, an expert on state constitutional law, estimated that between 1970 and the mid-1980s state high courts issued approximately 400 decisions based on the higher standards of the state constitutions as opposed to the minimum standards established by the U.S. Supreme Court in interpreting the U.S. Constitution.[12] As New Jersey Supreme Court justice Stewart G. Pollock suggests, "Horizontal federalism, in which states look to each other for guidance, may be the hallmark of the rest of the century."[13]

California Supreme Court justice Stanley Mosk argues that liberals and conservatives alike can support this trend—liberals because it is a continuing expansion of individual rights begun under the Warren Court, and conservatives because such decisions are being made in the state capitals rather than in Washington, D.C.[14] North Carolina Supreme Court justice Harry Martin feels that this trend also gives "the people of the individual states greater protection of their individual rights because of the way people live in the different states." He argues that the state constitutions were designed to respond to the needs of each state, while the U.S. Constitution must respond to the needs of all fifty states. He cites as examples Florida's protection of citizens from unreasonable searches and seizures on boats, Alaska's similar protection of passengers on airplanes, and the right of North Carolina's citizens to a system of inexpensive higher education—all critical parts of each state's economy.[15]

Not all legal scholars and participants agree that this activism will have positive results. Former Oregon attorney general David Frohnmayer argues that "superimposing new and different state doctrinal rules on top of federal law is an open invitation to confusion and error on the enforcement front." He says the movement also means a greater responsibility will now be placed on the state legislators who draft state constitutional provisions and pass the statutes that can be questioned under the constitutional provisions.[16]

Why does such activism develop in a state's supreme court? One study of six state supreme courts from 1930 to 1980 found that dramatic shifts by state high courts from a relatively passive role to an active role take place in a relatively short period of time and are due mainly to a change in the composition of the court. The appointment of a "maverick" judge to a state's supreme court begins a process in which that judge dissents from the previous consensual and passive court decisions, soon swaying some supporters to the minority position. With additional appointments of more activist-oriented jurists, the court changes direction. Of import is the fact that once a transition to activism occurred, none of these courts moved back in the direction of nonactivism, at least not during the period studied.[17]

However, there still may be a question as to whether federal or state court decisions will affect states more. In recent years the U.S. Supreme Court has been making significant decisions affecting state politics. In *Davis v. Bandemer* (1986), the Court changed the ground rules of reapportionment by allowing a losing political party in a redistricting plan standing in a court suit to challenge the plan. In *Tashjian v. Republican Party of Connecticut* (1986), the Court threw out a state law mandating a closed party primary, thereby allowing independents to participate in the party nomination process. In *Johnson v. Transportation Agency, Santa Clara County, Calif.* (1987), the Court upheld local government affirmative action plans and decisions that discriminate in favor of women and minorities. In *Rutan et al. v. Republican Party of Illinois* (1990), the Court narrowly ruled against the time-honored patronage system of hiring political supporters to work in a gubernatorial administration. Finally, in 1991 the "Court issued an unusually strong federalism decision in *Gregory v. Ashcroft*" by ruling "that the Missouri constitution's requirement that state judges retire at 70 does not violate" either the federal Age Discrimination Act or the equal protection clause of the U.S. Constitution.[18]

Changes are now afoot at the Supreme Court. One of the present Court's most conservative judges, Byron White, is retiring in June 1993 and will be replaced by an appointee of Democratic president Bill Clinton. While part of the strong conservative block, White was the only remaining justice to have been appointed by a Democratic president. As other justices leave the Court, Clinton will be able to make additional appointments and many guess that the Court will begin moving away from its very conservative stances on a range of issues. For the states, the interesting question is whether or not this could signal a turn of the tide in judicial policy making toward Supreme Court involvement in issues that the state courts have been handling.

The state courts have had to address some difficult issues over the past few years. The area of criminal procedure is in ferment now as more citizens are seeking stronger and more effective punishment of criminals and protection of victims. The 1986 California Supreme Court election fight discussed earlier indicates just how serious a political issue this has become to the voters.

State courts are also in the process of addressing school finance issues. With so much of the K-12 education financed by revenue generated from local property taxes, parents are finding that where they live determines the quality of education their children will receive. The courts are trying to develop ways in which educational equity can be achieved. For example, shifting money from affluent communities to poor communities and from rich school districts to poor school districts are ways in which equity may be achieved. Such actions, however, tend to lead to conflict with other branches of the government.[19]

The abortion fight has also shifted in part to the states as a result of the 1989 *Webster v. Reproductive Health Services* decision. Some state legislatures and governors have developed abortion policies with no middle ground on which prolife and prochoice advocates can agree. Such efforts go directly into the state courts. The author of a controversial abortion judicial decision in Florida found his retention election much more difficult as antiabortion groups sought to defeat him. He won, but the political message was clear: abortion politics can be lethal.[20]

Money Politics

A new version of an old problem has surfaced in some states with the fiscal problems in the state budgets. As governors and legislatures cope with the serious revenue shortfalls of the 1990s, they often turn to cutting department and agency budgets. One such "agency" is the state judiciary, the third branch of state government, with its own original powers and jurisdiction. A question arises whether the other two branches can cut the budgets of the state judiciary.

Sol Wachtler, the chief justice of the highest court of New York State, sued Governor Mario Cuomo and the legislature over budget cuts made in that state's judicial budget charging the governor and the legislature "violated the state's constitution by failing to provide the court system with sufficient funds." [21] The justice argued that "the governor made the statement that the courts have to get on line with all the other state agencies. . . . That is to demean the separation of powers and the independence of the judiciary. And it's intolerable." [22] Such cases were settled in favor of the courts in at least fourteen other states,[23] and so it was in New York in an out-of-court agreement that provided the funds necessary to reopen previously shutdown portions of the court system.[24] (One perverse note to add:

Judge Wachtler was removed from office in 1992 after being charged with extortion and harassment.[25])

Part VIII explores different aspects of the state judicial branch. Melvin Kahn in *Comparative State Politics* explores how the new judicial activism plays out within the state of Kansas. Brenda Wilson of *Governing* documents the sexual bias lodged within our state courts. John Kincaid and Robert F. Williams in *The Journal of State Government* look at how civil rights are faring in the new judicial federalism. Finally, Richard Lee Price and Evan Davis argue the merits of electing judges to office.

Notes

1. Katherine A. Hinckley, "Four Years of Strife Conclude with Ohio Chief Justice's Defeat," *Comparative State Politics Newsletter* 8:2 (April 1987): 13. Reprinted in Thad L. Beyle, ed., *State Government: CQ's Guide to Current Issues and Activities, 1988-89* (Washington, D.C.: Congressional Quarterly, 1988), 174-181.
2. "Mississippi Ruling Could Aid N.C. Suit on Judgeship Elections," [Raleigh] *News and Observer*, April 5, 1987, 32A.
3. The Voting Rights Act of 1965, extended in 1970 and 1975, banned redistricting plans that diluted the voting strength of black and other minority communities. The law suspended literacy tests and provided for the appointment of federal supervisors of voter registration in all states and counties where literacy tests (or similar qualifying devices) were in effect as of November 1, 1964, and where less than 50 percent of the voting age residents had registered to vote or voted in the 1964 presidential election. State or county governments brought under the coverage of the law due to low voter registration or participation were required to obtain federal approval of any new voting laws, standards, practices, or procedures before implementing them. The act placed federal registration machinery in six Southern states (Alabama, Georgia, Louisiana, Mississippi, South Carolina, and Virginia), Alaska, twenty-eight counties in North Carolina, three counties in Arizona, and one in Idaho.
4. "Federal Court Applies VRA to State Judicial Districts," *Intergovernmental Perspective* 16:1 (Winter 1990): 20.
5. Peter Applebome, "U.S. Declares Georgia Judge Selection Illegal," New York Times News Service, in [Raleigh] *News and Observer*, April 27, 1990, 3A.
6. Peter Applebome, "Texan Fight over Judges Illustrates Politics' Growing Role in Judiciary," New York Times News Service, in [Raleigh] *News and Observer*, January 24, 1988, 14A.
7. Sheila Kaplan, "Justice for Sale," *Common Cause Magazine* (May/June 1987): 29-32.
8. Jane Ruffin, "Texan Warns N.C. Commission to End System of Electing Judges," [Raleigh] *News and Observer*, November 12, 1988, 3C.
9. Quoted in Kaplan, "Justice for Sale," 29.
10. Applebome, "Texan Fight over Judges," 14A.
11. Quoted in Robert Pear, "State Courts Move Beyond U.S. Bench in Rights Rulings," *New York Times*, May 4, 1986, 1.
12. Cited in Lanny Proffer, "State Courts and Civil Liberties," *State Legislatures* 13:9 (September 1987): 29.
13. Quoted in Pear, "State Courts," 16.
14. Stanley Mosk, "State Constitutionalism: Both Liberal and Conservative," *Texas Law Journal* 63:6/7 (March-April 1985): 1081.
15. Quoted in Katherine White, "North Carolina's Constitution Comes of Age," *North Carolina Insight* 10:2/3 (March 1988): 118-119.
16. Quoted in Proffer, "State Courts and Civil Liberties," 28.
17. John Patrick Hagan, "Patterns of Activism on State Supreme Courts," *Publius* 18:1 (Winter 1988): 97-115.
18. "Court Calls Federalism Out of Retirement to Uphold Mandatory Retirement for State Judges," *Intergovernmental Perspective* 17:3 (Summer 1991), 25.
19. Larry Baum, "Making Judicial Policies in the Political Arena," in *The State of the States,* ed. Carl E. Van Horn (Washington, D.C.: CQ Press, 1993), 163-164.
20. Baum, 164-165.
21. Joseph F. Zimmerman, "The Chief Justice vs. the Chief Executive," *Comparative State Politics* 12:6 (December 1991), 32.

22. Quoted in Rob Gurwitt, "Sol Wachtler: See You in Court, Mario," *Governing* 5:4 (January 1992), 22.

23. "Judicial Budgets," *State Policy Reports* 9:19 (October 1991), 18.

24. Information provided by the office of Chief Justice Sol Wachtler in a telephone interview with the author, May 12, 1992.

25. "New York: There Goes the Judge—Wachtler Loses Chains, Job," *The Hotline*, November 11, 1992, 16-17.

Judicial Activism and Legislative-Executive Politics: From Conflict to Tenuous Consensus

by Melvin A. Kahn

Prospects for legislative-executive harmony appeared dim at the beginning of the 1992 session of the Kansas Legislature. The major problems of 1991 still loomed: a lower chamber with a bare Democratic majority of one led by a speaker at odds with the populist-maverick Democratic Governor Joan Finney; and a Republican-dominated Senate often opposed to both the House and the governor. The 1991 battle over rectifying the inequitable property-tax system had floundered amidst harsh charges and countercharges, and the prospects for a 1992 consensus were none too bright.

Conflict emerged quickly at the start of the 1992 session. First, the governor sought to both lower property taxes and raise revenue by eliminating many sales tax exemptions. Legislators accused her of reneging on her campaign pledge not to increase taxes, but she maintained that eliminating unfair "special interest" exemptions differed distinctly from raising taxes.

The challenge of resolving fiscal issues became even more complex because of several lawsuits (later combined into one suit) challenging the existing method of financing public education—which had resulted in local district expenditures that ranged from a high of

$10,843 per pupil in one district to a low of $2,720.[1]

Three months before the session commenced, District Court Judge Terry Bullock took the unusual move of summoning 75 persons connected with the pending suit that challenged the constitutionality of the state formula for supplementing school district property taxes. Those appearing included Governor Finney, top legislative leaders and the attorneys representing the districts that had filed the suits. He warned that the failure of the state to rectify the enormous inequities might very well lead to a finding that the Kansas public school system is unconstitutional; moreover, such a finding would probably cause a suspension of all state aid to Kansas public schools. He emphasized that the continuation of the gross disparities in per-pupil funding would be unacceptable and charged those present to work out an equitable solution during the legislative session.

Several legislators from affluent districts, despite the stern admonition from Judge Bull-

Melvin A. Kahn is professor of political science at Wichita State University in Wichita, Kansas. This article is reprinted with permission from *Comparative State Politics* 13:6 (December 1992): 1-5.

Florio Wins Pink-Slip Battle

New Jersey's GOP-controlled Legislature overstepped its bounds in ordering Democratic Gov. Jim Florio which employees to lay off, the state Supreme Court ruled.

The court ruled unanimously that legislators violated the state constitution's separation-of-powers provision with budget language directing the governor to dismiss 1,357 non-union managers earning more than $50,000 and protect rank-and-file service workers from layoffs.

"(T)he Legislature's attempt to 'micromanage' the staffing and resource allocations in administering the appropriated funds was a serious intrusion on the governor's authority and ability to perform his constitutionally delegated functions," Justice Marie Garibaldi wrote in the court decision.

The Communication Workers of America, the state's largest public employee union, and seven Republican lawmakers sued Florio for giving pink slips to more than 1,000 workers between July and October. About three-fourths were union employees, said Tom Vince of New Jersey's Department of Personnel.

Florio blames the job losses on the Legislature because it sliced $1.1 billion from his $15.7 billion spending proposal for fiscal 1993.

"My original budget would have avoided any layoffs, but the budget that emerged from the legislative process required layoffs," Florio said in a statement.

The court said although the Legislature cannot mandate a pecking order for layoffs, it may provide advisory guidelines to the governor.

This advisory power may be the basis for further legal action against Florio because he blatantly ignored the Legislature's guidelines, said Vince Trivellis, a CWA spokesman.

Source: State Government News 36:2 (February 1993): 33. © 1993 The Council of State Governments. Reprinted with permission from *State Government News.*

---

ock, desired to avoid adopting any school-aid formula that would increase the personal property taxes of their constituents. Solons from similar districts were willing to adopt a new school-finance standard, but demanded a phase-in spanning several years; this would prevent staggering tax increases in any one year and thus minimize the risk of unduly antagonizing their constituents.

Realizing that little progress was occurring, Judge Bullock wrote the governor on January 22 that the Constitution required implementation of equalization "now, not at some delayed or future time." [2] He concluded, "The reason we have a Constitution is so that the people of our state can place absolute requirements upon our government . . . against which no concerns of political or other expediency can ever prevail." [3]

The judicial prodding apparently worked with the house; it approved a school finance bill in early March. The Senate, however, failed to pass a bill. On April 6, Judge Bullock summoned the attorneys representing the school districts challenging the state formula and announced that the trial would begin on June 1, 1992, unless the legislature enacted a new school finance law that met constitutional criteria.

Judge Bullock underscored his intention to proceed to trial by sending the school district attorneys and, indirectly, the legislators an

April 10 memo on the process of closing every school in Kansas: "In order to halt all illegal tax gathering it may be necessary to enjoin not only the state but county treasurers, school districts and the like. In the event we get this far in the litigation, I hope you will have the names and addresses needed, as well as process servers on hand, in the event that is required." [4]

The legislature adjourned on April 11 for a two-week period. When it returned for the wrap-up session, it was obvious that Judge Bullock had made a decisive impact on the formerly recalcitrant Senate. It quickly approved a school finance bill on the second day after returning from the break.

Although each chamber had now passed finance-reform bills, the Conference Committee had difficulty in reaching agreement because of three primary obstacles: the view of some legislators that they had not provided revenue to adequately finance public education; the perception that the proposed tax rate for business was too high; and dissatisfaction with not adding enough days to the school year. After much discussion, the Conference Committee finally reached agreement. But the Senate exhibited great reluctance—on seven separate occasions it failed to approve the Conference Committee compromise. Following intensive bargaining, the Senate finally accepted the Conference Committee agreement.

Enter Governor Finney. Relations between her and the legislature had been acrimonious during the regular session in which she had issued 18 vetoes. The legislature overrode her on 15 occasions. But the governor surprised many by announcing her support of the compromise, even though it contained a sales tax increase.

The main components of the legislation consisted of the following:

• a statewide property-tax levy that would start at $32 million and progress to $35 million in 1994-95;

• an increase of $349 million in sales and income taxes to underwrite $300 million in first-year property tax relief;

• a distribution of $3,600 per pupil to individual school districts (the state would provide supplementary amounts to provide for transportation and for students involved in bilingual, vocational and counseling programs);

• a provision allowing school districts that would lose funds under the new formula to raise up to 25 percent in additional local property taxes to restore their previous budgets.[5]

While most school districts welcomed the changes, several districts in southwestern Kansas objected strenuously since the new state property tax levy would significantly increase their total taxes. Residents of these districts had previously paid minimal property taxes since the Hugoton gas field provided generous local tax revenues. Sentiment ran so high that they undertook petition drives to secede from Kansas and form their own state. They even discussed possible names: Heartland, Sunflower and Paine (the latter honored the great Revolutionary pamphleteer, Thomas Paine). After realizing the legal difficulty of secession, they decided that, should secession fail, they would apply to the United Nations for recognition as a separate nation-state. Ultimately, they filed a law suit challenging the constitutionality of the 1992 Kansas statewide property tax levy as did the Bluestem School District located in affluent Johnson County.

Because of the continuous prodding of Judge Bullock, Governor Finney, the legislators and the school districts accomplished major breakthroughs that had eluded them in 1991. The governor honored her pledge to reduce property taxes and the legislature enacted school finance reform that many veteran solons regard as the most significant achievement of their careers. They concurred with the assessment of Joan Wagnon, chairwoman of the House Taxation Committee, who described the new law as a ". . . forward-thinking distribution approach that will allow us to reform education, fund schools adequately and coincidentally, reform the tax system." [6]

Originally, it was believed that the 1991 Kansas legislative-executive stalemate would recur; for consensus does not readily arise from the mixture of a Democratic-populist governor, a slightly Democratic House and a conservative Republican Senate. A determined Judge Bullock demonstrated that adroit judicial activism can help transform imminent deadlock into viable public policy.

Notes

1. *Wichita Eagle,* May 3, 1992, 8B.
2. *Wichita Eagle,* May 15, 1992, 11A.
3. Ibid.
4. Ibid.
5. *Wichita Eagle,* May 3, 1992, 8B.
6. *Wichita Eagle,* May 6, 1992, 4A.

Verdict on the Courts: Sexist As Charged

by Brenda L. Wilson

The cherished image of justice is of a woman, balancing a pair of scales, blindfolded against bias. The reality, in America's state and local courts, is far from that ideal.

In 38 states and the District of Columbia, special task forces composed of judges, legal professionals, social scientists and community leaders have been at work over the past decade assessing the treatment of women by the courts—as victims, litigants, attorneys and judges. The 24 that have completed their investigations have concluded, with a near uniformity of findings, that bias against women permeates every aspect of the state and local court system. The studies suggest that, despite the growing presence and rising stature of women in the legal profession and the courts, judicial decisions are still being influenced as much by stereotypes, myths, and outdated customs and institutional procedures as they are by the substance of the law.

The state task forces have recommended, first and foremost, education for judges, lawyers and other court officers on a full gamut of issues—particularly such areas as family dissolution, domestic violence, rape, sexual harassment, prostitution, and employment and wage discrimination—to heighten their awareness of how bias influences decisions.

Many task forces emphasized the need for judges to maintain more current and accurate information about the costs of child raising, the availability of child care and the economic consequences of divorce. Still others called for changes in the laws, ranging from permitting liens to be placed on automobiles owned by delinquent parents in child support cases to allowing the use of deadly force as a defense against sexual assault.

The catalyst for the studies was a joint project of the National Organization for Women and the National Association of Women Judges. That the studies have been conducted at all is in itself a testimony to the growing stature of women in the legal system. It wasn't until the turn of the century that law schools and state bars began to admit more than a few token women. Now, women make up 43 percent of the enrollment in law schools accredited by the American Bar Association. While only 10 percent of the approximately 30,000 judges in state and local courts are women, that number can be expected to grow as women work their way up through the legal system.

Brenda L. Wilson is a staff writer for *Governing*. This article is reprinted from *Governing* 6:3 (December 1992): 18-19.

Even so, the level of presence of women in the courts has so far not been enough to alter the style of an institution long dominated by men, the task force findings show. Detroit Judge Clarice Jobes, who was appointed to the Wayne County Recorders Court in 1978, recalls the attitudes of male colleagues at that time. "They made jokes about sex, mothers-in-law. There were a million anti-female things."

The reports document a tendency of judges to be more lenient in sentencing women criminals, particularly when they are also guardians of young children; to award custody of children to their mothers but fail to require adequate child support regardless of the spouse's ability to pay; and to fail to issue and enforce protective orders in domestic violence cases.

Beyond such general trends, the reports indicate that gender bias is a very subtle issue, one that gets into the difficult-to-sort-out area of attitudes. Much of the evidence is anecdotal:

• In Kentucky, one judge ordered a woman to attend church with her husband, even after she testified that she was afraid her husband might kill her.

• In California, a young black woman attorney who specializes in antitrust law says a federal judge in a merger case asked her, "Do you really understand all the economics involved in this case?"

• In Connecticut, when a female defense counsel asked to examine a rape victim's clothes, a prosecutor asked her, "Do you want to try them on?"

Those stories may seem trivial, but the picture that emerges from the accumulation of hundreds of pages of such stories, in report after report, leaves little doubt that there are serious problems in the courts.

Women, not surprisingly, need less convincing than their male colleagues. In a survey of Minnesota male and female attorneys in 1988, 48 percent of the women but only 10 percent of the men said that gender bias in the courts was widespread. Sixty-three percent of the men who responded said that it existed in a few instances. "The rest," says Minnesota Supreme Court Justice Rosalie E. Wahl, "thought women were just being thin-skinned." A male judge responding to a Washington State survey wrote, "I hope that whoever tallies these results gives up his or her crusade and finds some honest work."

What the surveys underline is the fact that men often don't find anything objectionable about behavior that deeply disturbs women. The Minnesota survey, for example, indicated that most male judges don't see anything wrong with addressing a female witness by her first name while addressing male witnesses by their last names; most don't object to attorneys telling jokes that are demeaning to women in chambers, although they would intervene if a woman were present. Task forces in Connecticut, California and Minnesota all were told of instances where women serving as the lead attorney with a group of male attorneys were repeatedly ignored by judges who addressed their remarks to the women's male colleagues instead. Women in the profession say that such incidents harm the credibility of women attorneys, undermine the believability of female witnesses, destroy their clients' confidence and influence jury decisions.

Male attorneys are accused of behaving worse than judges. Since the idea is to win at all costs, they may justify the use of endearments, offensive language, disparagement of female witnesses and other forms of sexist behavior to discredit the adversary and throw the opposing attorney off balance. Yet, according to the reports, the same attorneys say they would never stoop to using ethnic or racial slurs to undermine opposing counsel.

It is in the area of courtroom decorum that the greatest improvement appears to have been made in recent years. Lynn Hecht Schafran, an attorney with the NOW Legal Defense and Education Fund, says most judges have been willing to take instruction on what she calls "the front yard issues," such matters as how a woman attorney or female client should be addressed. Most of the state task forces have recommended that the rules of conduct for judges and attorneys be amended to address sexual harassment and sex discrimination. In some instances, action by the courts, the state bar association or the state legislature may be required.

A new American Bar Association Model Code of Judicial Conduct—adopted only by Nebraska, Nevada and Wyoming so far—requires that judges intervene to stop biased behavior on the part of anyone under their authority. In May [1992], a New York City judge fined a male attorney $500 for offensive remarks to a female attorney. The male attorney had dismissed questions from the female counsel by shooing her away and saying, "I don't have to talk to you, little lady" and "Go away, little girl."

The growing presence in state and local courts of women as judges goes a long way to curb this kind of behavior. Judge Jobes says male attorneys are learning that the courtroom is no longer their own private club. "They want to argue with me and speak over me. I tell them, 'I'm dressed like this for a reason. I'm the judge.' "

Beyond the issue of courtroom decorum, the area of family law has become a focal point for many of the task forces. Many judges have been faulted for undervaluing the role of homemaker, not recognizing wage discrepancies between men and women, and punishing women who step out of stereotypical roles.

In most states, alimony has been all but eliminated, even where marriages have lasted 25 to 30 years. When awarded, it is usually of limited duration and amount. "Some judges took the position that women are liberated now and should get out there and take care of themselves," says U.S. District Court Judge George I. Harrelson of Marshall, Minnesota. "They don't understand that a woman in her 50s who has devoted her life to her family is going to have a difficult time supporting herself." In recent years, appeals courts in Vermont, Florida, California, Pennsylvania and Minnesota have indicated they do understand, and have ruled that support may be owed even after the children have grown up.

A number of state gender-bias reports cited separate studies on the awarding of alimony and child support which concluded that when families break up, the standard of living for women and children usually declines, while for men it improves. Although payments to custodial parents improved as a result of child support guidelines established by Congress in 1984, they are still considered inadequate by family law experts.

But despite high divorce rates and the increasing complexity of family law, state and local courts have not shifted resources to handle the increasing caseload. Family law remains a low priority among state board examiners and law schools. Some suspect that family law may not be more highly regarded because it is viewed as a "woman's issue"; in California, judges compared assignment to family law court to being sent to Siberia.

In areas such as domestic violence and rape, the momentum for change has come from forces outside the court. Highly publicized cases in which women were murdered by abusive spouses have heightened awareness of the problem. In some parts of the country, state legislatures began stepping in as early as the mid-1970s to provide assistance and protection against abuse. Protection orders have become easier to obtain, although violators often still go unpunished.

A decade after the first task force set to work, the issue of gender bias is solidly before the courts. Continuing-education programs are offered by state bar associations and organizations of judges, attorneys, law enforcement officials, prosecutors and defenders, even in states where there have been no official task forces.

The fear is that despite the long lists of recommendations they contain, the reports are destined to gather dust on the shelves of law libraries. One of the more hopeful signs is a trend toward incorporating gender issues into the curricula of law schools, whose classes are now almost equally divided between men and women.

The New Judicial Federalism: The States' Lead in Rights Protection

by John Kincaid and Robert F. Williams

Claus von Bulow, whose trial was popularized in the film *Reversal of Fortune,* might not be a free man today but for the protection afforded individual rights in Rhode Island's Constitution.

Incriminating evidence in his wife's death was thrown out by the state court under the state's exclusionary rule. That decision hinged on the state high court's interpretation of search-and-seizure provisions in Rhode Island's constitution. The U.S. Supreme Court later declined to review the state ruling because the decision was based on independent and adequate state grounds.

Rhode Island is not alone in going farther than the U.S. Supreme Court in protecting individual rights. The emergence since 1970 of many state high courts as assertive protectors of individual rights comes as a surprise to many people. The fact that state courts are expanding protections beyond those guaranteed by the Bill of Rights is even more surprising. This development, called the new judicial federalism, defies traditional theories of American federalism, which saw the states being eclipsed by the federal government in every field.

The new judicial federalism generally refers to the authority of a state court to interpret its state constitution so as to provide broader rights protections than those recognized by U.S. Supreme Court interpretations of the federal Constitution. As in the von Bulow case, such state decisions are immune from Supreme Court review when they are based on "independent and adequate" state constitutional grounds.

In a 1970 decision, for instance, the Alaska Supreme Court wrote:

> While we must enforce the minimum constitutional standards imposed upon us by the United States Supreme Court's interpretation of the Fourteenth Amendment, we are free, and we are under a duty, to develop additional constitutional rights and privileges under our Alaska Constitution. . . . We need not stand by idly and passively, waiting for constitutional direction from the highest court of the land.

The Power of Interpretation

It is one thing for the Supreme Court to hold that people have certain rights under the

John Kincaid is executive director of the U.S. Advisory Commission on Intergovernmental Relations, Washington, D.C. Robert F. Williams is professor of law at Rutgers University, Camden, New Jersey. This article is reprinted with permission from *Spectrum: The Journal of State Government* 65:2 (April-June 1992): 50-52. © 1993 The Council of State Governments.

federal Constitution. It is quite another for the Court to hold that people do not have certain rights. Because both kinds of decisions come from the "highest court in the land;" we tend to believe that both should have the same force in every court, police precinct and state and local office throughout the land. But, just because a government action is not prohibited by the federal Constitution does not mean that it is automatically permitted under a state's constitution. A state constitution is the supreme law of a state, so long as it does not contradict the U.S. Constitution.

The new judicial federalism allows state courts and legislatures to set rights standards that are higher, but not lower, than those established under the U.S. Constitution. States also may recognize rights such as privacy and victims' rights that are not even found, at least not explicitly, in the U.S. Constitution. As such, the new judicial federalism conforms to an old principle of American federalism: that states may act where the U.S. government has elected not to act, so long as state action does not violate the U.S. Constitution or federal law.

Actually, the new judicial federalism is no longer new. Since 1970, state courts have rendered at least 700 decisions providing broader rights than those recognized by the U.S. Supreme Court or new rights not found in the Bill of Rights. Partly in response to this development, the U.S. Advisory Commission on Intergovernmental Relations in 1988 issued *State Constitutional Law: Cases and Materials,* the first textbook of its type ever published.

Examples of new rights protections can be found in Florida whose constitution contains a privacy provision approved by voters in 1980. It reads: "Every natural person has the right to be let alone and free from governmental intrusion into his private life except as otherwise provided herein." Under this rule, the Florida Supreme Court struck down a state law that required minors to obtain parental consent before ending a pregnancy, and it voided a municipal ordinance prohibiting people from sleeping in their automobiles. The Florida court also used the provision to uphold a 1990 law that broadened the "right to die" for citizens of the state.

State vs. Federal

However, most state court decisions under the new judicial federalism involve interpretations of state constitutional provisions that are very similar or identical to provisions in the U.S. Bill of Rights. A state court may interpret its state provision more broadly than the U.S. Supreme Court interprets the companion federal provision. Thus, state courts can choose to follow federal precedent or take a higher road and expand rights protections.

For example, in 1988 the U.S. Supreme Court ruled in *California vs. Greenwood* that police do not need a warrant to search trash put out for collection. In 1990, however, the New Jersey and Washington high courts ruled that their state constitutions do require police to obtain a warrant to search curbside trash. If no warrant is obtained, then evidence gleaned from the search will not be admitted in state court.

However, federal agents operating under U.S. rules need not obtain warrants to search curbside trash in New Jersey and Washington. This revival of dual federalism in the judicial arena raises interesting intergovernmental issues. For example, will federal agents deliver evidence gathered without warrants to state police? Probably. Will such evidence be admitted in state courts? Possibly.

The New Jersey Supreme Court recently held in split decisions that such evidence can be admitted in state court so long as there was no active cooperation "between the officers of the two sovereigns." Thus, after decades of cooperative federalism, during which great emphasis was placed on getting states to cooperate with federal rights laws and rulings, state courts now are talking about "uncooperative federalism," and about the need to protect their citizens' rights against federal action. This development could disturb intergovernmental cooperation in law enforcement.

Another question is whether states can nullify federal action. If states can set rights standards that are stricter than federal standards, can they apply those standards to federal agents within their borders—despite the supremacy clause of the U.S. Constitution? If states cannot abridge rights protected by the U.S. Constitution, can the federal government come into a state and abridge rights protected by the state constitution? Must the federal government explicitly preempt a state rights protection in order to immunize itself from state nullification?

These kinds of questions were raised by Thomas Jefferson and James Madison against the Alien and Sedition Acts passed by Congress in 1798. Their Virginia and Kentucky Resolutions triggered a debate over state nullification and interposition thought to have been settled by the Civil War.

Until recently, the new judicial federalism generally was viewed as a liberal movement. Indeed, former Justice William J. Brennan Jr. helped spur the movement in a now famous *Harvard Law Review* article in 1977. Critics charge that the new judicial federalism is little more than a reflex liberal reaction to the conservative Burger and Rehnquist Courts. The activism of the Warren Court years (1954-69) is being kept alive by numerous "little Warren courts" in the states.

But conservatives have also had victories in state courts. In 1991, the Pennsylvania Supreme Court produced a conservative ruling based on a liberal reading of the "takings" clause in Pennsylvania's Constitution. The court struck down Philadelphia's historic pres-

ervation ordinance on the ground that its application in this case constituted a "taking" of the owner's property without just compensation. The decision sent shock waves through the historic preservation and environmental protection communities because of its constraining implications for government regulation of private property. The decision is being reconsidered, though, because several concurring justices believe the court went overboard.

The U.S. Supreme Court has upheld other preservation and environmental laws against challenges under the "takings" clause of the Fifth Amendment to the U.S. Constitution. However, the court is hearing several new "takings" cases this term.

Looking Ahead

The future of the new judicial federalism is hard to predict. If the U.S. Supreme Court resumes an activist rights role, it may again move ahead of state courts. Also, given that most state high court justices must face the voters periodically, activist justices may be unseated by a disgruntled electorate. In addition, state constitutions can be amended more easily than the U.S. Constitution. In 1982, for instance, Florida voters nailed their supreme court to the federal rights floor by approving a constitutional amendment requiring the court to adhere to the U.S. Supreme Court's view of the exclusionary rule under the Fourth Amendment. By 1982, the Court had narrowed its view of the Fourth Amendment compared to the view of the Warren Court. Thus far, however, voters have expanded rights as much as they have restricted them through state constitutional amendments.

Finally, the new judicial federalism revives some basic questions about rights. If rights are universal, should they not apply equally everywhere? If not, what rights are universal, and what rights can vary among states? Just as women once crossed state lines to obtain abortions, will ambulances carry people across borders to states with more liberal right-to-die laws? Will some ambulances go in the opposite direction, carrying patients away from relatives eager to "pull the plug" under liberal state rules?

Although universal rights may seem to be the natural order, independent state constitutions offer opportunities to entrench certain rights, at least in some places, when the nation or its highest court cannot agree on applying these rights. We have already seen signs of this with regard to privacy, victims' rights, wom-

en's rights and environmental rights provisions in some state constitutions. In this way, states can also serve as laboratories for rights experimentation.

The new judicial federalism may have implications for emerging democracies worldwide, as well. Often, ethnic, religious and linguistic hostilities preclude consensus on common rights. However, entrenching even a few common rights in the national constitution is a step in the right direction that can foster the trust needed to break down barriers to the recognition of more universal rights.

Point/Counterpoint: Should Judges Be Elected?

by Richard Lee Price and Evan A. Davis

Richard Lee Price: Point

Although accused of politicizing what should be the branch of government above politics, most states still maintain that the best way to select judges is at the voting booth. I agree.

Those opposed to judicial elections say elected judges are politicians, beholden to their backers and special interest groups. They fail to acknowledge that judicial appointees suffer from the same fate.

One does not become appointed to a judicial position without cultivating supporters among the politicians with the power of appointment.

Gubernatorial appointments, the most common method of merit selection, do not routinely go to unknowns who, though bright and industrious, have no ties to the governor's office. Similarly, the members of judicial screening committees, who sometimes pick the pool from which the governor or other appointing official may select, are themselves either politicians or chosen by politicians.

Once one admits that both elected and appointed judges are politicians, it becomes clear that the public is better off with an elected judge. Such judges are accountable to the public and may be removed from office if their constituency is dissatisfied with the performance.

Take the case of the 1986 defeat of California Chief Justice Rose Bird, who was appointed to her post by Gov. Jerry Brown. During her tenure, she voted to reverse all 61 death sentences she reviewed.

When she ran in a retention election, she was ousted from judicial office. The lesson to be learned is that although the governor agreed with her death penalty reversals, the public was dissatisfied with her apparent refusal to enforce a law that the people supported.

Opponents of judicial elections insist that the judiciary must be capable of making decisions that may not, in some cases, adhere to the majority's ideas. Elected candidates, they proclaim, may be forced to compromise justice for the sake of pleasing their constituency.

Richard Lee Price is an acting justice of the New York State Supreme Court in the Bronx and is president of the American Judges Association. Evan A. Davis is a partner in the law firm of Cleary, Gottlieb, Steen, and Hamilton. From 1985 through 1990, he served as counsel to New York governor Mario M. Cuomo. This article is reprinted with permission from *State Government News* 35:8 (August 1992): 12-13. © 1993 The Council of State Governments.

While this concern may have some validity, judges should be re-elected not on the basis of a few decisions but on the basis of the body of work performed during their term. Moreover, public debate about controversial or unpopular decisions is healthy and should not be discouraged simply because the office to be filled is that of judge.

Judges perform a constitutional, as opposed to a majoritarian, function, and it is constitutional for the public to vote out a judge who does not enforce the laws passed by the majority.

Another benefit is that judicial elections can be scrutinized for discrimination, thereby encouraging minority candidates. This especially has become the case since the U.S. Supreme Court determined in 1991 that Section 2 of the Voting Rights Act, which prohibits the dilution of minority voting strength, applies to judicial elections. Gubernatorial and other judicial appointments do not have to comply with the provisions of the Voting Rights Act.

The right to contest a judicial election that appears to discriminate against minorities is a legitimate method of redressing discrimination in the judicial selection process.

Elections force candidates to go public with their qualifications, allowing voters to select a candidate with the qualifications and attributes they believe necessary.

Running for judicial office has drawbacks, most notably the expense. But judges invest more than money in their candidacy; they spend years in many beneficial, professional and community activities earning a reputation that entitles them to run for a judicial position.

Once elected, judges base decisions on their best understanding of the law. Because all judges are influenced by their own values and opinions and have varying degrees of ability, each performs differently.

However, when a term expires and re-election is sought, once again the public has the right to consider the candidate's qualifications.

The third branch of government, not unlike the other two, represents the people and upholds the laws. Excluding the public from the process of judicial selection is anti-democratic. The importance of a judgeship mandates application of a critical constitutional right—the right to vote.

Evan A. Davis: Counterpoint

Judges should apply the law, not make it. They should apply it objectively—without regard to the status or popularity of the parties before them. Litigants should not need an ideologically "correct" position to get justice, nor should they feel they lost because the other side had political connections.

The way we choose judges has a lot to do with how well we live up to these goals of objectivity, of fairness in fact and appearance and of wise judicial decisions.

New York chooses its judges in two ways—some by election, some by appointment. The election of judges is riddled with politics. Indeed, the process is controlled by the leaders of the two political parties in each county.

This approach is one of the last vestiges of patronage for the party leaders, who are accountable only to the party committee. Their job is to keep the party strong, ensure enough workers to get the party candidates elected, and raise money for the party.

Although there is technically an election, it is really these party leaders who choose the judges. First, they control the process for getting on the ballot. They are naturally inclined to choose people who have been active and helpful in the party.

Second, with other party leaders in the state, they control the party organization, an important resource for getting elected. For example, in New York state judicial candidates generally have to run in large, multicounty, multimember districts.

It is hard for many of them to raise money and remain within the bounds of the Code of Judicial Conduct. But political parties can raise money, and they have access to volunteers who will ring doorbells, hand out fliers and get out the vote. So in upstate New York, which the Republicans control, the Republican candidate wins. The Democrats have the same good fortune in New York City.

The rare contested election for a judgeship, is not a pretty sight. The soundness of the law a judge is required to apply becomes grist for the political millstone. Aid to parochial education can become a hot topic, as well as labor vs. management issues and criminal justice matters. One campaign commercial featured the sound of jail doors clanging shut.

In light of such a history, the appointment process begun in 1979 for judges on New York's highest court, the Court of Appeals, was a breath of fresh air. A nominating commission composed of diverse members forwards to an accountable elected official a list of names. The official then chooses an appointee from the list with the advice and consent of the state Senate. The advantages of this process are numerous:

• Scrutiny. Interested applicants must pass scrutiny at three levels: the commission, the appointing authority and the confirming authority. The bar association and the public have an opportunity for input at each level.

• Accountability. The list of names forwarded to the appointing authority and the makeup of the nominating commission are matters of public record. The elected official responsible for choosing an appointee is accountable to the voters for his or her choices. And the Senate is accountable for its decision about whether to confirm the appointee.

• Diversity. The bench needs a mix of race and gender to maintain public confidence and to be true to our constitutional principles of pluralism and inclusiveness. If the nominating commission is diverse and under a mandate to consider the need for improved diversity—which should be the legal requirement—that goal is likely to be achieved.

On the other hand, with racially polarized voting all too prevalent, many parts of the state are unlikely to elect a minority judge.

• Judicial independence. Merit selection greatly improves judges' independence. Judges can apply the law without acting as if they are politicians writing it. They are chosen for their competence and not because of their opinions of certain laws.

They can pledge faithful and impartial performance of their duties as judges, without worrying whether the party leader will approve and accordingly support them in the future.

• Opportunity. A lawyer or lower court judge without political connections can aspire to become a judge or gain a higher judicial office.

This does not mean that those with political connections will not become judges. But it does mean more competition, and from this better choices emerge.

To set out these two approaches is enough. Now, you be the judge.

IX. STATE ISSUES

One might think that the goal of state government is to provide the services that citizens need and then raise the money to do so. Actually, the process is just the reverse: the governor and state legislature raise the money they can and then decide the extent of services the state can provide. It comes as no surprise, therefore, that financial issues are at the top of state policy agendas. How should revenues be raised—taxes, user fees, bonds, lotteries? What kinds of taxes should be imposed—sales, income, inheritance, property? Who will bear the burden of these taxes—the rich, the poor, the consumer, the property holder? These are the most important questions state governors and legislatures address.

The 1980s presented the states with a roller coaster ride in budget operation. In the early 1980s, there was a recession and state revenues dropped precipitously. The fiscal crisis necessitated layoffs, hiring limits, travel restrictions, and delays in expenditures. The budget crunch of the early 1980s greatly lowered expectations of what state government could and would do.[1]

At the same time, the states were waiting to see how the national government would handle the federal deficit, and how that decision would affect state and local finances. Then, in the mid-1980s, a major fear of state leaders' came true: the president and Congress decided to solve part of the national deficit crisis by letting the states pay for a considerable part of it. Saving a program that formerly was funded in whole or part with federal funds means increasing state and local taxes. And to many lawmakers, increased taxes can mean defeat at the polls.

During this time, however, the economy recovered and revenues flowed into state treasuries. No matter what the governor proposed and the legislature adopted, there was always a surplus at the end of the fiscal year. State decision makers were confident despite the major changes going on within the federal system.

However, by the end of the 1980s another problem developed in many states: the deterioration of their fiscal health resulting from reduced tax revenues. In 1988, eighteen states had to cut back their enacted budgets, and by April 1989, ten had to do so for fiscal 1989.[2] The states faced a new budget problem: keeping their budgets balanced. In October 1988, the National Association of State Budget Officers (NASBO) reported "states are in a precarious position" and cannot afford to have any bad economic news. "They have very little reserves to deal with shocks." [3] Note the irony here: the bad news for the states was their low budget surpluses; for the federal government it was the large budget deficit! But that is just the problem, according to a later NASBO report: the "federal government continues to try and solve its own problems by passing costs on to the states." [4]

What could the states do? As already noted, one option is to raise taxes. States also could seek new sources of tax revenue. For example, more and more states considered instituting a state lottery, which seemed to be a painless way to raise money. But recent research on state lotteries indicates that they amount to a "heavy tax"—one that is sharply regressive—because it is levied in part on those who cannot afford it. The economics of the state lotteries in 1988 indicated that of each dollar spent on a lottery ticket ($16 billion), 48 cents went for prizes, 15 cents for administration, including promotion and sales, and only 37 cents ($5.7 billion) for government purposes.[5]

In the 1990s, finances dominate the agendas of most state governors and legislatures.

After a couple of years of economists arguing whether the country was moving into a recession, it became clear that we had. State leaders observed that an economic slowdown had occurred, which translated into decreasing state tax revenues or in a decline of the revenue growth they had experienced in the mid-1980s. This often meant tax increases had to be considered if programs were to be maintained at their current levels, let alone starting new initiatives.

To cope with their fiscal distress in fiscal 1991, twenty-nine states reduced their already enacted budgets by over $7.5 billion, while twenty-six states were also increasing taxes by more than $10.3 billion. For fiscal 1992, thirty-one states enacted revenue increases of over $15 billion.[6]

Now, in a 1993 survey of the states and their fiscal condition, the National Governors' Association and NASBO report that states "have adjusted to the fiscal conditions of the last several years by holding the line on spending and dramatically lowering their revenue expectations." And prospects do not look good with a continuing "sluggish economy and prospects of slower growth in the 1990s" making state policy makers extremely cautious as they develop state budgets.[7]

Now, there are few states that are not facing serious budgetary problems. The budget deficits in some cases have been enormous; California's for 1992-93 was over $14.2 billion, and even shutting down the state's entire higher education and correctional systems would still have left a large deficit to handle. Governors and legislatures are trying to erase these deficits with all types of "revenue enhancements," program and governmental cutbacks, and even are reverting to what the federal government has been doing: shifting some responsibilities downward, toward the local governments.

After money, what are the issues of greatest concern to the states? Or, to put it another way, what do states spend the most money on? Funding levels are a good indication of commitment.

Large sums are spent each year on education, health programs, state highways, welfare, corrections, and other programs such as economic development and environmental protection. To put this in perspective, let's look at where state spending per $100 of personal income goes. The year is 1989 and the figures exclude spending paid for by federal aid and user charges. In 1989, $100 of personal income generated $7.80 in state tax revenue, which was spent by state governments for the following functions: $2.30 for elementary and secondary education, $0.91 on higher education, $0.64 for highways, $0.63 on health and hospitals, $0.61 for Medicaid, $0.40 on other welfare programs, $0.37 for corrections, and $1.94 on all the other functions of state government.[8]

Medicaid spending, called "the PAC-Man of state government," increased by 28 percent in fiscal 1991 and by 30 percent in fiscal 1992. By fiscal 1995, Medicaid is expected to account for 25 percent of total state spending.[9] These rates of increase clearly are outpacing the growth rate in state economies and are absorbing much of the growth in state revenues.

Of course, different regions of the country have different priorities. In the Southwest, water policy is a dominant issue. In the Midwest, farm problems, the declining industrial base, and lack of economic development are major concerns. In the Northeast it is an aging infrastructure that must be rebuilt so the economies can recover. And in California, which is a region unto itself, the state must cope with both in and out migration, a multicultural population, unpredictable weather pattern shifts, and a contracting economic base in addition to a myriad of societal problems.

Waste problems affect each of the states and their local communities, and none appear to be as intractable as disposing of hazardous waste. One example makes the point. Under the prodding of the U.S. Department of Energy, the states have been grouped into a series of regional interstate compacts (legal agreements) to seek processes and sites for the disposal of radioactive waste within each region. But as the time draws near to select the sites for locating this waste, the process appears to be close to collapse due to a lack of trust. In a nutshell, the question that state policy makers are asking is "which state will take their turn next and can we be sure that they will do so?" No state wants to be first in a line where no one stands second.

Issues also vary from one state to another. Policy makers in Florida must address the many social and environmental problems created by the state's population boom and breakneck development. Some of these problems have difficult age and ethnic aspects to them. Connecticut and New York have different troubles, such as the deterioration of public highways and bridges, which was made evident by the collapse of the New York State Thruway bridge into Scoharie Creek in 1987. These states have been suffering from a declining tax base as industry and people move out. And in Nevada and New Jersey the infiltration of organized crime in state gambling casinos has officials on the watch.

Setting the Agenda

How do particular concerns become priorities on the states' agendas? Although state constitutions provide for the education, health, and safety of citizens, events can trigger new interest in these issues. For example, the collapse of financial institutions such as insurance companies or state-chartered banks can lead to citizen despair and action by state regulators. Campaign promises and court decisions also influence policy making. A gubernatorial candidate who promises to lower utility rates will try to keep this promise once elected. And if a state court finds that some citizens, such as the mentally handicapped, are not receiving the state services to which they are entitled, chances are the governor and state legislators will pay closer attention to this issue.

Provisions of the U.S. Constitution also can force issues onto a state's policy agenda. Since the 1950s, there has been a series of U.S. Supreme Court decisions on "separate but equal" education, reapportionment, and criminal justice based on lawsuits challenging state and local government policies and actions as violations of the plaintiffs' constitutional rights. These decisions have caused state and local government lawmakers considerable anguish as they address and adopt often controversial and expensive new policies, which usually translate into tax increases.

Federal program requirements also can play a role in state policy making and administration. For example, in the early and mid-1980s, the states had to raise the legal drinking age to twenty-one and limit interstate highway speeds to 55 miles per hour or face the loss of federal highway funds. However, federal encroachment on setting speed limits came to a head in a highly publicized and controversial vote to override President Ronald Reagan's veto of a multibillion dollar transportation bill in March 1987. The override allowed those states that wished to raise the limit to 65 miles per hour on rural interstates.

Innovations and programs in other states can influence a state's agenda, as a new form of activity in one state may lead to similar action elsewhere. Some of the specific steps taken by the states that had to deal with the AIDS crisis in the early 1980s are now being copied by other states. Some states are copying other states' attempts to develop technology centers to attract industry. This "copycat" method of decision making has proved to be very popular: How did State X handle this? However, as some have noticed, what is "reform in one state may be the exact opposite of reform in another." For example, California made its insurance commissioner an elected official the same time as Louisiana was looking to make that office appointive rather than elective; and Georgia repealed no-fault auto insurance the same time as Pennsylvania added it.[10]

Events not only in another state but in another part of the world occasionally determine the issues that state governments must address. Although the recent decrease in tension between the United States and the former Soviet Union has raised hopes of a "peace dividend"—a budget windfall from cuts in the defense budget—the states will bear the cost of the dividend. Cuts in the defense budget mean the closing of military bases in some states, reducing military personnel, and cutting back or canceling contracts for military hardware and weapons systems and funding for military research. Many states and localities have greatly benefited from the defense budget in years past. Now, as times and concerns change, so will their economies and fiscal health.

Implementation

Once policy goals and priorities are set by governors and legislators, important decisions must be made concerning who will implement them. This not only means which agency in state government will have the responsibility, but which level of government—state, local, or both.

Implementation decisions are often made with the considerable interest and involvement of the federal government. State and local governments administer some federal programs: food stamps, child nutrition, social services, community action, and senior citizen centers. In other areas federal and state governments *share* administrative and fiscal responsibility: public welfare, Medicaid, interstate and federal highways, hazardous waste, and water supply and sanitation.

But in many program areas the federal presence is minimal or nonexistent—especially since the passage of the 1985 Balanced Budget and Emergency Deficit Control Act, commonly known as the Gramm-Rudman-Hollings bill after its sponsors. This legislation mandates extensive across-the-board federal budget cuts if deficit targets are not met. Even before Gramm-Rudman-Hollings, federal aid to state and local governments had declined 23.5 percent in real terms between 1980 and 1985.[11]

Even leaner times are ahead. The federal government is picking up a smaller and smaller share of the state tab for primary and secondary schools, state and community colleges, public hospitals, police and fire protection, state prisons and local jails, local streets and roads, public utilities, state and local parks, public libraries, and facilities for the disabled. As the new president, former Arkansas governor Bill Clinton, and the Congress battle over changes in policies, taxes, the national debt, and budgets, no one is exactly clear as to the outcome of the conflicts. If these issues were not so important we might enjoy the battle a bit more. But for state officials and their counterparts at the local level, the conflicts have a direct impact on their jobs and responsibilities. And by extension, the outcome of these conflicts will have considerable impact on citizens and on what they can expect from their state and local government.

Current Issues

To put today's issues into perspective, the top seven discipline problems in California public schools in 1940 were "talking, chewing gum, making noise, running in the halls, getting out of turn in line, wearing improper clothing and not putting paper in the waste baskets." In the 1980s, the top seventeen problems were "drug abuse, pregnancy, rape, assault, arson, murder, vandalism, gang warfare, venereal disease, alcohol abuse, suicide, robbery, burglary, bombings, absenteeism, extortion and abortion."[12] In the 1990s, many of the problems of the 1980s remain, but AIDs, racism, guns in school, and a few others probably should be added to the list.

More generally, a recent Council of State Governments survey of the upcoming agenda for the states suggested that "the most significant ideas being debated in state government include: site-based school management as a core of education reform; public and/or private school choice; health care rationing waivers to Medicare/Medicaid; multistate foreign trade initiatives; workfare and other restrictions on welfare entitlements; expansion of sales tax to services and mail order purchases; creating markets for recycled materials; alternatives to incarceration; restrictions on abortion; [and] redefining standards for lobbyist-legislator relations."[13]

The articles in Part IX focus on six issues currently on the states' policy agendas. Penelope Lemov of *Governing* provides two separate pieces, first looking at what the states are doing in health reform and then whether or not the states can get out from under the federal government's strictures on running prisons. Theresa Raphael in *State Government News* focuses on health problems created by AIDS in the states. David Rapp of *Governing* raises the interesting question of whether the states should really want a balanced federal budget. Next is an analysis by *State Policy Reports* on a current fad in the states—raising money through gambling and lotteries. And Jonathan Walters of *Governing* explores how land-use laws can be used in creative ways.

Notes

1. National Governors' Association, *The State of the States, 1985*, 6.
2. National Association of State Budget Officers and National Governors' Association, *Fiscal Survey of the States, 1989* (Washington, D.C.: April 1989).
3. *Fiscal Survey of the States, 1988* (October 1988).
4. Marcia Howard, author of *Fiscal Survey of the States, 1989*, quoted in John Bacon, "Strapped U.S. Passes the Buck," *USA Today*, May 10, 1989, 5A.
5. Peter Passell, "Duke Economists Critical of State Lotteries," *New York Times News Service*, reported in the *Durham Morning Herald*, May 21, 1989, 11A.
6. "Trends: Budget Cuts, Tax Hikes, Revenue Increases," *Governors' Weekly Bulletin* 25:43 (November 1, 1991), 1.
7. "Budgets Assume Modest Growth Spending: Prospects of Slow-Growth Economies Shape Governors' Decisions, Study Says," *Governors' Bulletin* April 26, 1993, 1.
8. Steven D. Gold, "The Story Behind State Spending Trends," Rockefeller Center *Bulletin* (Albany: SUNY-Albany, 1991), 4-5.
9. "Budgets Assume Modest Growth," 2.
10. "Ebb and Flow in State Policy," *State Policy Reports* 9:18 (September 1991), 12.
11. Congressional Research Service, "The Effect of Federal Tax and Budget Policies in the 1980s on the State-Local Sector," *Governors' Weekly Bulletin* 20:9 (March 7, 1986): 2.
12. Remarks of William Bondurant, executive director, the Mary Reynolds Babcock Foundation, to the National Development Conference in Dallas, Texas, June 12, 1987.
13. Dag Ryen, "The Challenge Ahead: The State Agenda for the Coming Years," *The Journal of State Government* 65:2 (April-June 1992): 56.

Health Care Reform: The States Get Serious

by Penelope Lemov

[Nineteen ninety-two] will go down in the annals of health care politics as a time when the federal government talked endlessly about the problem—and state governments began to do something about it.

States have been drawing up pilot programs in the health care field for more than a decade now. But [recently], three states—Minnesota, Florida and Vermont—have moved far beyond the pilot approach, passing comprehensive new laws aimed at insuring more people and keeping costs down. Several other states will be considering wide-scale reform. . . . Even in Oregon, where a wide-ranging program that included a Medicaid rationing plan ran into the buzz saw of federal disapproval, . . . the betting is that the law will be modified and resubmitted to Washington.

Meanwhile, well over half of the rest of the states have enacted smaller-scale changes, many of them centered on lowering the cost of health insurance for clusters of the uninsured, especially those who are employed by small businesses. New York State has enacted a law that makes it more difficult for insurance companies to price health insurance out of the reach of small groups and individuals.

The states have been impelled to act not so much by a notion that they can solve the

health care crisis alone, but rather by the idea that someone has to take the first steps. When the federal government finally gets around to legislating health care reform, many state legislators argue, the states, through the track record of their programs, will be able to shape and direct the debate. "We'll not only be able to show members of Congress how programs work, but what the public reaction is to what we offer," says Elaine Bloom, who heads up the health care committee in the Florida House.

Other legislators feel it is simply a waste of time waiting for the federal government to act. "None of us is going to live that long," sniffs Vermont Representative Peg Martin, who, as head of the state House health and welfare committee, fought to push Vermont's new health care bill through the legislature.

It is, after all, the states that have to deal directly with the two most devastating aspects of the health care crisis: the holes in the coverage and the exploding costs of treatment. Nationwide, about 35 million people—10 million of them children—remain uninsured.

Penelope Lemov is a staff writer for *Governing*. This article is reprinted from *Governing* 6:1 (October 1992): 27-29.

Most are too poor to buy insurance, not poor enough to qualify for Medicaid, and not lucky enough to work for companies that provide health insurance benefits. Meanwhile, health care costs are rising annually at a rate of about 20 percent a year—many times higher than the rate of inflation. That hurts the states, their localities, their businesses and their voters. And it is slowly creating a majority coalition for change.

"State policy makers do not prefer a state-based resolution on this question," notes Minnesota state Representative Paul Ogren, who was instrumental in fashioning his state's new "HealthRight" bill. "We simply understand that the economic and moral imperative is here, and we must act where we can."

For health care reform to garner public support, Ogren argues, it can't appear to be a welfare issue. That is, it can't deal only with coverage for the working poor and their children, as many of the state pilot programs born in the 1980s do. Real reform has to come to terms with problems that affect a broader range of the population. In Minnesota, where only a relatively small percentage of the population is uninsured, that group and those sympathetic with their plight lack the political influence to bring about meaningful change. "The thrust of legislation," Ogren says, "had to be about controlling costs for those currently insured."

The step that Minnesota, Florida and Vermont have all taken is to create special new health agencies and order them to figure out ways to contain health care costs. Few states have tried cost control before in any comprehensive way, but it is the underpinning of the current wave of state legislation.

Just how the cost controls will be achieved is a question that none of the new laws really resolve. They all approach the issue rather delicately. Minnesota is asking its new agency to look into limits on capital

expenses by health care providers; Vermont's legislature wants its newly created authority to create a statewide health care budget that would take into account all of the players in the health care system; Florida asks its new agency to seek ways of expanding caps on fees for health services.

The vagueness of the marching orders invites the criticism that none of these programs really does much—that they just make plans to make plans. In Vermont, critics joked about what they called "the leap-of-faith bill." Peg Martin, the health committee chairwoman, accepts that criticism, but says the new law is important nevertheless. "It's the only chance to go forward," she insists.

The fact is that all these new bills are a step, if only a tentative one, toward tighter state control over health care, its costs and the delivery of services. They might not authorize strict rationing of care, as Oregon would like to do, but they point ultimately to limits on service based on resources available. As the states move in that direction, they will be edging toward the type of behind-the-scenes rationing system used by many of the countries in the Western world.

On a more immediate and less controversial level, all three states have also charged their new agencies with some practical, specific cost-control missions: They have been told to develop uniform billing and claim forms (to cut down on administrative costs) and to set protocols for physicians to limit practices that lead to unnecessary surgery and other expensive abuses of the health care system.

On the access side of the equation, the impact of the new reform laws will be much more immediate. As of October 1992, Minnesota's HealthRight provides that children whose families cannot afford health insurance will have coverage for visits to doctors and clinics. The cost of their care—be it treatment for an ear ache or a spill on a playground—is covered by state insurance. By the summer of 1994, these Minnesota youngsters will be covered for hospital care as well, as will their parents and other uninsured adults who buy into the subsidized program. Enrollment is voluntary, but legislators are counting on reaching more than 40 percent of the uninsured with the program, which will be financed in part by premiums and in part by a tax on providers and an increase in the cigarette tax.

Fees will be based on a sliding scale, with charges as low as $13 a month for a family of three at the bottom of the income ladder. The program also stacks its benefits on the outpatient side: adult hospital care benefits will be capped at $10,000 a year, but everyone will be allowed a vast array of doctor visits, checkups, immunizations and illness-prevention tests.

Vermont and Florida are trying variations on that theme. Vermont is broadening its state-funded "Dr. Dynasaur" program for poor children, increasing the upper age limit from 7 to 18, and extending the scope of benefits. Florida hopes to expand coverage to the poorest of the currently uninsured by using state subsidies to pay premiums that allow them to use the Medicaid program.

What Florida wants to do, however, would require permission from the federal Health Care Financing Administration. And that brings up a crucial point about the whole health care reform movement: Nearly any important change a state wants to make will need federal approval—in the form of a waiver or exemption from existing federal law—at one point or another. Minnesota, for example, would ultimately like to take the whole gamut of public health programs, including Medicaid and Medicare, and put them into one state-administered program. The streamlining, the state believes, could save everyone a good deal of money. But that could never be done without approval from

Table 1 Federal Medicaid Expenditure Growth

Fiscal year	Total expenditures[a]	Total yearly growth[b]
1980	$14,069,421	16.77%
1981	16,681,025	18.56
1982	17,866,898	7.11
1983	19,326,227	8.17
1984	20,697,444	7.10
1985	22,685,387	9.60
1986	24,668,512	8.74
1987	27,528,933	11.60
1988	30,521,156	10.87
1989	34,350,182	12.55
1990	41,194,571	19.93
1991[c]	53,393,353	29.61
1992[c]	72,502,738	35.79
1993[c]	84,401,234	16.41
1994[c]	98,149,341	16.29
1995[c]	113,594,217	15.74
1996[c]	130,992,516	15.32

Source: Health Care Financing Administration. Reprinted with permission.

[a] Thousands of dollars.
[b] Growth compared to previous year.
[c] Figures from the President's fiscal 1993 budget proposal.

Washington. Even something as simple as developing uniform claim forms—a move that would save money for business as well as government—necessitates asking Congress for waiver of a federal law.

A few months ago, the states were relatively optimistic about getting waivers. Now they are less sure. Early in August [1992], the Bush administration rejected Oregon's request for a waiver for its plan to ration health benefits for Medicaid patients. Coming as it did after a year of negotiation between the state and the federal government, the decision initially cast something of a pall over Minnesota, Vermont, Florida and the other states preparing to join the wave of experimentation.

"It makes us wonder," says Florida's

Elaine Bloom, "if the federal government is serious when they say they want the states to experiment."

In the long run, though, the rejection of the Oregon plan is unlikely to slow things down very much. The administration did not reject cost controls or even rationing per se; it said only that Oregon had not done enough to protect the rights of the disabled. Other state reform laws would not necessarily be vulner-able to that complaint. In addition, it is not at all clear that a new presidential administration would take a similarly restrictive stand.

And perhaps most important, the political lesson of the 1992 reform efforts, especially in Minnesota, has been that the coalition of forces demanding change is gradually becoming strong enough to overpower those forces that are opposing it. In a climate like that, health care reform will be difficult to derail.

The AIDS Factor

by Theresa Raphael

The face of AIDS is changing. New cases among gay men are stabilizing while rates among intravenous drug users continue to grow, as they do for women, minorities and teenagers. Among those already infected, survival times have improved.

These changes create the potential for enormous impacts on the way states tackle AIDS issues and other public health problems.

IV Drug Use

States must pay close attention to the epidemic among IV drug users. The national figure—which indicates that IV drug users compose about 25 percent of all AIDS cases to date—can be misleading. It doesn't show that in New Jersey, by 1989, two-thirds of the state's reported cases were among IV drug users, their sexual partners and offspring. Nor does it tell you that the population of drug users contains two of the groups where AIDS is most rapidly growing: minorities and women. Seventy-one percent of all cases in women are related to drug use. African-Americans make up 45 percent of all cases involving drug users, while Hispanics account for 26 percent. Few of these victims have insurance or access to primary health care, and many are homeless.

Most states with large inner city areas, where the majority of drug users live, have extensive programs for people with AIDS and have tried to adapt those services to drug users. New Jersey, with the help of a grant from the Robert Wood Johnson Foundation, has established a hospital-based case management program as part of a strategy to bring AIDS patients into a statewide services network.

Under the program, each AIDS patient is assigned to a case manager who coordinates and monitors services that include day care, drug treatment, medical care and assistance with housing and everyday tasks. The program helps drug users and appears to save money because it provides AIDS patients with an alternative to hospital care. Also, case managers try to obtain money to help defray the cost of hospital care for AIDS patients. For those with AIDS and their families, the improvement in quality of care and quality of life is incalculable. Despite the savings and benefits, continued funding is uncertain. About 20

Theresa Raphael is a senior policy analyst for The Council of State Governments' Eastern Office in New York. This article is reprinted with permission from *State Government News* 35:6 (June 1992): 24-27. ©1993 The Council of State Governments.

states have introduced case management programs for people with AIDS, some through special Medicaid waivers.

Of the programs designed to prevent AIDS among drug users, the most controversial are needle exchange programs. In exchange for used needles, drug users can obtain clean ones in addition to counseling, and in some cases, treatment. Needle exchange reduces the risk of transmitting HIV, the virus that causes AIDS, and other blood-borne diseases via shared needles.

In the late 1980s, needle exchange programs began unofficially in a number of states. In 1990, Hawaii and Connecticut were the first to officially endorse such programs. Preliminary studies prove encouraging: Needle exchange has reduced sharing, increased the number of drug users in the health and social service system and has not resulted in more drug use.

The impact that the rise in HIV and AIDS among drug users has had on the states is hard to measure because programs are scattered among various departments: corrections, housing, social services, substance abuse, general health and hospitals, and of course, in AIDS departments. HIV-related programs are sometimes part of general drug user programs and other times part of programs for all people with AIDS.

Drug users and their families often need social services even before they become infected. Once drug users are infected, whole families can be infected. Male drug users transmit the virus to their sexual partners, who can then pass the virus to their unborn children. Children not infected often are orphaned, losing parents and siblings. It is estimated that by 1993, New York City alone will have more than 20,000 orphans of AIDS. Medicaid shoulders medical care costs for drug users and their families, further straining states' already strapped Medicaid budgets.

Table 1 Modes of Transmission of AIDS (in cumulative cases)

Homosexual contact (male)	58%
Intravenous drug use	23
Heterosexual contact	6
Multiple modes	6
Blood/tissue receipt	2
Hemophilia	1
Other	4

Even if AIDS were stopped in its tracks today, drug users and their families, half of whom already may be infected, would need basic support for living as well as medical care for many years to come.

Living Longer with HIV and AIDS

It is important to differentiate between HIV and AIDS: HIV is the virus that weakens the immune system and can be present for many years before a person develops AIDS; AIDS is the disease that results from the virus.

People are living longer through the use of drugs that delay the on-set of symptoms. Among people with AIDS, average survival time has almost doubled from one to two years, and many survive significantly longer with the use of AZT and other drugs. These longer survival times also mean that many AIDS patients need long-term care facilities such as skilled nursing homes.

Some states offer more money to nursing homes for HIV care. In New York, the state with the highest number of AIDS cases, nursing homes that accept HIV-infected individuals are reimbursed at rates two to three times higher than for non-HIV patients.

When possible, intensive home care is an alternative to nursing homes. New York pays 30 percent more for home nursing visits to HIV patients. An estimated 25 percent to 30 percent of all people with AIDS will need skilled home nursing care, and many states have responded by adding nursing care to their AIDS program.

For individuals who do not yet have AIDS but whose immune system has started to weaken, the news is encouraging: Use of AZT and other drug therapies have been found to delay the onset of AIDS, allowing them to live in relatively good health. But the drugs are expensive, about $5,000 per year, and well beyond the means of many patients. Private insurers limit prescription coverage, and while Medicaid covers AZT, most AIDS victims do not qualify.

Some states have established drug reimbursement programs. New Hampshire provides AZT for HIV-infected people who meet the financial qualifications. Joyce Welch, the state's AIDS director, said the program is a rest stop on the road to Medicaid eligibility.

For those in the early stage of HIV infection, early intervention with AZT is thought to delay the start of AIDS. However, many of these people do not even know they are infected, and among those who do, many do not have the means to pay for the drug.

"We need funds for early intervention" Welch said.

For early intervention, there must be increased access to counseling and testing. Michigan, like most states, faces the problem of trying to meet the increased demand, said Randall Pope, chief of AIDS Prevention. "Our counseling and testing sites are overburdened, with waiting lists of six to eight weeks."

The availability of drugs that slow the progression of HIV affects state and local health programs in two ways. First, AIDS is seen less as an acute illness requiring extensive hospitalization and is increasingly treated as a chronic disease in clinics, patients' homes or nursing homes. But, historically, hospitalization has been more readily reimbursed than other forms of care. As states shift the focus from hospitals to ambulatory care, they must find other means to fund AIDS care.

Second, as evidence mounts supporting the efficacy of early intervention, and as people seek testing in larger numbers, states are trying to expand and enhance their counseling and testing services. Also, an estimated 80 percent of the prescriptions for AIDS drugs are paid for out-of-pocket. In this recession, finding the extra resources to expand services is beyond the means of most states.

Financing Trends for HIV Care

States contend with AIDS on a number of fronts. Patient care leads the way in costs, followed by education, testing and surveillance. State, federal and private funds provide the financing.

Medicaid. Medicaid has assumed the role of chief payer for AIDS care, covering about 40 percent of people with AIDS. As HIV spreads among drug users and the health of those with full-blown AIDS deteriorates, this share is expected to increase rapidly. Individuals with private insurance lose their coverage as they become disabled, at which time they enroll in Medicaid. A major limitation of Medicaid is that people must be clinically diagnosed with AIDS to be eligible. Therefore those in the early stages of HIV cannot get treatment even if they are penniless.

Other barriers are the strict financial eligibility requirements and services covered, which vary greatly from state to state. Low reimbursement rates are another problem. Hospitals must cover much of the costs themselves, and many physicians refuse to treat Medicaid patients. In fact many physicians refuse to treat HIV patients no matter who is footing the bill.

States have responded to these problems by increasing the amount of money paid for HIV and AIDS care and devising schemes to keep people off the Medicaid rolls and on private insurance for as long as possible. In 1988, Michigan became the first state to enact an insurance continuation program that pays insurance premiums for people with AIDS who are at risk of losing their jobs and thus their insurance because of the illness. Currently the program pays the premiums of 140 people.

"The program is going exceedingly well," Michigan's Pope said. "For every dollar invested, $7 to $9 is saved in Medicaid costs. It is a good investment of limited dollars."

Twelve other states have implemented similar programs.

Private Insurance. Private insurance still plays a large role in financing AIDS care, but its portion is shrinking as publicly funded care increases. While estimates are difficult to come by, the Health Care Finance Administration figures that 29 percent of people with AIDS are privately insured. HIV-infected people who have private insurance tend to work for larger firms where much of the health care costs are paid for by the company. Those in smaller firms face restricted coverage, if it exists at all. As the composition of the HIV population continues to shift toward the poor and uninsured, and AIDS services shift from hospital to outpatient care, this trend away from private insurance will persist.

State Funds. A survey released in November 1991 by the Intergovernmental Health Policy Project (IHPP) showed that states had doubled funding for AIDS-related programs since 1989, a remarkable increase during this time of fiscal austerity. In New York, according to Richard Gottfried, chairman of the Assembly Health Committee, "The AIDS Institute (New York's AIDS program) budget was the only health program not cut this year. We actually increased it by $4.3 million." The enormous rise in case loads prompted the increase, he said.

AIDS programs in smaller states with fewer cases often do not fare as well at budget time. New Hampshire's Welch said her department's state appropriations had declined from $310,000 in 1988 to $132,000 for 1992. "New Hampshire does not have a system in place to provide care," she said. "We are totally reliant on federal money." Eighteen other states face the same problem, according to the IHPP survey.

Federal Funds. The 1990 Ryan White CARE Act is the most important source of federal AIDS funding for HIV-infected people. Originally authorized at $875 million, funding for fiscal 1992 dropped to $322 million. The act is divided into four parts: grants for care and services in the hardest hit cities, grants for care and services in each state, grants to each state for counseling and testing and grants for pediatric programs. (The last has yet to be funded.) The National Commission on AIDS, a bipartisan group, urged full funding of Ryan White to reduce the economic burden in states and cities and to avoid further state and local cuts in services.

A Crisis Response

States have been forced to respond in a crisis fashion to an epidemic that strains our patchwork system of health care. Each shift in the course of HIV has prompted states, local governments and those in health care to pay for services.

Our health care system is based on certain assumptions: that people work most of their lives, or are married to someone who does, and that most people die in old age of chronic, debilitating diseases. AIDS challenges each of those assumptions. We were simply not prepared for a disease that strikes young people in large numbers, is easy to transmit through difficult-to-change behaviors, is costly to treat from its earliest stages, and has quickly permeated a poor, uninsured population.

In the absence of a universal health care system, states will continue to provide and coordinate services to HIV-infected people through a hodgepodge of financing schemes. Meanwhile, despite gaps in care and financing and public debate about who should pay for what, we, as a society, shoulder the costs of our citizens' terminal illnesses, albeit in a less than perfect fashion. How to spread those costs equitably is the fundamental policy question that we have yet to answer.

Do the States Really Want a Balanced Federal Budget?

by David Rapp

"Save us," members of Congress were calling to the states. "Save us from ourselves."

It was a desperate plea from a large majority of Republicans and Democrats alike, staring blankly together at a deficit approaching $400 billion and an accruing national debt that has surpassed $4 trillion. Just how willingly states would have answered that plea is something we can't know at the moment; the constitutional amendment requiring the federal government to balance its budget fell nine votes short of winning the two-thirds majority it needed in the House. That kept it from going to the Senate and on to the states for ratification.

But it will be back. Anti-deficit sentiment is too strong all over the country for the amendment's sponsors not to make another try sooner or later. The deficit and the debt are certainly not going away. In the end, it may still be up to the states to decide whether a balanced federal budget is something that is necessary, desirable or even in their best interest.

Just about everyone in Washington believes that a balanced-budget amendment would sail easily through the 38 states that would have to ratify it to make it part of the constitution. After all, it is argued, the states

balance their own budgets; all except Vermont are legally required to do so. Wouldn't it be a simple matter for them to ask Washington to play by the same rules they play by?

Not as simple as it might seem. The whole balanced-budget issue presents states with some puzzles they probably want to think through before the amendment ends up in the legislatures' lap.

To start with, there is the dirty little secret of state fiscal policy: In most states, a balanced budget is more fiction than reality. Some regularly borrow from pools of money outside the "general fund," such as capital budgets or pensions. Others count revenue that won't really arrive until the next fiscal year. Many more simply delay making obligated payments—to suppliers, to salaried employees or to local governments.

But there is a far more important reason why states should think twice about whether to ratify a balanced-budget constitutional amendment, if the decision is given to them. The states—and their local governments—could not help but suffer under its consequences.

Congress has, after all, spent the past

David Rapp is a staff writer for *Governing*. This article is reprinted from *Governing* 5:10 (July 1992): 85.

What States Can Do

It is clearly in the national interest to stop runaway deficit spending and restore financial integrity to the federal government. The long-term benefits—lower interest rates and renewed investment, economic growth, and job creation—are clear.

How should states respond to the significant short-term disruption that will precede the long-term benefits?

First, states must play a significant role in framing the implementation of a balanced budget constitutional amendment in order to minimize the short-run disruption on state governments. The need for ratification may give states the leverage they need to insist upon such a role. States may even want to ask Congress for an implementation plan prior to ratification. Second, states must begin to develop a common position on key state implementation concerns, such as:

• Which programs would be shifted to the states—and how could states be protected from unrestrained federal mandates?

• What types of taxes would need to be increased and by what level of government?

• What programs are included in the balance? For example, will trust fund expenditures, such as Social Security and highways, be included? Will the federal government move toward a capital budget and only include depreciation in the operating budget? What about the savings and loan issue? Do actual revenues and expenditures need to be in balance at the end of a fiscal year or just the President's submission and the enacted budget?

Regardless of the approach, states need to play a major role in the implementation plan. Governors are deeply concerned about the impact of growing deficits on interest rates and, ultimately, long-run economic growth and the standard of living of all Americans.

Source: Raymond C. Scheppach, "How Would a Balanced Budget Affect States?" *Governors' Bulletin* 26:11 (May 25, 1992), 2. Reprinted with permission.

---

seven years trying to meet the terms of the anti-deficit Gramm-Rudman law. It has done so in part by cutting financial aid to states and cities and by imposing new and costly "mandates" on what the states must do to qualify for federal aid. Medicaid mandates, as every governor and state legislator knows by now, have become a favorite way for congressional Democrats to increase health care coverage for the poor without having to pay for it out of the federal Treasury.

Suppose Congress is suddenly forced to cut $400 billion from its $1.5 trillion budget. Where will that money come from? Remember this: Unlike the states, which separate their programs into many different funds for expenses such as capital projects, education, highways and pensions, the federal government must operate on a unified budget. A constitutional amendment barring outlays in excess of revenues would not allow Congress to borrow against future revenues, as 37 states now do with their capital budgets. To balance the federal books, Congress would have to cut spending and/or raise taxes—by more than 25 percent.

That's one-fourth of Medicaid, Community Development Block Grants, low-income housing assistance, aid to historically black colleges, sewage treatment grants, mass transit assistance. Or else it's a 15- to 25-cent increase in the federal gasoline tax. Either way, states, cities and counties would be the losers. The next time Congress considers a balanced-budget amendment, don't be surprised if it is the states that end up pleading with Washington to "save us from ourselves"—to avoid sending them a piece of legislation that legislatures would be pressured to approve but would very likely live to regret.

More public officials at the state level may realize this than the current wisdom suggests. A decade ago, after all, it was the states that were clamoring for a constitutional convention for the purpose of imposing the balanced-budget requirement on Congress and the president. Thirty-two state legislatures passed resolutions calling for a convention that has only one precedent—the original constitu-tional convention in 1787.

But the last state that passed such a resolution was Missouri in 1983. Since then, proponents have remained two states short of the two-thirds needed to approve a convention call. Conservative activists, led by the National Taxpayers Union, have tried to keep the idea alive, but they have found few sympathizers in the 18 remaining state legislatures. Indeed, three states—Florida, Alabama and Louisi-ana—have since voted to rescind their resolu-tions, taking most of the steam out of the convention drive.

There is a reason why all those states have acted the way they have. They have learned what is, for them, the most relevant truth about a balanced-budget constitutional amendment: They would be its first victims.

Gambling and Lotteries

The Spread of Legalized Gambling. Legal gambling is now easily accessible to nearly every American. By one count, some form is already available in every state but Hawaii and Utah. In many of the states that have been the slowest to move to modern legalized gambling, charity Bingo and casino nights are widespread.

As more states have adopted lotteries, racing, and other forms of gambling, it is increasingly clear that state prohibitions are not preventing state residents from gambling. Stories of lottery pools to invest in tickets of other states, bus charters to Atlantic City casinos and neighboring-state race tracks, and massive sales in tiny stores just across the border into a lottery neighbor of a non-lottery state are common. All strengthen the case that state access to gambling jobs and state revenue, not residents' access to gambling, is being restricted by gambling prohibitions. Public opinion polls and voter approval of gambling in other states is convincing reluctant elected officials of public support.

Changing Opposition to Gambling. Some state officials and religious groups have tried to buck the trend or at least slow the rush. There appears to have been a change in the source of opposition to new legalized gambling proposals. The importance of moral objections has shrunk considerably to a few bastions—the Mormon church in the West and Christian fundamentalists in the South. Now the strongest opposition to extension of legalized gambling comes from beneficiaries of old legalized gambling fearful of new competition.

Some of this opposition is formidable because it brackets the sources of influence in state policymaking. On the one hand are groups clearly representing large numbers of ordinary citizens—religious groups, volunteer fire departments, and other bastions of the community. On the other are the already legalized operators, such as race track owners, with their strengths in the behind-the-scenes atmosphere of campaign finance, as well as lobbyists who are established figures in their state capitols.

Gambling Appears Secure. It is conceivable that some event would turn back the current trends, but it is hard to imagine what it might be. So many people have vested interests in the continuation and expansion of present legalized forms of gambling that it is

This article is reprinted from *State Policy Reports* 10:14 (July 1992): 11-15.

Table 1 Per Capita Lottery Sales, CY 1991

Rank	State	Amount	Rank	State	Amount	Rank	State	Amount
1	Massachusetts	$267	12	New York	$113	23	Colorado	$64
2	South Dakota	198	13	Delaware	107	24	California	61
3	Maryland	169	14	Kentucky	95	25	Washington	59
4	Florida	167	15	New Hampshire	87	26	Arizona	56
5	New Jersey	165	16	Wisconsin	85	27	Iowa	56
6	Connecticut	163	17	Vermont	83	28	Idaho	50
7	Ohio	151	18	Maine	81	29	West Virginia	47
8	Illinois	140	19	Indiana	75	30	Missouri	42
9	Virginia	133	20	Oregon	69	31	Louisiana	38
10	Michigan	124	21	Rhode Island	66	32	Kansas	31
11	Pennsylvania	122	22	Minnesota	65	33	Montana	31

Note: Kentucky, Indiana, Minnesota, Idaho, and Louisiana established lotteries in 1989 or later.

most unlikely that the feared corruption of legalized gambling, even if it materialized in several states at once, would cause abandonment of gambling any more than evidence of corruption in Medicaid has caused its abandonment.

Lotteries Becoming Mature. With the Texas lottery now underway and Georgia and Nebraska . . . lotteries [approved] in November [1992], 37 states, including all the major industrial states, will be in the lottery business. Some of the Northeastern lotteries are now over 20 years old, meaning that a whole generation has come of age without any recollection of periods without lotteries. Only a few of the major lotteries are so recently established that their sales are subject to both the stimulus of start-up excitement and the lower per capita sales associated with start-up processes. Except for states which established lotteries in 1989 or later, per capita sales reflect long-term differences among states.

The disparities in per capita lottery play are substantial, with the Massachusetts total more than twice the national average. Six states are at half or less of that average. Many explanations are possible for the differences. They include factors under the control of state governments such as the variety of games available, the restraints states place on advertising, the percentage of revenues available for prizes, the prize structure (mix of small and large prizes), the size of the state (and thus the size of typical jackpots), and the skill of each state's lottery administrators. Other variables relate to the state's demographics. Some population groups bet more than others. States are unequally endowed with those populations. Finally, there are competitive factors beyond state control, such as whether neighboring states have lotteries.

Lottery Sales Growth. Over the past year, state lottery sales have grown by only 0.5%. When adjusted for the number of persons in lottery states, revenues [in the U.S.] shrank by half a percent.

While there is great variation among states (which [State Policy] Reports cannot explain), the budget message for the large industrial states is that lottery revenues didn't exhibit significant growth, and actually declined in many. The 1991 results are the first serious demonstration that state lotteries are not a powerful revenue engine that can be counted on to grow by at least the rate of inflation in good times and bad. The recession apparently had effects on the purchase of lottery tickets similar to its effects on other

Table 2   Percentage Change in Lottery Sales, CY 1990–CY 1991

Rank	State	Percent	Rank	State	Percent	Rank	State	Percent
1	Kentucky	81.9%	12	New Jersey	2.7%	23	Michigan	−2.9%
2	South Dakota	45.2	13	Delaware	1.6	24	Missouri	−3.3
3	Oregon	29.0	14	Illinois	1.6	25	Pennsylvania	−5.2
4	Colorado	27.3	15	New Hampshire	0.5	26	Montana	−5.3
5	Virginia	26.5	16	Connecticut	0.2	27	Florida	−5.4
6	Minnesota	16.2	17	Vermont	0.2	28	Idaho	−7.3
7	Washington	14.4	18	Maine	0	29	Iowa	−9.1
8	Kansas	12.6	19	Rhode Island	0	30	Indiana	−9.9
9	West Virginia	11.6	20	Ohio	−1.3	31	California	−20.7
10	Wisconsin	11.0	21	Maryland	−1.8	32	Arizona	−29.6
11	Massachusetts	2.9	22	New York	−1.9	33	Louisiana	N/A

Note: Kentucky, Minnesota, Idaho, Indiana, and Louisiana established lotteries in 1989 or later.

consumer purchases. Even in better economic times, the large-state lotteries have been unable to maintain the rapid growth of their early years. For example, declining lottery revenues for schools in California have strengthened the resolve of education interests to fight for the constitutionally guaranteed share of state revenues under Proposition 98.

Earmarking Lottery Revenues. The lack of growth in lottery revenues and the instability suggested by large gains and losses among individual states is not much of an argument against having lotteries. It is a substantial argument against earmarking lottery revenues for a stream of expenditures that exhibits a steady profile of growth. The resulting problems have been particularly severe in Pennsylvania. Most states earmark money for education. But Pennsylvania's earmarking is for programs for the elderly, particularly subsidizing the purchase of prescription drugs. As these costs have grown in some years much faster than lottery revenues, Pennsylvania decisionmakers have been confronted with the awkward choice of scaling back spending or financing a portion from general revenues.

Other Gambling Forms Advance. The states now appear to be moving quickly into new forms of gambling such as video

poker (called video lottery terminals) and casino gambling in special situations—ships to nowhere, riverboats, and historical towns. Colorado and South Dakota both have historical towns which are currently operating casinos. Illinois, Iowa, Louisiana, and Mississippi have all approved riverboat gambling. Missouri voters will consider riverboats in November. Gambling on Indian reservations is providing an impetus to gambling in some states, sometimes in peculiar and unpredictable ways (*see box*).

Many want their states to be among the leaders in the latest gaming innovation. [In 1992] the Louisiana legislature authorized a casino in New Orleans. . . . However, there will be litigation over whether the action conflicts with a state constitutional provision: "Gambling shall be defined by and suppressed by the legislature." Chicago business and government leaders are asking the Illinois legislature to adopt a multiple-casino plan for the Windy City. There are similar proposals for Cleveland, Detroit, Hartford, Milwaukee, and other large cities.

Iowa is offering "lottery" tickets in vending machines that let the purchasers buy paper tickets and pull off ticket coverings with the same results as pulling a slot machine lever—

matching fruits and other symbols for prizes. Other pull-tab games simulate blackjack and poker. The ads say, "CASINO ACTION! As close as you can get without being there."

Video lottery machines—video terminal versions of slot machines, computerized poker, and bingo—have been approved in at least five states. Other states are seeking to match South Dakota's success. Its revenues of $46 million in 1991 equaled the costs of its prisons and courts.

Sports betting has been approved in Delaware and Oregon in addition to Nevada which has allowed it for decades. The National Football League is so alarmed by the trend it is asking the Congress to outlaw the practice.

The bounds of ways to legalize gambling are tested by a tongue-in-cheek proposal in New England to take the controversial Seawolf submarine and convert it to underwater gambling, one-upping the riverboats of the Midwest. As one proponent puts it, "Far from being above the law, participants will now remain safely below it."

Gambling Economics. The state gambling proposals have produced extreme claims of economic benefits.... The different claims were recently exhibited in Louisiana with vast differences between opponents and proponents, and even among proponents, in predicted economic impacts of a new casino. Ironically, the site is a convention center area available because optimistic claims for it haven't been realized. Recent separate Illinois studies credited $1.4 billion in economic activity to horse racing and credited the proposed Chicago casinos with a $3.7 billion impact. The state and local tax impact was estimated at 5.7% of total impact in the horse racing study and 14% in the casino study.

The continuing caveat on all claims for

Indian Gambling, the Wild Card

The complex ground rules for gambling on reservations boil down to the concept that states cannot prohibit tribes from offering gambling opportunities that are legal anywhere in the state. The interaction of this rule with charity gambling statutes, the wording of lottery amendments in individual states, and conflicting interpretations of federal rules and state laws has created near chaos in some states.

Governors and legislatures are frequently getting crosswise on the issue, as has happened in Connecticut and Kansas. The situation in Wisconsin is so complex that it defies explanation in anything short of a book-length treatise. The speaker (D) offered the governor (R) an oblique compliment by commenting, "This is the only issue he has managed to totally screw up in his 5½ years as governor." The Wisconsin Taxpayers Alliance recently suggested that as a result of the decision to put a five-question advisory referendum on the April ballot, "Come April 1993, the gambling waters might be even muddier than now."

Source: State Policy Reports 10:14 (July 1992): 14.

extraordinary returns from legalized gambling is that competition among states and among forms of gambling will tend to reduce returns over time. Examples: the national movement to cut state taxes on horse and dog racing, pressures to reduce the state percentage from lotteries, and moves to end limits on riverboat gambling in Iowa because of Illinois competition.

Land Use Laws:
Handy Villain in Hard Times

by Jonathan Walters

New Hampshire residents don't care much for government land use controls: They would rather "Live Free or Die," as their license plates proclaim. To the west, however, across the Connecticut River, Vermonters look at the world differently. Most of them seem to favor land use planning. That way, they like to tell people, Vermont won't end up looking like New Hampshire.

The Granite State's pristine facade did indeed take some harsh hits through the 1980s, a decade of unrestrained strip mall construction and condominium development. Mountainsides became magnets for town houses. Along parts of once-bucolic Lake Winnipesaukee, there are areas where the houses are three deep, offering up more the aspect of Boston suburb than lakeside retreat.

Vermont, on the other hand, has managed to keep intact more of the natural beauty and unclutteredness that people love about it. A lot of the credit for that goes to Vermont's 22-year-old state land use law, known as Act 250. Under Act 250, nine regional commissions were organized to review any large-scale development falling within their jurisdictions. Before a development can proceed, it must win a permit from its regional commission. The commissions, supporters say, have done their best to balance economic growth with environmental and aesthetic sensitivity and planning practicality.

In the current climate of recession, however, some Vermonters have been pushing state officials to act a bit more like their libertarian cousins in New Hampshire. Act 250, and a companion statute, Act 200, which mandates local land use planning, came under intense attack from business interests during this year's legislative session. Business blames the land use laws for Vermont's inability to pull out of the economic stagnation of the past three years.

So far, the twin statutes have been successfully defended. But the attack fits a national pattern: When economies go sour, state land use laws become a target.

At the moment, Florida's tough growth control law and Maine's comprehensive state land use plans are both under fire. In both cases, opponents are using the weak state economies as their opening. "You can't blame the entire recession on land use laws," says James Burling, an attorney with the Pacific

---

Jonathan Walters is a staff writer for *Governing*. This article is reprinted from *Governing* 6:1 (October 1992): 24-25.

Legal Foundation, a private property rights advocacy organization. "But they are a significant factor in our inability to crawl out of it."

Land use planning advocates insist it is a false connection. In fact, they argue, strong growth planning laws help avoid the boom-and-bust cycles that characterize the economies of some large states, such as California and Florida. They cite Oregon, for example, where a strong state land use law is credited with helping the state's economy achieve modest but steady growth.

This is the argument that Vermont Governor Howard Dean and the pro-land use planning forces are making. Over the long run, they say, states with tough controls have more stable economies and are, not incidentally, nicer places to live. But the fight is far from over, there or in the several states where land use laws have come into being in recent years.

While it is not surprising that developers and real estate brokers would fight tough land use laws, such laws have also traditionally been resisted by one other key group: local officials, who see long-range growth plans as another example of states trying to dictate to them.

"The state is interested in land use planning and the localities are too, and on that basis we have alliance," says Karen Horn of the Vermont League of Cities and Towns. "But the question is: Who makes the decision? The trend in Vermont, from our point of view, is toward centralization, while we've been working hard to keep it locally based."

In Maine, some localities are flat-out refusing to comply with the state's new land use law, which mandates that all localities in the state come up with long-range land use plans that are consistent with planning goals set out by the state. But while local officials may view planning control as a turf issue, they, too, often parrot the developers' argument that tough planning laws stifle economic growth.

The truth is that, whether land use laws do anything to cause recession or not, they are easy to portray as culprits. The laws tend to be passed toward the end of the boom phase of an economic cycle, when voters are fed up with watching fields become strip malls and country roads turn into traffic jams. Not long after that, the bust comes. When it arrives, land use control opponents seize the opportunity to connect the two: It was the land use plan that caused the downturn. Let us loose, and prosperity will return.

That is the rallying cry in Florida, where the state's tough new "concurrency" law is being attacked by some in the development and real estate business. Under the law, new development cannot occur in any part of the state unless the roads, sewers and other infrastructure exist to handle it. Real estate brokers say the requirements frighten prospective developers away in an economically chancy time. "Baloney," retorts John DeGrove, director of the Joint Center for Environmental and. Urban Problems at Florida Atlantic University. "If anything, land use laws have helped soften the blow by holding developers back from overbuilding more than they did."

Recession or no recession, DeGrove insists, the real long-term national trend is not away from land use planning, but toward it. California, Connecticut, Massachusetts, New York, North Carolina, Pennsylvania and Virginia all have study commissions looking into the implementation of state land use plans. Some of those efforts, most notably California's, are stalled right now, a casualty of a prolonged budget crisis, but most seem likely in the end to generate new laws of one form or another.

The question is how strong those laws will be. Two states, New Jersey and Maryland, passed comprehensive land use plans [in 1992], despite their economic woes. But the two versions illustrate quite starkly the range

New Jersey Under Control

The New Jersey state land use planning commission last June [1992] adopted a tough new growth control plan. Implementation now depends on legislative and executive branch action. Here, the Center for Urban Policy Research at Rutgers University makes its case in favor of the plan, comparing the effect land use controls will have on the Garden State during the next 20 years with how the state could have developed in their absence:

Economic Growth. Overall growth remains unchanged with land use controls. But businesses will save $1.3 billion in capital infrastructure costs.

Jobs. The same number of jobs will be created overall, but 10 percent more of them (62,000) will be directed to cities. An additional 300,000 jobs will be directed to suburban and rural "centers," rather than scattered by sprawl across the entire state landscape.

Fiscal Impact. School districts and municipalities may save as much as $400 million a year in operating costs through more efficient use of existing infrastructure and service delivery capabilities.

Environment. The land use plan is expected to save 80 percent more acreage deemed "frail," including forests, slopes and sensitive watersheds.

Agriculture. One-third less farmland acreage will be given to development, saving 30,000 acres of "high-quality" agricultural land.

Air Pollution. Nitrogen oxides and non-methane hydrocarbons will be reduced by as much as 40 to 50 percent.

Water Pollution. A one-third reduction—4,560 fewer tons—in pollutants (including nitrogen, phosphorous, lead and zinc) in stormwater runoff by the year 2010.

Local and State Roads. The land use controls will save $740 million in road costs.

Water and Sewer. The controls will save $440 million in infrastructure costs.

School Capital Facilities. No significant difference. $5.1 billion under land use law, $5.3 billion without it.

Source: Jonathan Walters, "Land Use Laws: Handy Villain in Hard Times," *Governing* 6:1 (October 1992): 25.

of potency that exists among statutes that call themselves land use programs.

New Jersey's plan lays down a comprehensive and fairly tough planning template over cities, suburbs and rural areas. It places strictures on building density, and it directs growth toward areas that have transportation, water and sewer systems already in place.

Maryland's plan, by contrast, does little more than ask counties to plan responsibly. If Prince George's County wants to continue its haphazard development sprawl from one end to the other, it is free to do so under the new law, without formal penalty.

The difference, says Robert W. Burchell of the Center for Urban Policy Research at Rutgers University, is that the New Jersey effort, unlike the one in Maryland, was the result of years of consensus-building and millions of dollars in research and analysis. Planning proponents managed to convince local officials and the business community that it would cost everybody more in the long run to let the laissez-faire approach to land use run its course. In Maryland, even proponents of land use planning concede that they failed to make their case and build such a consensus. So in the end, they had to settle for what they could get. "I think we erred on the side of 'Let's get something passed,'" says Jane Nishida, Maryland's executive director of the Chesapeake Bay Foundation.

Making that case is crucial, argues Henry Richmond, executive director of a group known as 1000 Friends of Oregon, which was formed to fend off efforts at weakening that state's tough land use law. The Oregon law, passed in 1973, required 273 cities and 36 counties to develop comprehen-sive land use and zoning plans, and forced the rezoning of 26 million acres of land. Measures to overturn the law appeared on statewide ballots in 1976, 1978 and 1982, but it survived each time.

As in other states, however, the recession has revived the arguments against land use planning in Oregon, and brought new rhetoric from pro-development forces arguing that the state's economic climate would be better if there were not so many restrictions placed on new building. "If you have a land use program that is breaking the cycle of uncontrolled sprawl development," says Henry Richmond, "and you are using that policy against land-owner choice of where development goes, the boat is never going to stop rocking."

Taking Your Prison Back From the Feds

by Penelope Lemov

It wasn't exactly a moment for champagne and congratulations. But last month [December 1992], when a federal judge held hearings on an agreement to end *Ruiz vs. Collins,* the marathon Texas prison case, state correctional officials felt like celebrating. After two decades of running a prison system with the courts looking over their shoulder, they were on the brink of getting the operation back under their own management.

"It was something that had to be done," Assistant Attorney General Jay Aguilar said of the time and effort the state has spent laboring under court orders to improve its correctional facilities. But, he added, "after 22 years I think the people of Texas have a right to control their prison system."

The agreement gives state officials much more control over prison staffing and inmate discipline and more discretion in population management. There are strings attached. The court can still set limits on overall population in the 50,000-bed Texas prison system. But Judge William Wayne Justice has suggested that, since the system is running more efficiently now, the state would be able to add more inmates as long as the prisoners are given substantial recreation time. That is more leeway than the state has had in recent years.

Texas may not be back in complete charge, but there is no doubt that many states and localities would like to be where Texas is now. At this moment, 40 of the 50 state prison systems and roughly one-third of the 500 largest local jails remain under court supervision. They are required to comply with court orders or court-supervised consent decrees covering anything from the number of prisoners who can live in a 45-square-foot cell to the way in which inmates can be punished for breaking prison rules.

Some spell out very specific remedies—the number of days within which medical care must be provided to an ailing inmate. Others set out overall goals—clean kitchens, adequate recreational facilities. But whatever the language, the orders are mandatory, and the state or locality must figure out how to pay the costs of meeting them. The courts are no help with that. Nor have they been receptive to hindsight arguments that judicial demands go far beyond any constitutional ban on cruel or unusual punishment.

So far, only a few states and counties have

Penelope Lemov is a staff writer for *Governing*. This article is reprinted from *Governing* 6:4 (January 1993): 22-23.

been able to free themselves from federal fetters. But the 1990s could see more systems gain a good deal of autonomy. Some, after 10 to 20 years of supervision, have finally reached a point of acceptable improvement. Others, emboldened by recent U.S. Supreme Court language, will ask the courts to modify their court decrees so that it will be easier to comply.

Many of the federal court orders and consent decrees that control state prisons and county jails date back to the 1970s and early 1980s, when deplorable conditions were widespread. Some prisons did not have beds for every inmate or places for inmates to sit during daytime hours. Living conditions were unsanitary. Inadequate health care led to permanent disabilities. There were extremely high levels of violence among inmates. "Conditions were sufficiently shocking that even judges who in principle were opposed to intervention were unwilling to walk away from the issue," says Susan Sturm, an associate professor of law at the University of Pennsylvania.

The cases started with freedom-of-religion suits brought by Black Muslims, escalated into claims of due process violations and then exploded into a rash of actions covering systemwide abuse. "It became clear," Sturm says, "that there was breakdown of the system's ability to provide minimally adequate conditions." For a court to intervene, the plaintiffs had to prove that prison conditions were depriving inmates of the basic necessities of life—health care, food, adequate clothing, protection from violence. In a depressing number of places, it was all too easy to prove.

Some of the court-mandated goals or consent-decree standards were set so high or were worded so vaguely that systems were— and still are—unable to meet them. Or, as Robert C. Wood suggests in his book *Remedial Law,* it was not made clear just what it would take for the court to declare victory and turn a prison back to its regular managers.

Whatever the specific language, however, overcrowding was almost always at the heart of the problem. "Everything else falls apart when you have the numbers," says John Hale, a spokesman for the Alabama prison system.

In the past decade, systems have been trying to stay ahead of the overcrowding issue—and satisfy the courts—by building new prisons, releasing prisoners early or developing alternative sentencing programs to keep nonviolent criminals out of prison in the first place. Some have gained court permission to double up population in cells by adding recreational facilities or adding staff.

Over the course of the 1980s, a few of the states cited for the most egregious problems— Oklahoma and Alabama, among them—finally managed to reach a point where the courts were willing to give up day-to-day supervision.

All are agreed on one point: Morale improves when the court moves out. During Oklahoma's decade of intensive court supervision, says the prison operations chief, Steve Kaiser, "there was a defensiveness that's natural when somebody scrutinizes you and says you're doing something wrong. We'd say, 'Yeah, we fixed this.' The plaintiffs would say, 'Prove it.' Now we no longer have to prove everything." Oklahoma has essentially been out from under court control since 1983, although federal officials still monitor some technical aspects of prison management.

There is a downside to working free from court supervision, however: It's harder to keep up funding levels. Kaiser doubts the Oklahoma legislature would have approved the dollars needed to improve and maintain a more professional system "unless we had a federal judge breathing down our neck saying we had to do it." Among other things, Oklahoma's legislature came up with the money to build and run three new prisons. Now, though the need for funds is as pressing and the prison population continues to increase, legislators aren't as amenable to pleas for money. "Legislators come and go. They forget the days when the courts took over," Kaiser says. "The threat doesn't seem as real."

But it is.

Inmates continue to keep officials on their toes. They write letters of complaint; they sue. In Texas, the judge studying the agreement to loosen federal supervision warned state officials that they must be vigilant to ensure that, once free from the courts, political pressure does not erode prison reforms. And overcrowding is a constant threat to those reforms.

Alabama worked itself largely free of court control by building three new facilities to alleviate crowding. But now, state corrections spokesman John Hale admits, things are crowding up again. "The more you overcrowd, the more conditions tend to break down. We're nowhere near the bad shape we were in prior to the court case in the 1970s, but overcrowding is a serious problem." As it gets worse, the specter of a federal court seizing control again begins to seem more and more real.

However fragile the successes have been, quite a few jurisdictions are anxious to join the ranks of those emancipated from court scrutiny. While most have not been able to comply with all the details in the consent decrees or court orders under which they operate, several are asking the courts for relief anyway. Two events [in 1992] have set a new round of requests in motion. First, U.S. Attorney General William Barr offered Justice Department help to states seeking relief from consent decrees. In particular, Barr had his eye on making more room in state facilities for new prisoners.

Then the U.S. Supreme Court announced a decision [in] January [1992] in *Rufo vs. Inmates of Suffolk County Jail* that seemed to suggest that federal judges should be more willing to reopen consent agreements, particularly if there has been a significant change in a jurisdiction's circumstances. Coming on top of Barr's announcement, the case was seen as one that would encourage more states and counties to go to court and seek modification of their decrees.

"Both sides have been uncomfortable with the idea that you reach an agreement at the beginning and regardless of needs and circumstances, you're stuck with it," says law professor Susan Sturm. Now the Supreme Court has given some incentive to state and local governments to push for change.

It is too soon to tell whether there will be an avalanche of petitions to revisit. And what will happen to those that do reach the courts is even more unpredictable. Meanwhile, however, the pressure to keep prisons and jails up to constitutional standards will remain formidable, especially as crowding becomes more and more intense and prison systems operate, as many do, at 130 percent of capacity. So court supervision is going to be a fact of life in many state systems for years to come.

Officially, sheriffs and prison wardens will continue to complain about that, and to express their resentment at a court's intrusion into their facilities. Unofficially, however, more than a few of them agree with Jim Gondles, the former sheriff of Arlington County, Virginia. Gondles, who is now executive director of the American Correctional Association, admits that during the 1980s, when he was overseeing 400 inmates in a jail built for 168, he sometimes "wistfully thought" that it would be nice for an inmate to sue him and force the county and the state to comply with the population cap. Court orders, he says, are a way of getting help. "It's hard to get anything done without that hammer."

Reference Guide

SOURCES FOR ALL STATES

Advisory Commission on Intergovernmental Relations
Changing Public Attitudes on Governments and Taxes (1992)
Intergovernmental Perspective (published quarterly since 1975)
The Question of State Government Capability (1985)
Significant Features of Fiscal Federalism (1993)
State Constitutional Law: Cases and Materials (1990)
State Constitutions in the Federal System (1989)
The Transformation in American Politics: Implications for Federalism (1986)

Center for the Study of the States, Rockefeller Institute of Government, SUNY-Albany
State Fiscal Briefs (published monthly since 1991)
State Revenue Reports (published quarterly since 1990)

Congressional Quarterly
Congressional Quarterly Weekly Report (published weekly since 1954)
Governing (published monthly since 1987)

Council of State Governments
The Book of the States (published biennially since 1933)
Spectrum: The Journal of State Government (published bimonthly from 1986 through 1989, quarterly since 1990)
State Government News (published monthly since 1956)
State Government Research Checklist (published bimonthly since 1968)
Suggested State Legislation (published annually since 1941)

Government Research Service (Topeka, Kansas)
State Legislative Sourcebook (published annually)

The Heartland Institute
Intellectual Ammunition for State Legislators (published monthly since 1992)

Legislative Studies Center, Sangamon State University (Illinois)
Comparative State Politics (published bimonthly since 1979)

National Association of Attorneys General
State Constitutional Law Bulletin (published monthly since 1987)

National Center for State Courts
State Court Journal (published quarterly since 1977)

National Civic League
Campaign Finances: A Model Law (1979)
A Model Election System (1973)
A Model State Constitution (1968)
National Civic Review (published bimonthly)

National Conference of State Legislatures
Capital to Capital (published biweekly from Washington)
The Fiscal Letter (published bimonthly)
Mason's Manual of Legislative Procedure (1989)
State Legislatures (published monthly since 1975)

National Governors' Association
The Budgetary Process in the States (1985)
Fiscal Survey of the States (published biannually)
Governors' Bulletin (published weekly through 1991, biweekly since 1992)
State of the States Report (published annually)

State Policy Reports
State Budget and Tax News (published biweekly since 1981)
State Policy Reports (published bimonthly since 1983)
The State Policy Reports Data Book (published biannually 1984 through 1989)
States in Profile (published annually since 1990)

SOURCES FOR INDIVIDUAL STATES

State Blue Books (usually published by the secretaries of state)

State Journals
California Journal (published monthly since 1970)
Empire State Report (published monthly since 1975)
Illinois Issues (published monthly since 1975)
The Kentucky Journal (published ten times a year since 1989)
New Jersey Reporter (published since 1971, currently six times per year)
North Carolina Insight (published quarterly since 1978)

State Textbooks
The following texts are from the State Politics and Government Series of the Temple

University Center for the Study of Federalism and the University of Nebraska Press.

Blair, Diane D. *Arkansas Politics and Government.* 1988.

Krane, Dale, and Stephen D. Shaffer. *Mississippi Government and Politics.* 1992.

Miewald, Robert D., ed. *Nebraska Government and Politics.* 1984.

Morgan, David R., Robert E. England, and George G. Humphries. *Oklahoma Politics and Policies.* 1991.

Palmer, Kenneth T., G. Thomas Taylor, and Marcus A. LiBrizzi. *Maine Politics and Government.* 1992.

Salmore, Barbara G. and Stephen A., *New Jersey Politics and Government.* 1993.

Thomas, James D., and William H. Stewart, *Alabama Government and Politics.* 1988.

GENERAL SOURCES

Alexander, Herbert E. *Reform and Reality: The Financing of State and Local Campaigns.* New York: Twentieth Century Fund, 1991.

Barone, Michael, et al., eds. *Almanac of American Politics.* Washington, D.C.: National Journal. Published biennially since 1972; by National Journal since 1983.

Benjamin, Gerald, and Michael Malbin, eds. *Legislative Term Limits.* Washington, D.C.: CQ Press, 1992.

Beyle, Thad L., ed. *Governors and Hard Times.* Washington, D.C.: CQ Press, 1992.

Beyle, Thad L., and Lynn Muchmore. *Being Governor: The View from the Office.* Durham, N.C.: Duke University Press, 1983.

Cronin, Thomas E. *Direct Democracy: The Politics of Initiative, Referendum, and Recall.* Cambridge, Mass.: Harvard University Press, 1989.

Duncan, Phil, ed. *Politics in America.* Washington, D.C.: Congressional Quarterly. Published biennially since 1981.

Elazar, Daniel J. *American Federalism: A View from the States.* 3d ed. New York: Harper and Row, 1984.

Gray, Virginia, Herbert Jacob, and Robert B. Albritton, eds. *Politics in the American States: A Comparative Analysis.* 5th ed. Glenview, Ill.: Scott Foresman, 1990.

Herzik, Eric B., and Brent W. Brown, eds. *Gubernatorial Leadership and State Policy.* Westport, Conn.: Greenwood Press, 1991.

Jewell, Malcolm E., and David M. Olson. *Political Parties and Elections in the American States.* Homewood, Ill.: Dorsey Press, 1988.

Key, V. O., Jr. *Southern Politics in State and Nation.* New York: Alfred A. Knopf, 1949.

Legislative Drafting Research Fund, Columbia University. *Constitutions of the United States: National and State.* Oceana, N.Y.: Oceana Press, 1985.

Pierce, Neal R., and Jerry Hagstrom. *The Book of America: Inside Fifty States Today.* New York: W. W. Norton, 1983.

Price, David E. *Bringing Back the Parties.* Washington, D.C.: CQ Press, 1984.

Rosenthal, Alan. *Governors and Legislatures.* Washington, D.C.: CQ Press, 1990.

Rosenthal, Alan. *The Third House: Lobbyists and Lobbying in the States.* Washington, D.C.: CQ Press, 1993.

Sabato, Larry. *Goodbye to Good-time Charlie: The American Governorship Transformed.* 2d ed.

Washington, D.C.: CQ Press, 1983.

Van Horn, Carl E., ed. *The State of the States.* 2d ed. Washington, D.C.: CQ Press, 1992.

Wright, Deil S. *Understanding Intergovernmental Relations.* 3d ed. Pacific Grove, Calif.: Brooks/Cole, 1988.

SELECTED TEXTBOOKS

Adrian, Charles R., and Michael R. Fine. *State and Local Politics.* Chicago: Lyceum Books/Nelson Hall, 1991.

Berman, David R. *State and Local Politics.* 6th ed. Dubuque, Iowa: Wm. C. Brown, 1991.

Bingham, Richard D., and David Hodge. *State and Local Government in a Changing Society.* 2d ed. New York: McGraw Hill, 1991.

Bowman, Ann O'M., and Richard Kearney. *State and Local Government.* Boston: Houghton-Mifflin, 1990.

Burns, James M., Jack Peltason, Thomas E. Cronin, and David B. Magleby. *Government by the People: State and Local Politics.* 7th ed. Englewood Cliffs: Prentice-Hall, 1993.

Dresang, Dennis L., and James J. Gosling. *Politics, Policy, and Management in the American States.* New York: Longman, 1989.

Dye, Thomas R. *Politics in States and Communities.* 6th ed. Englewood Cliffs, N.J.: Prentice-Hall, 1988.

Grant, Daniel R., and Lloyd B. Omdahl. *State and Local Government in America.* Madison, Wis.: Brown and Benchmark, 1993.

Gray, Virginia, and Peter Eisinger. *American States and Cities.* New York: HarperCollins, 1991.

Harrigan, John J. *Politics and Policy in States and Communities.* 4th ed. New York: HarperCollins, 1991.

Hill, Kim Quaile, and Kenneth R. Mladenka. *Democratic Governance in American States and Cities.* Pacific Grove, Calif.: Brooks/Cole, 1992

Jewell, Malcolm E., and Samuel C. Patterson. *The Legislative Process in the United States.* 4th ed. New York: Random House, 1986.

Leach, Richard H., and Timothy G. O'Rourke. *State and Local Government: The Third Century of Federalism.* Englewood Cliffs, N.J.: Prentice-Hall, 1988.

Lorch, Robert S. *State and Local Politics: The Great Entanglement.* 4th ed. Englewood Cliffs, N.J.: Prentice-Hall, 1992.

Luttbeg, Norman R. *Comparing the States and Communities.* New York: HarperCollins, 1992.

Press, Charles, and Kenneth Verburg. *State and Community Governments in a Dynamic Federal System.* 3d ed. New York: HarperCollins, 1991.

Ross, Michael J. *State and Local Politics and Policy: Change and Reform.* New York: McGraw Hill, 1993.

Saffell, David C. *State and Local Government: Politics and Public Policies.* 6th ed. New York: McGraw Hill, 1993.

Schultze, William. *State and Local Politics: A Political Economy Approach.* St. Paul, Minn.: West Publishing Co., 1988.

Staufer, W. B., Cynthia Opheim, and Susan Bland Day. *State and Local Politics.* New York: HarperCollins, 1991.

Index